THE ENCYCLOPEDIA

SHATNERICA

THE ENCYCLOPEDIA

SHATNERICA

BY ROBERT SCHNAKENBERG

QUIRK BOOKS
PHILADELPHIA

INTRODUCTION

"**W**elcome to the final frontier of Shatnerology." When I first wrote those words, in 1998, I believed them to be true. Little did I know that there would one day be a second edition of this book—still the world's only comprehensive guide to the complex, multidimensional universe of William Shatner. A lot has happened in the ten years since the publication of the first edition. Shatner has undergone yet another amazing career renaissance. He's back in prime-time and bigger than ever. His mantelpiece is now crowded with Emmy Awards. Priceline.com has hired him, fired him, and brought him back. He's built an online presence, married a fourth time, even auctioned off his kidney stone. Not bad for a man who titled his own comeback CD *Has Been*.

With so much tachyon activity in the Shatnerverse, the time seemed right for a new edition. This edition represents a comprehensive revision of the original contents. Other books may cover Shatner's life and career, or the fictional universe of *Star Trek*, his most celebrated professional achievement, but in no one place can you find A-to-Z coverage of the whole wide world of William Shatner. This Millennium Edition provides expanded, enhanced coverage of all of Shatner's major television series and feature films, along with selected stage productions and notable TV guest appearances. Special emphasis is given to trends, recurring

themes in his life and work, and revealing personal anecdotes. What Shatner says about himself and what others say about him are given a full and fair airing.

The world of William Shatner is an unfolding text. No one book—no one author—can contain it all. But over time we gain focus, and the meaning becomes clearer. If you're reading this, you, like me, have struggled with the riddle that is Shatner, squeezed your hands around this unruly Rubik's Cube of a man, and failed to put the colored sides together. I am here to tell you there is a solution. It starts with the magical book you now hold in your hand. So come with me into the Shatner chamber. Sit down on the toilet seat shaped like a captain's chair and discover what I have uncovered. Without a guide to shed light on the shadowy places, this dark forest of a man will swallow you whole. Our mission here is a simple one: to boldly go where no book has gone before. To unlock the secrets of Shatnerica . . .

A NOTE ON THE ENTRIES

Items in boldface are cross-references to other entries in *The Encyclopedia Shatnerica*.

For Shatner films and television appearances, a handy "Six Degrees of *Star Trek*" guide has been included to alert fans of that TV show to *Star Trek* regulars and notable guests who appear in the entry under discussion.

A rating system has been provided to help you prioritize your Shatner consumption. Each Shatner film, series, book, album, TV appearance, and Web-accessible video clip has been rated as follows:

✳ ✳ ✳ ✳	Essential viewing/reading/listening for all Shatnerphiles.
✳ ✳ ✳	Worth a look. Rent, borrow, or download only.
✳ ✳	Minor Shatner. Feel free to skip it.
✳	Car wreck territory. For masochists/obsessives only.

ACTING

"I don't have a technique for acting," Shatner told the *New York Daily News* in 1982. That revelation will come as a surprise to some—especially those, such as comedian **Kevin Pollak**, who have made a living imitating Shatner's unmistakable mannered acting style. But it's true: Shatner has never had any formal performance training. Rather, he approaches his craft as a visceral endeavor in which learned responses have no place. "An actor's emotions are just below the magma of his sophistication," he has said. Despite this idiosyncratic approach, he has influenced several other talents, including **Jason Alexander** of *Seinfeld* fame. When Jim Carrey is asked what other actor makes him laugh, he replies, unhesitatingly: William Shatner.

What do Jason and Jim see that others don't? Let's break down the celebrated "Shatner Approach." Often imitated but never duplicated, it is marked by his use of urgent, hurried phrasing, placing the emphasis on unexpected words and syllables; a tendency to linger on words midsentence; and a curious habit of overrunning logical voice stops and careening into the next sentence in defiance of English syntax. Another characteristic is his trademark shrug, usually accompanied by open arms that are bent at the elbows; upturned palms; and wide, beseeching eyes. This pose works especially well when, as Captain Kirk, he confronts an adversary appearing on the viewscreen of the starship *Enterprise*.

The origin of this performance style can be traced to one of Shatner's earliest professional experiences. While serving as an understudy at the **Stratford Shakespeare Festival** in Ontario, **Canada**, Shatner had to play the title role in Shakespeare's *Henry V* on only a few hours' notice and without the benefit of rehearsal. His hastily cobbled performance—full of abrupt stops and inappropriate pauses when he forgot the dialogue—was hailed by critics as remarkably

As intrepid veterinarian "Rack" Hansen, Shatner shows his fellow thespians how it's done in the 1977 insect invasion shocker *Kingdom of the Spiders*.

intuitive and full of passion. Always quick to respond to positive feedback, Shatner began to incorporate these techniques into subsequent performances.

The apotheosis of the Shatner acting style came in his most famous role as Captain Kirk, which he played on TV's **Star Trek** from 1966 to 1969. In a 1989 interview with *Playboy*, Shatner explained his reasons for employing these devices. "There were two things at work. One was what I do naturally. Because it [*Star Trek*] was a series, and because fatigue means you have no time to separate yourself from the character, I tried to retain in Captain Kirk what was the essential me, I guess. I'm dimly aware that Captain Kirk phrased things in a certain way, and I'll do that on occasion. But I try not to be deliberate or even cognitive about it. It's all just part of me." More recently, Shatner has become somewhat less analytical. In a 2002 interview with *Maxim* magazine, he chalked his acting style up to "shallow breathing, allergies, and owning a dog that won't listen."

The final piece to the puzzle that is Shatner's acting style is his relationship with the audience. In a 1979 interview with authors Sondra Marshak and Myrna Culbreath, Shatner likened the interplay between a performer and his paying customers to an act of group **sex**: "I have had visions, dreams, before an opening night of actually encompassing a whole audience, of actually making love to a whole audience and making them my lover, and I theirs." Kind of gives a whole new meaning to the old show business term *flop sweat*.

"I sometimes think of myself as an acting machine."
—*Shatner, in 1967*

ADVENTURES OF TOM SAWYER, THE

Shatner played the title role in this Mark Twain classic in his first public performance, for the Montreal Children's Theatre in 1939. He was eight years old. He remained with the group for five years, appearing in children's plays every weekend.

AIRPLANE II: THE SEQUEL ✷✷✷✷

This 1982 follow-up to 1980's enormously popular movie *Airplane!* may have fallen flat with critics and audiences, but it gave Shatner an early opportunity to poke fun at himself on-screen. As Buck Murdock, the commander of a moonbase where a distressed space shuttle must land, Shatner mugs shamelessly and spoofs his heroic

Shatner chews the scenery as moonbase commander
Buck Murdock in 1982's *Airplane II: The Sequel.*

Captain Kirk persona. Actors Raymond Burr, Sonny Bono, and Hervé Villechaize also have cameos in the generally unfunny film, which marked the end of the line for the *Airplane!* franchise.

ALEXANDER, JASON

Best known for his portrayal of pint-sized neurotic George Costanza on *Seinfeld*, this multitalented performer maintains a profound—and largely unexplained—reverence for Shatner. "I became an actor because of Shatner," Alexander told *Entertainment Weekly* magazine. "Everywhere I went as a kid, I was doing the best Shatner you've ever seen." In 1994 the two performers bumped into each other for the first time on a crowded elevator at an entertainment-industry convention in Miami. "I broke into a huge sweat," reported Alexander. "I don't know if he knows who I am." Shatner had no reported comment on the brief encounter, although the pair subsequently reunited in 2001 for an episode of Alexander's short-lived TV sitcom *Bob Patterson*. Alexander also served as roastmaster for Comedy Central's *Roast of William Shatner* in 2007.

ALEXANDER THE GREAT ✳ ✳ ✳

No relation to **Jason Alexander**. This one-hour **television** pilot, filmed in 1963, featured Shatner as the Macedonian conqueror of the ancient world. The epic program sat on a shelf in the ABC network vaults until January 26, 1968, when it earned a one-time-only airing in the wake of ***Star Trek***'s success. The all-star cast includes a pre-*Batman* Adam West as Cleander, Alexander's lieutenant; a pre-*Faces* John Cassavetes as his ambitious rival Karonos; and a post-everything Joseph Cotten as the venerable Antigonus. All the actors wear extremely short togas—a shameless attempt to divert viewer attention from the bad **acting**. Filmed on location in the state of Utah (substituting for the country of Syria), this telefilm was the first of many costume dramas in which Shatner would boldly partake.

Critics panned the show. None was harsher than that notorious voice of reason, Adam West: "It just didn't work. The audience and Madison Avenue just weren't ready for orgies with Shatner and West lying there on their backs, eating grapes, with belly dancers beside them." Apparently, overseas audiences *were* ready for such an advanced entertainment concept, and *Alexander the Great* was a great success as a European theatrical release.

Shatner, at least, found a silver lining in this misbegotten small-screen project. "The nine months I spent working on *Alexander the Great* came in handy for *Star Trek*," he admits. "Captain Kirk is in many ways the quintessential hero, and the

A suntanned Shatner shows off some cutlery in this promotional
still from the 1963 TV production *Alexander the Great*.

Greek heroes in literature have many of the same qualities I wanted to explore."

ALFRED HITCHCOCK PRESENTS ✳ ✳ ✳

Shatner appeared twice on the legendary director's anthology TV series, each time in a memorable installment. The first, "The Glass Eye," aired on October 6, 1957. Shatner plays Jim Whitely, the brother of a recently deceased spinster. In a cool monotone, he narrates certain unnerving events regarding his late sibling, a dwarf, and a ventriloquist named Max Collodi. The final scene of this understated half-hour shocker is a must-see for fans of suspense.

Almost three years later, on April 10, 1960, Shatner made his second Hitchcock appearance in "Mother, May I Go Out to Swim?" This time he plays John Crane, a weak-willed mama's boy whose fiancée urges him to do away with his meddling mother. Again, there is a surprise ending in the grand Hitchcock tradition.

Shatner gets his motor running on a mid-60s motorcycling trip.

ALIENS

He confronted, killed, cajoled, and seduced them as the captain of the *Enterprise*, but did he also meet one in real life? Shatner has long promoted the idea that we are not alone in the **universe**. "I believe in UFOs," he told an interviewer in 1968. "The time is long past when the Air Force or the scientists or the government can say what people are seeing in the sky are nothing but hot air balloons or the planet Venus. That kind of double-talk won't wash any longer. There has been too much evidence over the years that UFOs exist." In a separate interview he added, "There's a strong possibility that these UFOs may be scouting our earth."

He may have been speaking from personal experience. In the summer of 1967, Shatner reportedly had a close encounter with a visitor from outer space while on a motorcycling excursion in the Mojave Desert. It wasn't the first time the actor's thoughts turned to space aliens while he was out riding his hog. With nothing but the sand and the sun to occupy his mind, Shatner often found himself gazing at the heavens. "I'd say to myself; 'Well if I were a little green man in a flying saucer and wanted to get publicity, who would I contact faster than Captain Kirk of the Starship *Enterprise*?'" In subsequent interviews, he coyly denied trying to send telepathic messages to extraterrestrials.

On this particular afternoon, however, the alien transmission apparently got through. While biking with friends, Shatner got separated from the group and mysteriously disappeared for several hours. Some of his fellow bikers later reported that an unidentified stranger had replaced him in their convoy. Shatner apparently hit a ditch and wiped out, the bike collapsing on top of him. When he awoke a minute or so later, he experienced a weird apparition—"like when you have a nightmare and you feel something crawling over your body or wrestling with you"—but he was unable to pinpoint its source. He managed to extricate himself from the overturned **motorcycle**, but he couldn't get it to start. Disoriented and dehydrating in 130-degree heat, Shatner was on the verge of collapse. Just then he saw, or thought he saw, another cyclist in the distance, beckoning him. He lugged his Harley toward this vision, which led him to a gas station and the chance to get a drink and recuperate. Then he saw an object "glistening in the heavens"—an object he would neither confirm nor deny was a flying saucer. No matter what its origins, Shatner remains convinced the unknown force saved his life.

In fact, he was so moved by this experience that he planned to make a half-hour film about it. While that project never came to fruition, Shatner used the alien encounter as a point of departure for many future works, including his 1968 album **The Transformed Man** and a series of **one-man shows** in the late 1970s.

ALLEY, KIRSTIE

This buxom Scientologist steamed Shatner's girdle as the Vulcan Lieutenant Saavik in **Star Trek II: The Wrath of Khan**. Formerly married to TV "Hardy Boy" Parker Stevenson, the actor allegedly endured the amorous advances of "hard boy" Shatner during filming in 1982. When, at one point during production, a playful Shatner stepped on a round styrofoam prop and shouted "I've crushed a ball," Alley lamented that it wasn't one of his own. She reportedly found the experience of working with Shatner so distasteful that she refused to appear in **Star Trek III: The Search for Spock** unless she was paid as much as he was. Paramount refused to give in to her salary demands and replaced her with actress Robin Curtis. Alley went on to a successful career as a sitcom actor and **weight**-loss icon.

ANDERSONVILLE TRIAL, THE ✳✳✳✳

Shatner gives a commanding performance—arguably the finest of his career—in this 1970 television film. *The Andersonville Trial* dramatizes the 1865 war crimes trial of Henry Wirz, commander of a notorious Confederate prison camp in Georgia where barbaric conditions resulted in the deaths of nearly 15,000 Union soldiers. Actors Richard Baseheart, Jack Cassidy, and a young Martin Sheen

In one of his most powerful performances, Shatner plays a spit-and-polish JAG officer in the 1970 TV movie *The Andersonville Trial*.

also appear in the production, directed by legendary actor George C. Scott. In one of his first major post-*Star Trek* roles, Shatner plays Colonel N. P. Chipman, the JAG officer who prosecuted the trial on behalf of the U.S. government. Broadcast by PBS on May 17, 1970, *The Andersonville Trial* earned rave reviews and won Emmys for Outstanding Single Program and Best Adapted Teleplay.

Sadly, the high quality of *The Andersonville Trial* was not a harbinger of things to come for Shatner. He almost immediately plummeted into the professional death spiral known as his **lost years.** Coincidentally, he met his future wife (and future ex-wife), **Marcy Lafferty**, on the set of this production.

SIX DEGREES OF *STAR TREK*

Harry Townes (Colonel Chandler in ***The Andersonville Trial***) plays Reger in the first-season classic "The Return of the Archons."

ARCHERY

This ancient sport is one of Shatner's longtime hobbies. For an early 1970s segment of the outdoor sports series *The American Sportsman*, Shatner hunted bears armed with only his bow and arrow. He eventually killed a nine-foot-tall Kodiak bear and kept the skin as a rug in his Los Angeles home. In a separate hunting expedition, Shatner led a large wild boar chase on Southern California's Catalina Island and—again relying only on his bow and arrow—bagged both a huge boar and a wild goat.

As with horsemanship, **flying**, and numerous other activities (see **Sex**), Shatner finds in archery a profound sexual metaphor. "What could be more sexual than archery as a phallic symbol?" he has said. "I mean, it's like an act of sex." Perhaps this explains why, on the ***Star Trek* blooper reel**, Shatner can be seen clowning around with an arrow sticking out of the crotch of his spacesuit.

"Looking back on the things I've done, I must be a little crazy. But I'm constantly testing myself both in athletics and acting. I've always believed that if you don't define your limits by trying everything, you'll never know your capabilities."

—*Shatner, on his passion for adventure*

ARDREY, ROBERT

The theories propounded by this controversial American anthropologist had a profound effect upon Shatner. Ardrey's two most impor-

Ready…aim…fire! Shatner stalks his prey on one of his occasional bowhunting expeditions.

tant books, *African Genesis* (1965) and *The Territorial Imperative* (1966), greatly influenced the actor's thinking about society and the male ethos. The author believed that man is an innately aggressive creature, a "killer ape" driven by a desire to protect his property and gain dominance over others. "His theories are illuminating and dazzling to me," Shatner has said.

Originally a playwright, Ardrey became fascinated with the theories of Raymond Dart in the late 1950s. Dart's killer ape theory held that our earliest ancestor was aggressive and violent, and that violence is the driving force behind human evolution. Ardrey soon developed his own thesis based on this idea. "Man is a predator whose natural instinct is to kill with a weapon," Ardrey wrote in *African Genesis*. "The sudden addition of the enlarged brain to the equipment of an armed already-successful predatory animal created not only the human being but also the human predicament."

Over the decades, Ardrey's theories have been used by fundamentalist Christians and other traditionalist thinkers as an intellectual basis for male dominion over society. "The time will come when the male will lose all interest in **sex**; but he will still fight for his status," Ardrey wrote. He argues that male instinct for domination reveals itself in three ways: first, in property instinct and territoriality; second, in status and a drive to establish rank in hierarchical order; and third, in survival and the manipulation of social order as a means of survival. Shatner has applied these ideas to the ongoing war over screen parts in Hollywood, which may explain his obsession with **line counting** and his other territorial drives. "I loved Ardrey's stuff about males stamping out a little territory there, fighting other males off, and the females coming because the males have a little area," Shatner once said.

ASHETON, RON

This punk rock guitarist, a founding member of Iggy Pop's band The Stooges, once claimed that Shatner made a pass at him in a Los Angeles bar. According to Asheton, in the summer of 1975 an inebriated Shatner approached him in the Hyatt House pub, where the axeman had gone to listen to some jazz. "He wanted me to sit down, and then he got kind of grabby," Asheton claimed. Horrified at the prospect that Captain Kirk might be anything less than 100 percent straight, Asheton promptly fled the scene. "Probably if I'd been drinking I would have sat down just for the weirdness of seeing what would happen," the reluctant boy toy remarked. Asheton, whose aggressive guitar chops can be heard on such seminal Stooges albums as *Funhouse* and *Raw Power*, ranks 29th on *Rolling Stone* magazine's list of the 100 Greatest Guitarists of All Time.

ASS KICKING

Shatner received his first proper butt whuppin' while a child at summer **camp** on a farm in **Canada**. "I got my ass, literally, kicked—hard—for pulling up carrots out of a farmer's field," he told biographers in 1979. "I couldn't make it over the fence like the other kids did and dive over the top. The farmer caught me with a good kick. That was his way of teaching children not to steal." The pain was severe and it lingered, although Shatner ranked its intensity "somewhat short of getting kicked in the balls"—an experience for which he has yet to relate a comparable anecdote.

"Very few people have actually gotten their ass kicked with a hard, hobnailed boot by a strong, angry man. That hurts."

—*Shatner, on his first ass kicking*

ATOMIC SUBMARINES

Shatner says he learned a lot about the "loneliness of command" through discussions with the captains of atomic submarines. "[I] talked to those guys about it, the skippers. . . . I said, what about . . . when you're alone? I mean, you can only be so familiar with your executive officers. There comes a point when you come back to this little cubicle—you're really alone, man." Shatner claims he used his personal experience of loneliness in his portrayal of Captain Kirk, the archetypal commander married to his ship, the *Enterprise*.

AUTO RACING

Shatner took up auto racing for a brief time in the late 1970s. He was asked to try his hand at driving a Formula One car after a friend saw him racing go-carts on a TV special. Never one to back down from a challenge, Shatner took classes on driving competitively and actually competed in a grand prix race in Long Beach, California. However, it wasn't until he was on the course going 110 miles per hour that Shatner came to a crucial realization: "You know, I could get hurt. Killed." Thus ended his brief love affair with racing—until he was lured back to the pits for the 2007 reality **television** series **Fast Cars and Superstars**.

BABYSITTER, THE   ✳ ✳

Don't let the title fool you. This 1980 TV movie is actually about a housekeeper, not a babysitter, but that's a minor complaint in the grand scheme of things. Shatner and Patty Duke Astin are Jeff and Liz Benedict, a troubled married couple who fall under the spell of their creepy live-in nanny, played by Stephanie Zimbalist. She wants Astin out of the way and Shatner in her bed. When she can't have either one, she decides to murder the entire family. Quinn Cummings, the delightful gamin from the 1977 film The Goodbye Girl, graduates to obscurity here as the Benedicts' gawky, precocious daughter. Venerable John Houseman is wasted in a thankless role as the ancient town physician. The film builds up to what we're led to believe will be a bloody climax—but it is neither bloody nor climactic.

BACCHUS

At the 1987 Mardi Gras Parade in New Orleans, Shatner assumed the role of King Bacchus, the mythical Roman **god** of wine. The Krewe of Bacchus is one of the most spirited Mardi Gras parade organizations. Spectacular floats, a massive supper dance, and a national celebrity chosen yearly as the ceremonial monarch are a few of the signatures of the Bacchus organization. Other celebrities who have played the giddy god of the grape through the years include Bob Hope, Jackie Gleason, Charlton Heston, Kirk Douglas, and James Gandolfini.

> "Bacchus is anything you want him to be. I want him to be wild and woolly and to have a great time."
>
> —Shatner, on his role as the god of wine at the 1987 Mardi Gras Parade

BARBARY COAST, THE   * *

This short-lived **television** western series starred Shatner as Jeff Cable, a master of disguises. Set in the lawless Barbary Coast district of San Francisco in the 1870s, the hour-long adventure drama followed two special agents who spent their time collecting information on local criminals. Doug McClure played Cable's partner, Cash Conover.

Loosely modeled on the popular *Wild Wild West*, which was itself a kind of sagebrush *Star Trek*, *The Barbary Coast* debuted with a

An avid horseman, Shatner looks right at home atop his steed in a scene from his 1970s TV series *The Barbary Coast*.

two-hour pilot on May 4, 1975. Bill Bixby (who later played Dr. David Bruce Banner on *The Incredible Hulk*) directed, with a script from *Twilight Zone* veteran Douglas Heyes. In this showcase, Shatner donned a variety of costumes, including a pirate, a Ku Klux Klansman, and a sightless vagrant. The pilot did well enough to warrant a network series commitment. However, critics decried the lack of chemistry between the two stars and the show's obvious and tortuous plots.

Ideally, ABC would have given the struggling *Barbary Coast* the time to grow and find its audience, but instead it did all it could to undermine the already floundering show. Programming it in a family hour time slot (opposite CBS's popular sitcoms *Rhoda* and *Phyllis* and NBC's adventure show *The Invisible Man*), the network insisted that violence and conflict be kept to a very discrete minimum. For a show that was supposed to be about two-fisted western action, this executive decision was a death sentence.

"We can't have any man-to-man combat, even for the fun of it," Shatner wailed. "We're throwing mud pies at each other in an effort to get in some action. . . . However, mud in the face works only for a while. We need more tension in the stories and that comes from conflict between stalwart people."

Unfortunately, ABC never heeded Shatner's urgings. It canceled *The Barbary Coast* as of January 9, 1976, after only thirteen episodes. All that remained to remind Shatner there had even been a series were his scratches and bruises, the painful consequences of doing all his own stunts.

"[It] took me months to recover from *Barbary Coast*," Shatner later recalled. "I mean physically, literally physically. I had to stop working. I'd get out of bed tired. I'd have nine hours sleep and I'd get up—I couldn't move. Took me three months."

SIX DEGREES OF *STAR TREK*

Michael Ansara (Diamond Jack Bassiter in the pilot of *The Barbary Coast*) played Kang the Klingon in the third-season *Star Trek* episode "Day of the Dove."

BASTARD, THE ✳

This bizarrely cast two-part 1978 TV movie was adapted from John Jakes's potboiler novel about life during the American Revolution. Always dreamed of seeing Tom Bosley play Benjamin Franklin? How about William Shatner as Paul Revere? Done and done. Made under the auspices of Operation Prime Time, a joint endeavor by independent television stations to create highfalutin' dramatic programs, *The Bastard* emphasizes soap opera shenanigans rather than authentic history. Andrew Stevens struts as the eponymous bastard, Phillipe Charboneau, a hunky French nobleman who assumes a new identity as Philip Kent and meets all the leading figures in colonial America. William Daniels, who previously capered as John Adams in the Broadway musical *1776*, plays Adams's beermaking brother Samuel here. Peter Bonerz, the wacky dentist from TV's *The Bob Newhart Show*, spouts a homily about the benefits of democracy. "Haven't we seen all this before?" asked a cynical *Variety* critic. Yes, the year before in *Testimony of Two Men*. Shatner passed on the popular telefilm's sequels, *The Rebels* (1979) and *The Seekers* (1979), also based on Jakes's novels.

Shatner girds himself for a midnight ride as Paul Revere in the 1978 TV movie *The Bastard*.

BECK

This elfin alternative rocker (born Bek David Campbell) paid tribute to Shatner's infamous 1978 performance of **"Rocket Man"** in a 1996 **music** video. In the video for the song "Where It's At," from Beck's critically acclaimed album *Odelay*, the singer mimics the "three Shatner" motif from the actor's misbegotten performance at the 1978 Science Fiction Film Awards. Never pausing to explain this obscure visual cue, Beck leaves it to the initiated to recognize the insider's reference.

BELIEVE ✳ ✳

This historical novel, written by Shatner and **Voice of the Planet** author Michael Tobias, was published in 1992. The speculative tale concerns an imagined battle of wits between world-renowned American magician Harry Houdini and British physician, novelist, and detective-story writer Sir Arthur Conan Doyle. Shatner hoped to produce a **stage** version of *Believe* with himself as Harry Houdini and **Leonard Nimoy** as Sir Arthur Conan Doyle, but he could not conjure up enough money to cover the cost of production. It should be noted that, in September 1994, a playhouse owner in New Hope, Pennsylvania, attempted to sue Shatner because he failed to appear, as he had reportedly agreed to do, in a play based upon this book.

BELLE REVE

This sprawling 360-acre farm is found in the lush bluegrass country near Versailles, Kentucky, where Shatner raises his **horses**. (In French, the name means "beautiful dream.") Shatner began breeding American Saddlebreds in the early 1980s, and, by the close of the century, he owned more than one hundred of these expensive high-stepping **horses**. "You might say I put myself pretty deep into the business," he said of his passion for breeding. "When I'm not acting or directing, I'm at the farm."

BICYCLE STORY

See **Practical Jokes**.

BIG BAD MAMA   ✳

This trashy 1974 feature stars Shatner and curvaceous '70s sexpot Angie Dickinson. She is Wilma "Mama" McClatchie, a machine-gun-toting, bank-robbing mom in Depression-era Texas. He is William J. Baxter, an effete Southern drifter who takes up with Mama and her gang. Tom Skerritt, who went on to play Shatner's brother in **The Devil's Rain**, is his rival for Angie's affections. Although given star billing, Shatner really has little to do in this tedious Bonnie and Clyde knockoff. *Big Bad Mama* is notable only for Shatner's three **nude scenes** with Dickinson, stills of which were subsequently published in men's magazines. Produced by B-movie impresario Roger Corman, the film also features actors Joan Prather, Dick Miller, and Royal Dano. The Shatnerless sequel *Big Bad Mama II* appeared in 1987.

BILL AND TED'S BOGUS JOURNEY   ✳ ✳

This 1992 comedy movie, a sequel to the 1989 hit *Bill and Ted's Excellent Adventure*, features Shatner in a cameo as Captain **James**

Shatner appears to be eating his cigarette in this publicity still from the 1974 film *Big Bad Mama*.

T. Kirk. The lowbrow romp stars Alex Winter and Keanu Reeves as the eponymous nitwits. They travel back and forth in time and meet up with a gaggle of strange characters—including the commander of the *Enterprise*. The general critical consensus: not as good as the first movie.

BLOOPER REEL

This notorious reel of foul-ups, bleeps, and blunders caught by cameras on the *Star Trek* set began circulating in 1969. Shatner has admitted that seeing the blooper reel for the first time alerted him to the growing popularity of *Star Trek* after its cancellation in 1969. Among the Shatner highlights are the numerous scenes in which he keeps kissing a female guest star long after the scene has ended. He also initiates a number of famous bloopers. In one instance, Spock shoots an arrow, and the next scene calls for Kirk to be carried into a cave. Unaware that the cameras are rolling, a playful Shatner strolls through the sequence with the offending arrow sticking out of the crotch of his spacesuit.

BOSTON LEGAL   ✦ ✦ ✦ ✦

Shatner copped his second Emmy and first Golden Globe Award in 2005 for his portrayal of **Denny Crane** on this ABC legal drama. A spin-off of **The Practice**, where the characters of Crane and **James Spader**'s oleaginous Alan Shore originated, *Boston Legal* veered more toward comedy than its mother series. It was also designed to be much less of an ensemble piece and more of a showcase for its two lead actors. "There are at least two reasons to watch *Boston Legal*," opined the *Los Angeles Times* shortly after the series premiered in 2004, "and their names, in alphabetical order, are William Shatner and James Spader." The paper's TV critic was just the first of many to detect a Kirk-and-Spock dynamic in the byplay between Spader's blithe sociopath and Shatner's egocentric blowhard.

From the beginning, *Boston Legal* has been a veritable feast of insider references for the attentive Shatnerphile. A host of former Shatner costars and **Star Trek** players have made guest appearances on the program, including one-time **T. J. Hooker** regular **Heather Locklear** in a two-episode arc in 2005. Scripts are often larded with **Star Trek** allusions, and one memorable 2007 show features footage of Shatner from the 1957 Studio One drama **The Defenders**, refashioned as a **Denny Crane** flashback sequence.

A hit with audiences and critics alike, *Boston Legal* may turn out to be the crowning achievement of Shatner's **television** career. Credit for the show's enduring popularity must go to

As the lascivious lawyer Denny Crane, Shatner unleashes his id on America in the TV series *Boston Legal*.

Shatner's delightfully self-aware performance, and to creator David E. Kelly's clever dialogue—two elements that, in Shatner's mind, go hand in hand. "David Kelley is a genius," he has said. "I mean that literally. . . . David himself has said that by watching me work, he writes for me, and I, by watching him write, am able to perform it. So there's an unusual, if not unique, arrival of two forces that seem to combine, a synthesis of two forces—a writer and actor—that's just very unusual."

"I read what he's written and see where he's pointing the character and try and invest the things he writes with a solidarity, an anchoring point, so that the buffoonery is serious and the serious parts are buffoonery."

—*Shatner, describing his collaborative process with writer/producer David E. Kelley on* Boston Legal

SIX DEGREES OF *STAR TREK*

René Auberjonois (Paul Lewsiton on ***Boston Legal***) played Odo, the shape-shifting chief of security, on ***Star Trek: Deep Space Nine***.

BROKEN ANGEL ✳

Shatner and Susan Blakely play Chuck and Catherine Coburn, the shocked parents of a teenage gang leader, in this 1988 TV movie. The alarmist melodrama features comely Erika Eleniak as the couple's wayward daughter, who entices other affluent suburban kids into a hedonist cult called "Live for Now." Enter Shatner as the obsessed dad, who descends into a seamy underworld of gang-bangers and runaways to haul his little princess back from the abyss. "Shatner struggles," observed the *Variety* critic kindly, going on to lament the film's "cardboard characters cut out to fit a thesis." There's a thesis here?

BROTHERS KARAMAZOV, THE ✳ ✳ ✳

This 1958 film, based on the classic Fyodor Dostoyevsky novel, features Shatner in support of actors Yul Brynner, Lee J. Cobb, and Claire Bloom. Producer Pandro S. Berman personally cast Shatner in the role of Alexei, the monastic youngest of the three Karamazov siblings. At a meeting to discuss the part, Berman reportedly took one look at the handsome young actor and proclaimed "Yes, he's the

"Wig? What wig?" Shatner shows off a new lid in the 1958 feature *The Brothers Karamazov*.

one." Shatner's performance earned strong notices in the trade press. "William Shatner has the difficult task of portraying youthful male goodness," *Variety* reported in its review, "and he does it with such gentle candor it is effective." Less effective is the ludicrous **toupee** Shatner wears in this 147-minute philiosophical potboiler. The helmet-like wig may have been modeled on a Hummel figurine.

BURMESE SAILOR

No stranger to portraying racial stereotypes, Shatner once played a Burmese sailor on an episode of the TV drama **Naked City**. The episode, "Without Stick or Sword," aired on March 28, 1962. As

Maung Tun, a devout Buddhist seaman lately returned to shore, Shatner stabs several people to death in revenge for the killing of his brothers. However, he is wracked by guilt and turns himself in during the funeral of one of his victims. To research his character, Shatner visited the Burmese consulate and talked at length with natives of the Southeast Asian nation (now Myanmar). However, his principal contribution to the role—aside from racially offensive eye makeup—was a preposterous Charlie Chan accent. In 1968, Shatner labeled the Burmese sailor the one part he has played "that was completely and utterly foreign to me."

BUTLER'S NIGHT OFF, THE　　　　　✳ ✳

Shatner made his big-screen debut with a small role as a crook in this little-seen 1951 Canadian feature, starring Peter Sturgess as the titular manservant.

BUTT TIGHTENING

Demanded by Shatner, this airbrush technique helped make his rump look narrower in 1991's **Star Trek VI: The Undiscovered Country**. Shatner was especially distressed by the width of his caboose during a scene in which he walks across the *Enterprise* bridge in full view of the widescreen camera.

CAMP

The man whose career offers such distictive camp value learned to value camp at an early age. Summer camp was a childhood haven for Shatner while growing up in **Canada**. He spent his months off from school on working farms in French-speaking Quebec. Activities included tending to the animals and watching the farmer slaughter his pigs. It was on one such farm that Shatner received his first **ass kicking**, an experience he would not soon forget. Shatner also excelled in many camp activities. He was an accomplished swimmer and won many boxing matches with other boys.

Camp also provided the setting for one of Shatner's earliest **acting** experiences. In 1937, six-year-old Shatner was spending the summer on a farm owned by his aunt in the Laurentian Mountains about two hours north of Montreal. He starred in *Winterset*, a camp production about a persecuted Jewish family living in Europe between world wars. In a poignant scene, Shatner, playing a young boy not unlike himself, bid goodbye to his beloved dog. Desiring a pet of his own in real life, but forbidden by his parents to own one, Shatner was able to conjure up actual tears that left the audience bawling along with him. He later recalled the moment: "I looked out, and they were weeping. I thought, something I did made them weep. And I got a little crazy. Wow, I did that!" It was a turning point in the impressionable youngster's life. From then on, he had the **acting** bug.

CAMPUS, JAKE

Original name of **Jake Cardigan**, protagonist of Shatner's *Tek* book series.

CANADA

While Shatner has never shied away from his Canadian heritage, many people don't know he hails from the Great White North. Part of the reason is his complete lack of a Canadian accent, something he worked hard to eradicate after making the decision to pursue an **acting** career in America. Shatner toplines an impressive list of Canadians who have excelled in the performing arts. Why such a high success rate? "I think we Canadians do well in acting because we have the technique of the English and the virility of the Americans," Shatner once remarked to an interviewer. "We're in an advantageous position by being in the middle of the two."

CANADIAN NATIONAL REPERTORY THEATRE

Shatner worked for this touring theatre company, based in Ottawa, from 1952 to 1954. Relying on a professional reference from the **Mountain Playhouse** in Montreal, Shatner secured a job as the assistant manager for $31 a week. However, he quickly moved out from behind the scenes and onto the **stage**, often playing children and teenagers. During the summer months, Shatner returned to the **Mountain Playhouse** to appear in stock productions.

CANADIAN URANIUM

Shatner paid a heavy price for his interest in this heavy metal in the 1950s. In an interview with *Money* magazine in 2007, Shatner related a cautionary anecdote from his days at the Stratford Shakespeare Festival in Ontario. One of the older actors approached him with a tip on investing in Canadian uranium. Shatner quickly rushed out and sunk $500 into it—his only savings at the time. "The following day, the Canadian prime minister said the country would no longer buy uranium. I was wiped out," Shatner confessed. "Since then I've led a very conservative financial life."

CARDIGAN, JAKE

This oddly named character is the hero of Shatner's futuristic *Tek* book series. Originally called Jake Campus, Cardigan is a hard-boiled ex-cop turned private eye who is falsely convicted of trafficking a mind-altering brain stimulant called "tek." He spends four years in suspended animation for this crime, then emerges to find his private life turned upside down and the world in the grip of the drug-dealing teklords. Cardigan joins forces with the mysterious philanthropist Walter Bascom in a bid to clear his own name and rid the planet of tek. *B. J. and the Bear* hunk Greg Evigan played Cardigan in the *TekWar* cable television series.

In both his book and TV incarnations, Cardigan bears more than a passing resemblance to several of Shatner's own on-screen creations. "In the beginning I planned *TekWar* as a screenplay for myself to star in," the actor/author told *Entertainment Weekly* magazine in 1993. "I had this idea of putting T. J. Hooker into a futuristic milieu." Cardigan's many travails in the *Tek* cycle include wrestling robot bulls, deactivating android doubles, and staving off homicidal hockey players. His loyal partner through it all is Sid Gomez.

CAROL CHRISTMAS, A   ✳ ✳

Shatner's performance as the Ghost of Christmas Present in this 2003 holiday TV movie reportedly inspired **The Practice** creator David E. Kelley to cast him in the role of orotund attorney **Denny Crane** on the popular ABC legal drama. A distaff re-do of Dickens's *A Christmas Carol*, *A Carol Christmas* features a veritable pantheon of TV has-beens. *Beverly Hills 90210*'s Tori Spelling plays the eponymous miser, Carol Cartman, who learns the true meaning of Christmas at the hands of Gary Coleman (the Ghost of Christmas Past), Empty Nester Dinah Manoff (the Jacob Marley analog), and Shatner. Watching at home, Kelley was so taken with Shatner's antic take on his ghostly character that he proceeded to devise a similar character to play off **James Spader**'s ethically challenged Alan Shore on **The Practice**.

CAT ON A HOT TIN ROOF

Shatner was in the running to play Brick Pollitt in the 1958 film version of Tennessee Williams's hit Broadway play, *Cat on a Hot Tin Roof*. Newspaper reports even pegged Shatner as the top choice for the lead opposite Elizabeth Taylor. But the plum role went to Paul Newman instead, the start of a trend in which Shatner lost choice movie parts to more bankable film actors. "My dream of success was hollow," Shatner confided to *TV Guide* in 1968. "I started losing parts, something that had never happened to me before." Shatner's failure to establish a foothold as a big-screen actor eventually led him to accept the part of Captain Kirk on TV's **Star Trek** in 1966.

CHRISTIAN, CLAUDIA

This bodacious actress, best known for her portrayal of Commander Susan Ivanova on the sci-fi TV series *Babylon 5*, excoriated Shatner in a 2007 interview with the pop culture website retrocrush.com. Christian accused Shatner of manhandling her while they were filming an episode of **T. J. Hooker** together in 1982. "I do remember [him] trying to shove his tongue down my throat in his dressing room after eating Thai food," Christian claimed. "He was a bit of an ass. He was already wearing the **corset** back then, so I should have punched him in his stomach." It wasn't the first time Shatner had faced these kinds of aspersions from a female costar. Actors **Kirstie Alley**, **Vira Montes**, and **Heather Locklear** have all made similar allegations.

> "Well, who am I to tell a lady that she's a liar? I have no recollection. I'm sure it was memorable for her, though."
>
> —Shatner, on actress Claudia Christian's allegation that he groped her on the set of T. J. Hooker

COLUMBO: BUTTERFLY IN SHADES OF GREY ✳ ✳ ✳

This 1995 TV movie stars Peter Falk as the rumpled, intrusive Lieutenant Columbo. Shatner is the villain, Fielding Chase, a

A forlorn Shatner fights a losing battle with Peter Falk and his own false moustache in the 1994 TV movie *Columbo: Butterfly in Shades of Grey*.

pompous **radio** talk show host clearly modeled on Rush Limbaugh. Shatner gets to wear a comical wig and a false moustache that changes position from scene to scene. His dirty deeds include murdering one of his broadcast assistants and framing the deceased man's gay lover for the homicide. The mystery is unraveled when he uses a ***Star Trek*** communicator-shaped phone to make a 911 call! Shatner had previously tangled with Falk's detective in a 1976 episode of the *Columbo* TV series, "Fade in to Murder."

COMMODORE VIC-20

Shatner hawked this so-called "wonder computer of the 1980s" in a series of **television** commercials beginning in 1982. Trading on his

Star Trek persona, Shatner is "beamed in" to the ad via some unspecified, but presumably Commodore-controlled, agency. The thrust of the pitch was the VIC-20's supposed superiority to the then-popular Atari 2600 video game system. "Unlike games, it has a real computer keyboard!" Shatner gushes at one point.

C.O.R.E. DIGITAL PICTURES

Shatner cofounded this Toronto-based computer animation firm with business partner Bob Munroe in 1994. Utilizing the talents of animators hired to work on effects for the mid-1990s *TekWar* cable TV movies, the company has provided special effects for both theatrical films and **television**, including the Canadian-made *Johnny Mnemonic*, starring Keanu Reeves, and Disney's **The Wild**, featuring Shatner himself as the king of the wildebeests.

CORSET

See **Weight**.

COSTUME DRAMA

Over the decades, Shatner has excelled at playing heavily costumed characters in both period movies and **television** specials. Some of the actor's memorable roles in this vein include Paul Revere in **The Bastard**; a nineteenth-century Pennsylvanian in **Testimony of Two Men**; a colonial Satanist in **The Devil's Rain**; and Jo March's husband in a **television** adaptation of Louisa May Alcott's classic **Little Women**.

One of Shatner's most personally rewarding costume roles was **Alexander the Great**, which he essayed for a failed ABC pilot in 1963. He reminisced about the experience in a *TV Guide* interview: "One day we were on location in the wilds of Utah where the geological formations, mesas, and fauna and flora were remarkably similar to Syria where Alexander conducted his military campaign. The director and I were alone, off in the distance from the company. We discussed a great dilemma we had, namely, what to do about the creaking of the leather uniforms." After all, Shatner ruminated, wouldn't the noisy duds give the soldiers away as they crept forward to surprise the enemy? "There I was, dressed in the costume of ancient Greece with my horse beside me and the panoramic view around me. I was discussing a problem that Alexander must have discussed with his own soldiers. Suddenly, in a flash, I came to the awareness of how bound we are to history and how universal our problems are. That insight was also the solution to the problem of the creaking uniforms. I realized that Alexander could do nothing about it, so why should we! Anything we feel, they felt. This fact makes me understand men anywhere, any time."

> "It was like Combat in drag."
> —*Shatner, describing the experience of filming* Alexander the Great

CRANE, DENNY

Other than Captain Kirk, this bloviating attorney from the TV dramas **The Practice** and **Boston Legal** may be Shatner's most iconic portrayal. A brilliant, pompous, infuriating blowhard whose mannered speech patterns (including the repeated, out-of-context intonation of his own name) suggest some kind of early-onset brain disease, Crane resembles no one so much as Shatner himself, written times larger for maximum effect on the small screen. Just as Marlon Brando's performance in *Last Tango in Paris* helped revitalize his late career and cast everything that came before it in a new light, so Denny Crane has rescued Shatner from the post–**Star Trek** oblivion into which he had sunk in the eyes of America's TV critics.

From the beginning, Crane was tailored to Shatner's peculiar talents. David E. Kelley, the executive producer of **The Practice**, saw him playing an over-the-top ghost in the 2003 TV movie **A Carol Christmas** and believed a similar character would play well off **The**

Practice's ethically compromised junior partner Alan Shore, played by **James Spader**. Kelley immediately phoned Shatner, "and when David Kelley calls, trumpets sound, tympanis," Shatner later recalled. "So I met him for breakfast." Kelley proceeded to describe the part he envisioned for Shatner, who had to overcome his reluctance to get involved in another weekly **television** series. "I had seen with mine own eyes what devastation it wreaks on your life," Shatner reported. "But there is a siren song played by trumpets from David Kelley, and soon I was lured to brake my barque on the islands of his talents."

An older, wiser Shatner returned to the A-list with his portrayal of Denny Crane on *The Practice* and *Boston Legal*.

The two men then worked collaboratively to fine tune the character of Crane, who was introduced to viewers in **The Practice** episode "War of the Roses" on March 21, 2004. The result was a man who is equal parts macho paragon and deranged mountebank. "We discuss how much delight we take in the character, and how much seriousness," Shatner has said. "There's a balance, in order for the audience to continuously take him seriously and not as a buffoon. That's the fine line." Shatner even devised a backstory to account for Crane's overbearing demeanor. "I think he was in the military," he opined. "The way I stand, bark orders, change certain words. . . . I think he was in combat somewhere, mayhem, and had to stand up for his men and took up law as a result." Certainly Shatner's own unique combination of virility and dementia had a lot to do with his fitness for the part. Of selecting Shatner for the role, David E. Kelley observed, "I wanted someone who was physically robust and yet I wanted to get into his budding senility. [Crane] is a character that we want to always walk that line. We're never quite sure. He's either a genius or quite crazy."

The true origin of Crane's eccentric affect remains a mystery. "My vote would be for a man who's fighting, if not Alzheimer's, then a certain amount of senility," Shatner once said. Of Crane's habit of incessantly blurting out his own name, he theorized: "I think it's like the snake that sticks out its tongue to sense the world around it. It's a sensory apparatus in the snake, and I think this is a testing of the winds by the character." Later episodes of **Boston Legal** suggested a more prosaic explanation: mad cow disease.

Whatever the source of his weird behavior, Denny Crane touched a chord with TV viewers—not to mention Emmy voters, who awarded Shatner the coveted statuette for playing the character in 2004 and 2005. The actor's lusty, winking portrayal propelled him back, if not to the A-list, at least to the high B-list among **television** performers. Gone were the dark days of constantly pimping his Captain Kirk persona for periodic guest spots on **3rd Rock from the Sun** and movies like **Lil' Pimp**. Shatner ran with the big dogs once again. He could have been speaking about his own career when he observed, in response to an interviewer's question about the secret of Denny Crane's appeal: "Whatever forces have [made him] a loon, somewhere in that person there's humanity. And that humanity commands respect and that's what I'm going for all the time in these loony moments that this character has."

CRASH OF FLIGHT 401, THE   ✳ ✳

This made-for-television airline disaster movie features actors Shatner, Adrienne Barbeau, Sharon Gless, and jazz bandleader Artie Shaw. Released to video as *Crash*, the 1978 quickie is based on the real-life crash of a jet plane in the Florida Everglades in December 1972. Shatner stars and narrates as Carl Tobias, an FAA investigator sent to look into the disaster. This was the second of two 1978 TV movies based on the same incident. Ernest Borgnine starred in the other, *The Ghost of Flight 401*. Just to confuse things further, Shatner and Borgnine had previously locked horns in the 1975 satanic cult theatrical feature *The Devil's Rain*.

CROSS COUNTRY JOURNEY

Together with a friend from **McGill University**, Shatner hitchhiked across the United States and **Canada** in 1951 when he was twenty years old. The pair left Toronto with only $200 between them and a sign that read "Two McGill Students Seeing America." They proceeded down the Eastern Seaboard to Washington, D.C. From there, it was due west to Los Angeles, north to Vancouver, and back east to Chicago. The trip ended back in Shatner's native Montreal.

DEAD MAN'S ISLAND   ✳ ✳

This 1996 TV movie stars Shatner, Christopher Atkins, and a diverse trio of blondes: Barbara Eden, Morgan Fairchild, and former porn queen Traci Lords. Shatner wanders listlessly through the proceedings as Chase Prescott, a wealthy businessman who journeys to a remote Pacific island retreat to find out which one of nine guests staying in his mansion is trying to kill him.

Ask Shat

Q: What's your favorite cocktail?

A: I really don't have a favorite cocktail. I'm fascinated by good wines, particularly a deep red.

"CRASH" OF THE TITANS

OK, it's four in the morning and you can't sleep. You flip on the TV and find out that *The Ghost of Flight 401* and **The Crash of Flight 401** are playing on different channels. Which one would you watch? Think carefully. Each has an all-star cast. Here are your starting lineups:

THE GHOST OF FLIGHT 401
Ernest Borgnine ("Marty")
Kim Basinger (Alec Baldwin's real-life ex-wife)
Howard Hesseman ("Dr. Johnny Fever" on *WKRP in Cincinnati*)
Russell Johnson (*Gilligan's Island* Professor)
Meeno Peluce (Soleil Moon-Frye's brother)

THE CRASH OF FLIGHT 401
William Shatner ("Toughy")
Adrienne Barbeau (*Maude*'s TV daughter)
Ron Glass ("Det. Ron Harris" on *Barney Miller*)
Sharon Gless (Lacey's partner in *Cagney & Lacey*)
Artie Shaw (famous bandleader)

DEFENDERS, THE ✳ ✳

Ralph Bellamy and Shatner play a father-son legal team in this

Years before Denny Crane, Shatner played a different kind of legal eagle in the 1957 TV drama *The Defenders.*

1957 *Studio One* drama. E. G. Marshall and future *Brady Bunch* paterfamilias Robert Reed took over the roles when the concept was adapted as an hour-long series by CBS in 1961. In 2007, footage from the original, Shatnerific *Defenders* was incorporated into a **Denny Crane** flashback sequence on ***Boston Legal***.

DENTISTRY

Rumors have abounded for years that Shatner has a background in dentistry. The probable source of the confusion is *New York* magazine movie critic David Denby, who inexplicably began referring to Shatner as a dentist in his film reviews. For example, in his critique of ***Star Trek V: The Final Frontier***, Denby wrote: "William Shatner, that muscular dentist who unaccountably wandered into acting, has now wandered into directing." Shatner has never studied dentistry. He has a business degree from **McGill University** in Montreal.

DEVIL'S RAIN, THE   ✳

This grisly 1975 horror movie combines the mismatched talents of
Shatner, Eddie Albert, Tom Skerritt, and Ernest Borgnine. Shatner
has a juicy **dual role**. As Martin Fife, a pony-tailed Puritan Satanist,
he is burned at the stake in the seventeenth century. As Mark
Preston, Fife's modern-day descendant, he is tortured and killed by
a cadre of devil worshippers—including a very young John Travolta.
Borgnine is the vindictive Corbis, the leader of the ritualistic cult
who crucifies Shatner, removes his eyes, and makes him atone
mightily for betraying the group in his past life. Keenan Wynn and
Ida Lupino are among the other victims. "Satanic effects are piled
on at every possible juncture," opined *Variety*, "with gore virtually
used to plaster over every gaping loophole." Anton Lavey, a real-life

Satan's minions render judgment on an unrepentant Shatner in 1975's *The Devil's Rain*.

devil worshiper, served as the technical advisor. This celluloid burnt offering was shot on location in Mexico.

"Blasphemer! Blasphemer!"

—the single line uttered by John Travolta as Danny the Satan Worshiper in The Devil's Rain

DIRECTING

"Directing has been a lifelong dream," Shatner once admitted. "My business is to entertain people, and to communicate my feelings to them, so I find the best way is to direct. Directing is the pinnacle of our business. . . . I'm under the impression that I can gather all my skills around me to make people laugh and cry."

Actor **Nichelle Nichols** saw a less altruistic motive behind Shatner's passion for directing. "Bill needs to control the action and be the center of attention," his *Star Trek* costar once observed. In fact, it was Shatner's pronounced tendency to direct even while **acting** that irked his fellow crew members the most on the *Star Trek* set. Nonetheless, for whatever reason, Shatner has not pursued directing as aggressively as he has his acting career. His directorial efforts comprise a handful of **stage** and **television** credits and only two feature films to date: 1989's execrable *Star Trek V* and the 2002 cheapie *Groom Lake*.

The creative failure of *Star Trek V* has often been laid at the feet of Shatner the director. However, as **Leonard Nimoy** has noted, the film's problems went way beyond the man behind the lens. "He was riding a bad script," Nimoy observed, "and as I've said at other times and places, when you're riding a bad script, there's not much that can be done to salvage a film." In fact, while they went into the project expecting the worst, Shatner's *Star Trek* costars emerged with nothing but praise for his directorial style. "Bill turned out to be among the finest, most respectful directors I've ever worked with," **Nichelle Nichols** concluded, to her own astonishment.

DISASTER ON THE COASTLINER ✳ ✳

Shatner plays a con artist on board a runaway passenger train in this 1979 TV movie. Old Hollywood heavyweights Lloyd Bridges and Raymond Burr also star, with E. G. Marshall and the curvaceous Yvette Mimieux in support. As Stuart Peters, Shatner places his own life on the line to save his fellow passengers after a deranged engineer sets two trains on a collision course. Reportedly, he performed some of his own stunts.

SIX DEGREES OF *STAR TREK*

Michael Pataki ("Tate" in *Disaster on the Coastliner*) played Korax the Klingon on the second season episode "The Trouble with Tribbles."

DOBERMANS

Shatner is a dedicated breeder of Doberman pinschers, those fiercely loyal short-haired dogs of German origin. He began acquiring the daunting canines soon after achieving his first success as an actor in the 1950s. "The first thing I did when I got married was I bought a dog," Shatner told biographers in the late 1970s. As a child, he had always wanted one, but for a long time his parents resisted. "They'd say, 'You can have a hobby horse, but you can't have a dog!'" Shatner once recalled. "I did have dogs as I got older but never for any length of time . . . [and] not the kind of dog and the way I wanted a dog in some inchoate way."

One anecdote from Shatner's days on **Star Trek** illustrates the special place his Dobermans have in his daily life. Paramount's

Business Affairs office became concerned after Shatner submitted an expense account containing a $15 bill for breakfast. Producer Fred Freiberger was dispatched to confront his star with the then-exorbitant meal charge. Shatner calmly listed the items in his breakfast, which totaled $7.50. When Freiberger reminded him he had billed Paramount for twice that amount, Shatner was nonplussed.

"Right. $7.50 for me and $7.50 for my dog. My dog and I always breakfast together and we usually order the same things." For the record, Freiberger approved the expense.

THE SHATMINSTER DOG SHOW

Shatner has had a number of beloved **Dobermans** over the years. A round-up of some of the more notable:

DUNHILL One of Shatner's early favorites, Dunhill would accompany him and his first wife to expensive restaurants. Shatner even made sure the pooch was provided with his own place at the table.

STIRLING A strapping male **Doberman**, Stirling once devoured a twenty-pound Thanksgiving turkey; Shatner was forced to serve cheese and crackers to his bewildered dinner guests.

KIRK In the 1970s, Shatner named one manly dog after his most famous character.

CHINA The so-called "Beauty Girl," this bitch loved to lie in the shade and was a special favorite of her master. Shatner had China interred alongside other celebrity canines at the **Los Angeles Pet Memorial Park** following her demise in 1988.

DODGEBALL: A TRUE UNDERDOG STORY

Shatner has a cameo role as the Dodgeball Chancellor in this 2004 comedy starring **Ben Stiller** and Vince Vaughn as rival gym owners vying for a $50,000 prize. Shatner previously met Stiller on the set of *The Barbary Coast* in 1975.

DOOHAN, JAMES

This burly character actor played Chief Engineer Montgomery Scott on *Star Trek*. A native of Vancouver, British Columbia, **Canada**, Doohan was a master of dialects who worked steadily in **television** throughout the 1950s and 1960s. His facility with a Scottish accent impressed **Gene Roddenberry**, who created the role of Scotty to accommodate Doohan's vocal talents. Always a **fan** favorite, the genial Canuck was long considered one of the most accessible stars in the *Star Trek* universe.

Doohan was also one of Shatner's harshest and most outspoken critics. In fact, he was the only member of the original *Star Trek* cast to refuse to be interviewed by Shatner for Shatner's 1993 memoir, *Star Trek Memories*. The long-brewing antipathy came as a shock to Shatner, who for decades had remained blithely unaware of Doohan's dislike for him.

What caused the rift? Doohan may have resented Shatner's oft-stated claim that he was the one who kick-started Doohan's TV career. "I believe I was instrumental in getting him his job [on *Star Trek*]," Shatner told biographers in 1979. "I can't remember exactly whether I first suggested his name or they mentioned it to me and asked me if I knew him. But I knew him as a fine actor from Toronto and I had worked with him. I recommended him!" According to various reports, the two men reconciled shortly before Doohan's death from pneumonia and Alzheimer's disease in 2005.

> "Jimmy went around and said nasty things about me, but I know he didn't mean it. I have no idea why he said those mean things. Do you?"
>
> *—Shatner, to **Leonard Nimoy**, at a 2006 convention appearance*

SCOTTY POPS OFF

Here are just a few of the verbal grenades that **Jimmy Doohan** lobbed at his longtime nemesis, William Shatner:

"Bill has a big, fat head. To me, Bill is selling Paramount a bill of goods which is rotten. I don't know why. He's got power somewhere. He shouldn't have it."

"There is really only one person on the show that nobody can stand. . . . He can't even act. He doesn't act: he makes faces. He'll wrinkle his nose like a rabbit and that's supposed to mean, 'Oh look, I'm about to cry.'"

"Bill doesn't like anyone to do good acting around him."

DR. KILDARE

Shatner turned down the title role in this hour-long medical drama, which ran on NBC from 1961 to 1966. Stolid actor Richard Chamberlain instead won the plum role of Dr. James Kildare, an intern at metropolitan Blair Hospital who turns for counsel and advice to the more experienced Dr. Leonard Gillespie (Canadian native Raymond Massey). The series helped make Chamberlain a star, while Shatner had to wait in the wings until 1965 for his next crack at a network series lead. Ironically, Shatner agreed to six guest appearances on *Dr. Kildare* over the course of its five-year run, often playing a physician.

DUAL ROLES

Shatner has always relished playing dual roles and bringing split personalities to life. "It gives the viewers twice as much of me!" he once gleefully observed. More often than not, the two sides of Shatner's character war with one another, providing dramatic conflict, as in the otherwise forgettable feature **White Comanche**, in which he plays feuding Indian twins.

Some of Shatner's most memorable dual performances occurred in **Star Trek** episodes. In "What Are Little Girls Made Of?" a deranged scientist bent on populating the **universe** with androids creates a perfect duplicate of Captain Kirk. The lookalikes have a very civilized dinner conversation thanks to a surprisingly well-executed split-screen effect.

In "The Enemy Within," a transporter malfunction splits Kirk into two physically identical individuals. In one scene, Shatner must play both halves of Kirk as they fight for control of his personality. Finally, in "Turnabout Intruder," the last episode of the original series, Shatner takes on the ultimate **acting** challenge, playing a woman inhabiting Kirk's body for the purpose of taking over starship *Enterprise*. Shatner's decision to play "female" Kirk as an indecisive, nailbiting hysteric comes off as sexist today, but critics at the time gave him credit for his versatility.

EGGPLANT PARMIGIANA

Traditional Italian-American dish Shatner cites as "my favorite" in the 1982 "meat is murder" documentary, **The Vegetarian World**.

EGO

Shatner has long had to deal with accusations from the media and the public that he is a rampant egomaniac. Many of these charges originated with his fellow **Star Trek** cast members. "Bill's the epitome of the star in many negative ways," **Walter Koenig** once remarked. "He's totally preoccupied with himself and his career and his work on the show." Shatner's personal pest, **James Doohan**, repeatedly made reference to the actor's "big, fat head." But, as exemplified by his **toupee**, Shatner exists in a state of deep denial about the widespread perception that he is full of himself. "I don't understand that," he once told an interviewer. "I'm not even aware of it, quite frankly."

> "I don't know what ego means. It takes a certain amount of chutzpah to think that writing something on paper will interest you or standing in front of a camera will entertain you, so if that's ego, I have one."
>
> *—Shatner, in a 1995 online forum, responding to a fan who accused him of having "an ego bigger than Texas."*

ELLISON, HARLAN

This diminutive science fiction writer, essayist, and self-promoting crank has feuded with Shatner for decades. In 1966, Ellison penned the classic **Star Trek** episode "The City on the Edge of Forever," accepted numerous awards for it, then spent the ensuing thirty years complaining about the changes that were made to his original script. This ridiculous controversy culminated in the 1996 vanity publication Harlan Ellison's *The City on the Edge of Forever*, which reprinted several drafts of the **Star Trek** teleplay—for anyone who still cared— and had room left over for a characteristically windy forty-six-page

Ellison essay on the topic. In it, Ellison relates his version of a story about Shatner visiting his Hollywood home and reading the "City" script in 1966. Accusations of Shatner's **line counting** are the least of Ellison's insinuations. Not surprisingly, Shatner gives a markedly different account of their meeting in his 1993 memoir *Star Trek Memories*.

What may have started as the clash of two colossal egos has become exacerbated by Ellison's gleeful willingness to savage Shatner in print. Evaluating Shatner's performance in *Star Trek: The Motion Picture*, Ellison pulled out all the stops, accusing the actor of being "stuffy when he isn't being arch and coy; hamming and mugging when he isn't being lachrymose; playing Kirk as if he actually thinks he is Kirk, overbearing and pompous." While it's hard to challenge that assessment on its merits, one can't be surprised by Shatner's wounded reaction. "Harlan Ellison is a surly young man," he said, "who has spent years saying awful things about me, while I find him admirable. In fact, 'City on the Edge of Forever' is my favorite of the original Star Trek series because of the fact that it is a beautiful love story, well told."

> "I don't agree with his adjectives. They're a little strong, but then, so is Harlan Ellison. He's little and he's strong."
>
> —Shatner, responding to criticism leveled by his pint-sized nemesis, Harlan Ellison

EXPLOSIVE GENERATION, THE ✳ ✳ ✳

This woefully low-budget 1961 movie stars Shatner as a high school teacher who is suspended for teaching his students about **sex** education. As progressive educator Peter Gifford, Shatner draws the ire of the conservative PTA when he assigns his class an unusual paper topic: their **sex** lives. The students protest his suspension. The all-weird cast includes Ed Platt (the Chief on *Get Smart*), Stafford Repp (Chief O'Hara on *Batman*), and a young Beau Bridges. Frequent *Gilligan's Island* player Vito Scotti has a small role as a janitor. Commented *Variety*: "Canadian actor William Shatner . . . has a

Young Shatner shows his hat to *Get Smart's* Chief,
Ed Platt, in 1961's *The Explosive Generation.*

pleasant screen personality and brings a moving power of oratory to his speech about students protesting all over the world." The actor returned to the "ripped from the headlines" theme the next year with the racial-strife drama ***The Intruder***.

FAMILY OF STRANGERS, A ★★

Shatner plays the adoptive father of a young woman facing life-threatening brain surgery in this lachrymose 1993 TV movie. When his on-screen daughter Melissa Gilbert demands her medical history, a dithering Shatner is forced to admit he is not her biological papa. The well-intentioned weepfest was based on Jerry Hulse's 1976 novel *Jody*.

FANS

Shatner has long had a love-hate relationship with his fans, that vast army of Spock-eared souls who people the science fiction conventions of this land. "It's a fandom I don't know who else has," the actor once observed. While the names **Leonard Nimoy**, **DeForest Kelley**, **George Takei**, **Nichelle Nichols**, **Walter Koenig**, and **James Doohan** immediately spring to mind, Shatner is right that there is a special regard reserved for the once-and-future Captain **James T. Kirk**. "I may be becoming an institution without my even knowing it," he once mused. "There's a touching quality. There's something touching about the way people look to me."

Shatner has not always found public adulation so poignant. "Those fans are like greyhounds racing to see who can get the rabbit," he reportedly groused of his followers in the late 1960s. "They only want to touch you or maybe get a souvenir, but if it gets out of control and reaches a flash point—well! They start pushing and grabbing, and then it becomes hysteria." Asked by *Playboy* in 1989 to provide the "early warning sign of a Trekkie," Shatner replied: "It's the wild-eyed look, the hands lifted above the ears and the shambling walk that breaks into a run as they approach me."

Shatner exacted the ultimate revenge on his fans with a December 1986 appearance on **Saturday Night Live**. The guest-hosting gig drew the ire of **Star Trek** followers for a brief sketch in which Shatner poked fun at Trekkies, who seem to have no life outside the world of fandom.

FAST CARS AND SUPERSTARS ✳ ✳ ✳

Shatner indulged his "need for speed" on this **auto racing** reality show, which aired for six nights in June 2007. The former *Enterprise* captain was one of twelve celebrities (if rodeo champion Ty Murray and former Pittsburgh Steelers coach Bill Cowher truly merit that appellation) taking to the track at Lowe's Motor Speedway in North Carolina for a stock car race. Shatner competed in a heat against Cowher and volleyball champion Garbrielle Reece, but he did little to burnish his NASCAR legend. Employing a Taoist abdominal breathing technique designed to release his chi, or spiritual energy, Shatner hooted like an owl on his trip around the oval at 160 miles per hour. He achieved a time sufficient to move on to the next round, but was disqualified for broaching the track's white line on three separate occasions.

> "I saw moisture on my bottom lip and a variety of bodily changes. I had more hair on my hands. It was miraculous."
>
> —*Shatner, on the transformation he experienced on the NASCAR oval while filming* Fast Cars and Superstars

FAVORED NATIONS CLAUSE

During the production of **Star Trek**, a clause was added to the contracts of Shatner and Leonard Nimoy that mandated to each actor the same salary and benefits won by the other. Shatner used the favored nations clause in his pact to secure the directorial reins on 1989's **Star Trek V: The Final Frontier**. (Nimoy had already directed installments *III* and *IV*.)

FIGHTS

As a child, Shatner got into his share of scraps with other young-sters. "I recall them as always being one-sided," he later recalled. "I remember the fights used to be where two or three kids would jump me and I'd be fighting them off and a group would gather around and be chanting, you know 'fight, fight, get him, get him' against me, for the attackers. But I also have a recollection of being rather good, and not really ever getting badly beaten up and doing more harm than getting harmed. In fact, there came a time when they stopped jumping me, because it was a problem for them." Young Shatner earned the nickname "**Toughy**" for his willingness to duke it out despite the odds.

For all his macho bluster, Shatner claims he hasn't been involved in a fight since childhood. "The only way I could possibly get into a fight would be in my self-defense or self-defense [sic] of somebody I love," he has said. Nevertheless, he has come close to blows on a number of occasions. During his years on *Star Trek* he was constantly confronted by tough guys who wanted a piece of TV's famous Captain Kirk. Invariably these encounters occurred in bars. Luckily, one of Shatner's drinking buddies, *Star Trek* bit player David L. Ross, was a former marine. He stepped in several times to help defuse a potentially ugly situation.

It is when Shatner is left alone without adult supervision that he gets into the most trouble. One such incident occurred during a theatrical production early in his **acting** career. A scene called for one of his supporting players to appear drunk. Some time after the opening night, the actor began to hit Shatner on the shoulder dur-ing the scene—although this action wasn't called for in the play. Eventually, these blows became painful, and Shatner asked the man to stop. When the actor refused, Shatner complained to the director, then the producer, even to Actors Equity, but no one was able to help. Finally, Shatner took matters into his own hands. One night, during the scene, after the man had clobbered him yet again, Shatner struck back, sending his fellow thespian reeling to the **stage**. When the curtain came down at the end of the first act, the actor attacked Shatner, cuffing an elderly prop man in the head before the other performers broke up the scuffle. The next day, the enraged actor continued his assault in Shatner's dressing room before the performance.

Shatner picks up the story from there: "Suddenly the veneer of civilization left me, and I saw in my mind's eye—me, going toward him like an animal—like a cat, really, my thumbs toward his eyes, and my teeth towards his jugular . . . I was an animal, and I was going to kill him. And when I look back on it, I could have killed him, if I had done what I had envisioned in that split second of seeing what I was going to do." Luckily for Shatner, and the man's family, the producer was able to separate the two. But the experience was revelatory for Shatner. "I realized there that I could have killed somebody," he explained. "It is within me to kill somebody, and by that primitive means of biting through the jugular vein."

Shatner's bloodlust cooled somewhat by the late 1960s, when he had his next close call. The setting was a miniature racecar track where he had gone with his children. As he told *TV Guide* in December of 1989: "Some eighteen-year-olds, verging on being hoodlums, kept banging into us [in our mini racecar] and I was trying to avoid them. Finally, everybody stopped and one of those young punks came at me and I was so angry, I picked him up, held him above my head and flung him to the ground. Then his friends came at me and I realized that there was a line between fiction and nonfiction that I had crossed and that when four muscular young kids come at you, you're gonna have the crap beat out of you. So I said, 'Please don't hit me.' I was so embarrassed. I'd wanted to act brave in front of my kids." There ensued an **ass kicking** to rival the one Shatner received from a Canadian farmer during his days at summer **camp**. "All three came at me and began to pound on me. Blood was spurting all over. One of them kept yelling: 'Don't get your blood all over me!' Captain Kirk was all over the floor."

Why is this self-professed alpha male so reluctant to throw down? According to Shatner, it boils down to economics. An actor simply cannot afford the consequences of disfigurement. "A broken face, a broken hand, a toe, a scratch—I mean, I can't deal with those things. Do you know, if I get a scratch on my face, the way I work I'd be out for what? Three, four weeks. A broken nose? Forget it. Six months. . . . All you need is one karate blow to the neck and it's all over. . . . A kick in the balls? I mean, you could die. And I as an actor can't afford to be put out of business that way."

FIRST LOVE

Shatner's first love was a college sweetheart whose name he has never revealed. They dated all through their years at **McGill University**, where Shatner was studying business. However, when he expressed his desire to become an actor, the girl—whom Shatner describes as "much more practical than I"—decided to marry a businessman and move to New York.

FLYING

"Flying is the skill of the twenty-first century," Shatner once opined. "Driving and sailboating, of the twentieth." Indeed, long before the calendar read "Y2K," flyboy Shatner was declaring himself master of skies and issuing pronouncements like "When in the air, I feel that the plane and I are one."

Shatner first learned to fly in the 1960s, the apex of his daredevil period. He reportedly flew solo in a Cessna 150 after only eight hours of training. The experience terrified him, but managed to arouse his macho sense of adventure. "I had to fight fear, but I conquered it," Shatner boasted. "Every aviator has to do that, especially while practicing stalls." Shatner likened the experience to his first attempt to ride a horse, when he "was dreadfully afraid that I'd fall off and that the animal would fall on me."

FOLDS, BEN

This North Carolina–born pianist, singer, and songwriter emerged as Shatner's principal musical coconspirator in the run-up to **Has Been**, the actor's 2004 "comeback album." Best known as the front man of Ben Folds Five, crafters of such tuneful mid-90s pop hits as "Brick" and "Kate," Folds has long been a **fan** of Shatner's groundbreaking 1968 LP **The Transformed Man**. Enthralled at the prospect of working with one of his idols, he wrote Shatner out of the blue, proposing that the two work on a song together. Shatner has admitted to having no idea who Folds was, considering him too "avant garde." But an enthusiastic endorsement from Shatner's children persuaded him to give the Tar Heel piano man a try. Their first studio collaboration resulted in the song "In Love," which appeared on the debut album by Folds's experimental side band Fear of Pop. On January 22, 1999, Shatner joined the band on *Late Night with Conan O'Brien* for its first and only **live television** appearance. **Has Been** followed in 2004 (see that entry for more details). In 2006, Shatner and Folds joined forces yet again on a remake of Folds's 2001 hit "Rockin' the Suburbs" for the **Over the Hedge** movie soundtrack. On the track, Shatner assumes the role of a furious bourgeois homeowner ranting at a neighbor for not picking his newspapers up off the driveway.

FOR THE PEOPLE

This hour-long crime drama, Shatner's first television series, ran for thirteen weeks on CBS from January 31 to May 9, 1965. Shatner played David Koster, a headstrong New York City assistant district attorney who was always butting heads with his superiors. "I like to stamp on any toes that get in my way," Shatner told the *New York Post*, speaking in the Koster persona; "I do a regular Spanish Flamenco heel dance on the toes of anybody who crosses my way." Shatner/Koster's dance partners on the short-lived show included Howard Da Silva as his boss and Jessica Walter as his wife. Shatner had high hopes for this show. "If I'm successful, the series will be," he predicted. "But there's something more immediate about it. The people I'm working with, feel fondly toward, will be employed if it is. . . . I hope any optimism they may have felt will be justified." Sadly, it was not. *For the People* earned plaudits from critics but had the misfortune of sharing a time slot with the NBC hit *Bonanza*. The audience's verdict was cancellation.

FOUNDATION: THE PSYCHOHISTORIANS ✶ ✶ ✶

In 1976, Shatner was nominated for a Grammy Award for his reading of Isaac Asimov's classic science fiction novel *Foundation* for Caedmon Records. Set in deep space thousands of years in the **future**, in the closing centuries of a vast Galactic Empire modeled on the Roman Empire, *Foundation* and its companion novels chronicle the evolution of a colony full of brilliant humanoids over several hundred years of psychohistory.

FREE ENTERPRISE   ✶ ✶ ✶

A rapping Shatner drops some science on a pair of **Star Trek**–obsessed filmmakers in this 1998 comedy, which has attained minor cult status in the years since its unheralded original release. Loosely based on the real-life experiences of cocreators Mark A. Altman and Robert Meyer Burnett, *Free Enterprise* casts Shatner as an amped-up, buffoonish version of himself. A chance encounter with two Hollywood wannabes—played by Eric McCormack and Rafer Wiegel—inspires him to pursue his dream of producing a one-man musical version of Shakespeare's *Julius Caesar*. The wry film is most notable for its spirited finale, in which Shatner recites Mark Antony's funeral oration to a hip hop beat. Oddly enough, Altman and Burnett actually wrote the script without first getting Shatner to commit to the project. He turned down the part four times before accepting—only after changes were made to make his character less godlike. "I had played my (Kirk) persona as far as I wanted to go and probably as far as anybody wants me to go," Shatner told *USA Today* in 2006 "What they had written had me as a guru who dispensed advice, and I kept turning this down." The changes won him over. He was so stoked by the finished project that he suggested an idea for a sequel.

FRESH PRINCE OF BEL-AIR   ✶ ✶

"Throw your hands in the air if you's a true player!" An overdose of laughing gas turns Shatner into a rapping fool in "Eye, Tooth," a May 1996 episode of this fish-out-of-water sitcom starring Will Smith. The hilarity ensues after Will accidentally chips Shatner's tooth with a pool cue shortly before he is scheduled to appear on Will's cousin Hillary's TV talk show. A visit to the dentist and an exposed valve of nitrous oxide create comic mayhem. Gags involve Shatner mistaking various characters for members of the *Enterprise* crew. Someone should have informed the writers that laughing gas is not a hallucinogen. Shatner's appearance was timed to coincide with the publication of his novel *Man o' War*, which is plugged on the show.

"Scotty! You're black!"

—*Shatner, during an embarrassing guest spot on* Fresh Prince of Bel-Air

FRIEDRICK, EVA MARIE

This personal assistant filed a $2 million **palimony** suit against Shatner in 1989. The former model joined Shatner's staff in 1986, ironically on the recommendation of his then-wife **Marcy Lafferty**. The two became lovers, but reportedly the relationship soured after Friedrick was injured in a car accident in October 1988. According to some sources, Shatner had all her possessions removed from his trailer and placed on the roof for her to retrieve.

FRUIT SALAD

Shatner detests fruit salad; he has disliked it since his "starvation years" as a young actor in Ontario, **Canada**. In those days, when he was earning a scant $31 a week at the **Canadian National Repertory Theatre** in Ottawa (and spending most of that on rent), Shatner would eat the twenty-seven-cent fruit salad at Woolworth's as often as he could, sometimes twice a day.

FUTURAMA   ✳ ✳ ✳

Shatner raps Eminem's 2000 hit "The Real Slim Shady" on an April 2002 episode of Matt Groening's animated sci-fi comedy series. **Star Trek** alumni **Leonard Nimoy**, **George Takei**, **Walter Koenig**, and **Nichelle Nichols** also provide voice-overs for the episode, entitled "Where No Fan Has Gone Before," which involves an attempt to rescue the remnants of the original **Star Trek** cast from an eternity of servitude to an alien Trekkie on a barren and forbidden world. **James Doohan** and **DeForest Kelley** were too sick and too dead, respectively, to take part in the episode, which contains a font of spot-on **Star Trek** references for the savvy **fan**.

An animated Captain Kirk dukes it out with the
redoubtable Turanga Leela on *Futurama*.

FUTURE

A self-proclaimed futurist, Shatner has embraced an increasingly
pessimistic view of humankind's ultimate prospects. This shift is
reflected in his ***TekWar*** book and **television** series, which depict a
future where powerful cartels use advanced technology to control
society. "The world hasn't really changed," Shatner mused in 1996.
"We're more likely to destroy ourselves than we ever were. We're a
technological world, and we're blind to the terrible toll that technology is exacting all around us." Shatner has even proposed modify-
ing the mission statement he once promulgated on ***Star Trek*** in the
1960s: "To cautiously go where everyone has gone before."

Ask Shat

Q: What was it like wearing panty hose during the filming of *Star Trek: Generations*?

A: It's a rather pleasant feeling, akin to scratching yourself all the time.

WILLIAM SHATNER, PROPHET OR BLOWHARD?

Soothsaying is hardly an exact science. Even the most prescient
seer is just blowing smoke (or merely guessing) 99 percent of the
time. William Shatner is no exception. He has used his access to
the media to issue periodic forecasts on the state of humankind
and technology. Here are a few of his bolder prognostications,
with date of utterance:

"We are headed for a computerized and automated civilization."
(1967)

"By the year 2540, we'll have a device that will disintegrate
the atoms of a human being. These atoms will be sprayed
through millions or billions of miles to some planet and then
reassembled, just the way our TV signals are today." (1967)

"Human beings always act as they have. That hasn't changed
since Shakespeare's day, so certainly it won't have changed by
the 23rd Century." (1989)

"All matter is part of Mother Earth and we have to start clean-
ing our act up immediately or we're all going to die." (1990)

"There is every reason to believe we will be in a catastrophic situation [fifty years from now]. Our population will increase by billions—to the point where the planet can't take the load. We can only hope that mankind will steer a different course than we are now." (1994)

"In defiling our planet, we have given ourselves a life term, and the electric chair is slowly coming our way. . . . It won't happen suddenly; we're all going to expire in a rather ugly way unless we do something about it." (1994)

"All of us will find ourselves pushed out of our comfort zones more often as time goes on. If you think you don't like change, you'll like irrelevance even less." (2007)

GALAXY QUEST

Home Improvement star Tim Allen took time off from grunting like an ape to perform a spot-on Shatner send-up in this 1999 comedy feature, which has attained minor cult status—especially in the ***Star Trek*** fan community. As Jason Nesmith, an egomaniacal actor who plays brash, two-fisted spaceship commander Peter Quincy Taggart on a fictional sci-fi **television** series, Allen gets to spoof both Shatner the man and his most famous TV alter **ego**, Captain Kirk. While Nesmith exhorts **fans** to "get a life" and treats his costars with imperious, diva-like hauteur, Taggart gets to vanquish **aliens** in hand-to-hand combat and take his shirt off with alarming frequency. The other cast members are all rough analogs of the original series ***Star Trek*** crew as well.

Asked for his take on the film, Shatner mockingly professed bewilderment at Allen's performance. "I thought it was very funny, and I thought the audience that they portrayed was totally real, but the actors that they were pretending to be were totally unrecognizable. Certainly I don't know what Tim Allen was doing. He seemed to be the head of a group of actors and for the life of me I was trying to understand who he was imitating."

GAME SHOWS

Shatner cut a bloody swath through the TV game show circuit in the mid-1970s. In fact, game show appearances provided one of his only steady sources of income during his **lost years**. From 1975, when he first appeared on *Masquerade Party* with Richard Dawson, to the career revival sparked by the 1979 release of **Star Trek: The Motion Picture**, Shatner made the rounds on *Don Adams' Screen Test*, *Rhyme and Reason*, *Celebrity Sweepstakes*, *Tattletales*, *Liars Club*, *Match Game*, *Celebrity Bowling*, *To Tell the Truth*, and *Cross Wits*. He seemed to get special pleasure from appearing on **$20,000 Pyramid**, the site of his infamous chair-throwing freakout in 1977.

By the 1980s, Shatner's star had once again grown too large for daytime game shows. He preferred to confine his appearances to prime-time athletic competitions like *Battle of the Network Stars*, *Celebrity Challenge of the Sexes*, and *Circus of the Stars* (for which he gave a martial arts demonstration). By the 1990s, he was through with these kinds of exhibitions entirely. The next time he appeared on a game show, it was as the host of ABC's short-lived **Show Me the Money** in 2006.

GIRDLE

See **Weight**.

GO ASK ALICE　✴ ✴

This 1973 TV movie aired a scant eleven days after Shatner's previous telefilm, **Incident on a Dark Street**. In this one he dons a false moustache and glasses to play the father of a teenage girl who gets hooked on hard drugs and suffers a bad LSD trip. Based on the real-life diary of a teenager, the film also stars Jamie Smith-Jackson, Ruth Roman, and Andy Griffith. Shatner and Griffith reunited the following year in **Pray for the Wildcats**. Shatner went on to play a similar "concerned dad" role in the 1988 telefilm *Broken Angel*.

GOD

Shatner has long harbored a profound metaphysical streak. He has tried to bring these concerns to bear in his work, from early films like **Incubus**, in which evil forces tempt a saintly man, to the quest for God that serves as the centerpiece of 1989's **Star Trek V: The Final Frontier**. Even Shatner's 1968 LP **The Transformed Man** addresses the ultimate questions of human existence. Its title track, with words by Frank Devonport, concerns a man who breaks free from the mundane concerns of everyday life in hopes of reaching "the eternal now." After much struggle, in which he must wait "for the hand of faith to lift the darkness," his vision is cleared and he is able to attain his goal. Or, as Shatner powerfully bellows to the accompaniment of strings and a soaring choir, "I had touched the face of God!"

> "I'm a Jew. But I do not believe in your God. . . . I do know that we are all afraid of dying . . . we are all afraid of loneliness. Those are universal truths. Are you scared? I'm scared. . . . I love you. . . . I need you."
>
> —Shatner, to the National Conference of Christians and Jews convention in 1968

GOLDEN BOY

This 1937 play by Clifford Odets was a favorite of the teenaged

Shatner. The drama concerns a moody Italian-American youth who longs to be a violinist, but instead settles for a more lucrative career as a prizefighter. Shatner has said that he empathized with the young man's dilemma, having had to choose between football and **acting** at **West Hill High School**. In fact, he has described filing past his jock buddies on the way to a play rehearsal as "tantamount to carrying your violin case while passing the school. Because the jocks at high school would say: 'Whaddya mean going to a play? What are you, weird or something?'"

GOULART, RON

This venerable science fiction and mystery writer served as a "consultant" to Shatner on his *Tek* book series. The prolific Goulart is the author of more than sixty novels of his own, including *After Things Fell Apart* (1970), *Even the Butler Was Poor* (1990), and *Now He Thinks He's Dead* (1992). But he eschews the term "ghostwriter" when discussing his role on the *Tek* project. "I'm just an adviser," he told *Entertainment Weekly*. "I just give Shatner my opinion from time to time. I help with timing and tone and other technical things." "Goulart doesn't actually edit me," Shatner contends, dismissing the consensus opinion of the science fiction community that their relationship is akin to that of a ventriloquist and his dummy. "He just sort of suggests things and does some rewriting. He's a great help, and I've tried to give him as much credit as possible—short of putting his name on the covers."

"Whatever Bill told you, I'll go along with that."

—*Ron Goulart, when asked to define his role as a consultant on Shatner's* Tek *novels*

GRITZ, BO

This colorful soldier of fortune, the reputed real-life model for Sylvester Stallone's Rambo character, received $10,000 from Shatner in the early 1980s as part of a development deal with Paramount Pictures. According to published sources, Gritz may have used this money to finance an illegal mission to rescue American POWs trapped in Laos.

See **Operation Lazarus**.

GROOM LAKE ✳

This 2002 UFO thriller marked Shatner's first turn in the director's chair on a feature film since ***Star Trek V*** in 1989. A low-budget effort released under schlockmeister extraordinaire Charles Band's Full Moon Video banner, the film mixes elements of *E.T.*, *Hangar 18*, and *Close Encounters of the Third Kind* to no discernible effect. Double threat Shatner steps in front of the camera as John Gossner, a project manager at a top-secret government UFO facility who works feverishly to get a stranded space alien back to his home planet. The words "Dick Van Patten also stars" should tell you all you need to know about the advisability of renting this cheaply made shocker, which makes ***Star Trek V*** look like *2001* by comparison.

GUTHRIE, TYRONE

This renowned English theatrical director founded the **Stratford Shakespeare Festival** in Ontario, **Canada,** and subsequently took Shatner under his wing. According to Shatner, Guthrie told him he "would be a great actor in the tradition of [Sir Laurence] Olivier." In 1956, Shatner was awarded the Tyrone Guthrie Award as the Festival's most promising actor. He used the $750 prize to pay for his move to New York, where he embarked on a career in **theater** and **television**.

HAS BEEN   ✳ ✳ ✳ ✳

This 2004 studio album represented a major comeback for Shatner as a recording artist. He has called it "the culmination of all that I have tried to do" musically. Produced by frequent Shatner collaborator **Ben Folds**, *Has Been* consists of 11 tracks, the majority written or cowritten by Shatner himself. He employs his customary spoken-word delivery throughout.

Invigorated by their work together on his *Fear of Pop* side project five years earlier, Folds (who also cowrote seven of the tracks) was eager to play McCartney to Shatner's Lennon on a full-length CD. On *Has Been*, he surrounded Shatner with a strong cast of supporting performers, each of whom lends the record added musical credibility. Guests include muscle-bound punk icon Henry Rollins, ungainly New Wave relic Joe Jackson, "'Til Tuesday" chanteuse Aimee Mann, guitarist Adrian Belew, and pop country star Brad Paisley. The album opener and debut single "Common People" is a cover of the mid-'90s hit by the U.K. pop band Pulp.

At a shade under forty minutes, the CD is brief by contemporary standards, but it packs an outsized emotional wallop thanks to the inclusion of a number of candid, confessional compositions. "What Have You Done" is a moving elegy on the drowning death of Shatner's third wife, **Nerine Kidd**, while "Ideal Woman" celebrates the impeccable sartorial sense of his fourth wife, **Elizabeth Anderson Martin**. "That's Me Trying" is Shatner's "She's Leaving Home," a heartfelt letter from a father to his estranged daughter cowritten by British novelist Nick Hornby (and containing a creepily worded request to "get a little dad/daughter action going"). Other tracks are more characteristic of Shatner's earlier recordings. On "I Can't Get Behind That," Shatner and guest vocalist Henry Rollins take turns spewing out a litany of modern inconveniences that infuriate them, including global warming, student drivers, and The Clapper. "I can't get behind a fat ass!" Shatner screams at the song's conclusion, though it's unclear whether he's talking about his own or someone else's.

Critical response to *Has Been* was almost universally positive. "Remarkably, the album coheres," wrote the *New York Times*, expressing the general feeling of shock and awe that Shatner could produce a record of such quality. The UK's *Guardian* took a Nietzschean view: "This CD is beyond good or bad. It is from a world where concepts such as 'unique' and 'indispensible' live happily alongside 'hilariously, brain-tearingly wrong.'" **Ben Folds** himself seemed to agree with that assessment, commenting after its release that "I've never heard a record quite like it." In February 2007, Shatner received the ultimate compliment when the Milwaukee Ballet Company performed a ballet, *Common People*, set to six songs from the *Has Been* CD. Can a light opera staging of **The Transformed Man** be far behind?

HIGH CHAIR CONTROVERSY

In 1967, a conflict emerged on the set of **Star Trek** over the size of the folding chairs provided to the cast. The so-called "Big Three"—Shatner, Leonard Nimoy, and DeForest Kelley—all had towering canvas seats with special receptacles for their scripts and personal effects. The supporting cast members, whom Shatner later labeled the "**seven dwarfs**," had noticeably shorter furniture. However, resentment over the chair situation did not reach a fever pitch until **Walter Koenig** joined the cast in the fall of 1967. The popularity of his Ensign Pavel Chekov character emboldened Koenig to demand a chair as high as the three established stars. He won a high chair and jealously guarded his new perk, but his lofty position was short-lived. The other cast members all demanded high chairs as well, and soon the entire *Enterprise* crew was breathing the same rarefied air. Ironically, a third-season **Star Trek** episode, "The Cloud Minders," concerns a rebellion by worker drones who toil in underground mines against an elite class of overlords who dwell in an ethereal cloud city. A veiled commentary on the high chair controversy, perhaps?

See **Phone Controversy**.

HOLLYWOOD WALK OF FAME

Shatner received his star on the Hollywood Walk of Fame—the 1,762nd star issued—on May 19, 1983. **Leonard Nimoy** joined him for the ceremony. For those visiting Hollywood, Shatner's cement marker is located outside the legendary Mann's Chinese Theatre between the stars of German-born movie director William Dieterle and comedian/singer Danny Thomas of TV's *Make Room for Daddy*.

> "Life is full of surprises, both uplifting and degrading. The Walk of Fame, with its bubble gum and doggy doo and its steps of admiration, is also the way of life."
>
> —*Shatner, at his induction ceremony for the Hollywood Walk of Fame*

HOME OF THE FUTURE

While Shatner has been lucky with his own domiciles, he found his credibility tested when he tried to peddle homes to others. In 1997, he provided narration for a marketing video touting Lennar Realty Corporation's voice-operated Home of the Future. "If you're not living in Lennar's Home of the Future, you're living in the past," Shatner intones on the video, which promises prospective buyers a high-tech domicile complete with an electronic butler to respond to every whim. Unfortunately, reality fell far short of fantasy, as ABC's *Good Morning America* reported in January 1998. Homeowners found the Home of the Future full of bugs that made everyday living irritating, even dangerous. "Our dog would bark, it would make long-distance calls," one dissatisfied customer reported. "Stereos would blast in the middle of the night . . . it's like living with a poltergeist." The electronic butlers repeatedly ignored their masters' commands, or carried out the wrong commands. Promises of lower utility bills and a life free of inconvenience went unrealized. "We thought we were buying the Jetsons, instead we got the Flintstones," groused one unlucky householder, who had put down nearly $200,000 for the high-tech money pit. "All they saw was a demo, and they saw William Shatner's video," explained *Good Morning America*'s consumer correspondent Janice Lieberman, who cautioned against buying futuristic products sight unseen. The aggrieved homeowners subsequently filed a $5 million class action lawsuit against the Florida-based Lennar Corporation.

HORROR AT 37,000 FEET, THE ⨰

Shatner has carved a nice niche for himself playing passengers aboard haunted airliners. A hysterical passenger aboard a jet being sabotaged by a gremlin in the similarly titled **Twilight Zone** episode "Nightmare at 20,000 Feet," Shatner ups his altitude for this 1973 TV movie starring Chuck Connors, Buddy Ebsen, France Nuyen, Roy Thinnes, Paul Winfield, and Tammy Grimes. The hackneyed plot concerns a first-class cabin in a jumbo jet that is being haunted by ghosts because of a druid stone in the baggage hold. Look for a brief cameo from Russell Johnson, the beloved Professor from *Gilligan's Island*.

SIX DEGREES OF *STAR TREK*

France Nuyen (Annalik) sparred with Shatner in the third-season **Star Trek** episode "Elaan of Troyius." Paul Winfield (Dr. Enkalla) went on to play Captain Terrell, a casualty of the Ceti Eel, in **Star Trek II: The Wrath of Khan**.

HORSERADISH

This ancient herb is one of Shatner's favorite condiments. He ate horseradish for the first time as a small child during a Jewish holiday celebration in Montreal. Having subsisted on baby food until then, Shatner saw ingesting the pungently spicy root as a rite of passage. "I was given a small portion of the red, mushy substance but took too much on my fork. My eyes welled with tears, my face flushed, my nose ran, my ears burned. It was the Queen's Coronation, Fourth of July, and Simchas Torah, all rolled into one." Horseradish is one of the five bitter herbs of the Passover festival, and is usually grated, added in sauces, or used as a condiment for fish or meat.

> "If you eat enough horseradish, nothing matters in the world,
> except the explosion in the center of your head."
> —*Shatner, on the palliative effects of horseradish, in 1975*

HORSES

Shatner is a dedicated breeder of quarter horses, with ranches in the bluegrass country of Kentucky and California's Simi Valley. In 1983 and 1985, he rode his own mounts along a three-mile stretch of Sunset and Hollywood Boulevards as part of the annual Christmas Lane Parade, held on the Sunday after Thanksgiving. In recent years, he has enjoyed his most notable success with American Saddlebreds, the high-stepping, five-gaited mounts. Shatner likens the ownership of these horses to a religious experience. Frequently, He appears in charity fund-raisers at the Equestrian Center in Burbank, California, some 15 miles north of downtown Los Angeles.

Shatner first learned to ride in 1963 while filming the failed

TV pilot **Alexander the Great**. In the beginning, he was terrified his mount would rear up and fall on top of him. However, he quickly overcame his fears. By the close of the shooting, Glen Randall, cowboy movie star Gene Autry's own trainer, was telling Shatner, "You have more natural ability as a horseman than anyone I've ever worked with." By his own admission, however, Shatner did not do much more than "hack around" on horses until the mid-1980s. That's when he caught the saddlebred bug, after visiting a stable while on location for an episode of his TV series **T. J. Hooker**. "It was one of those enchanted moments," Shatner told the *New York Times* of this encounter. "I fell in love from across a crowded room, a

A saddlebred's seed became the crux of a lawsuit
involving Shatner and his ex-wife in 2003.

crowded barn, really." He subsequently purchased the world champion stallion Sultan's Great Day to stand as stud at his **Belle Reve** farm in Versailles, Kentucky. His horse **Kentucky Dream** won the National Horse Show in 1986.

Shatner has spoken at length about his passion for riding. "The beauty of the horse, the feeling of two entities joining. The athleticism, the competition, the excitement of a galloping horse and the art that is needed to control and yet be free." He often compares horses to **women**. "A pretty girl is certainly comparable to a good horse," he informed an interviewer in 1996. That same year, he told a convention audience in Atlanta about another part of horse rearing that appeals to him. "I love to birth the babies," he said. "I love to take the babies out of the mother's womb."

Beyond the sensual aspects of horsemanship, Shatner has recognized the sport's utility in serving his favorite causes. Over the years, he has given time and money to Ahead with Horses, a therapeutic group that uses horseback riding to rehabilitate disabled children. In 1991, he started the Hollywood Charitable Horse Show, which annually raises close to $50,000 for various children's charities. The show combines quarter horse competition with western style barbecue, celebrity contests, and raffles—including one in which Shatner auctions himself off for dances to the highest bidder. In 2006, he brought therapeutic riding to one of the world's most troubled regions, partnering with the Jewish National Fund to form the William Shatner/Jewish National Fund Therapeutic Riding Consortium Endowment for Israel. The program aims to fund riding centers throughout Israel, raise money for scholarship funds, and facilitate cooperation between Israelis and Palestinians.

Like many equestrians, Shatner has had his share of riding accidents. On the set of his 1975 TV series **_The Barbary Coast_**, he suffered a broken ankle when a horse stepped on his foot. Then, in 1993, his mount was startled by a golf cart and reared unexpectedly, collapsing on top of him. Shatner suffered torn ligaments and had to be rushed to the hospital for treatment. At the time, the leg injury seemed the least of his problems. "It wasn't like my television show **Rescue 911**," he said afterward. "It was much messier. This guy, the EMT leaning over me, was sweating and perspiring and dripping on me."

In a case of art imitating life, Captain Kirk rides horses extensively in the feature film **Star Trek: Generations**. To relieve the chafing on his legs, Shatner wore **panty hose** throughout the filming.

> "Being around this breed of horse is just like
> show business, only better."
>
> —Shatner, on the charms of the American Saddlebred

HORSE SEMEN

This substance served as the sticky center of a breach-of-contract lawsuit brought against Shatner in 2003 by his ex-wife, **Marcy Lafferty**. In her suit, Lafferty claimed that Shatner violated the terms of their divorce settlement by providing her with frozen equine ejaculate from their stallion, Great Days Came the Son, rather than the "fresh cooled" variety she preferred. "Potential buyers of the breeding privileges do not want the semen in frozen format," Lafferty hissed in legal papers served to the actor. Claiming loss of income as a result of the improperly chilled jizz, she asked for a jury trial and undisclosed financial damages. The suit was eventually dismissed when Shatner's lawyer persuaded a judge that the couple's divorce settlement did not contain any restriction on how the semen was to be delivered.

HOUND OF THE BASKERVILLES, THE ✶ ✶ ✶

Stewart Granger plays Sherlock Holmes and Bernard Fox is Dr. Watson in this 1972 TV movie based on Sir Arthur Conan Doyle's novel. Shatner has third billing as the villainous George Stapleton, whose "abrupt and limp demise" was lamented by the reviewer for *Variety* magazine. Abrupt and limp are two words no man ever wants to hear. The telefeature served as the pilot for a proposed detective anthology series that was never consummated.

HOUSES

The type of home an actor owns is often a barometer of his status in show business. Thus, the chronology of Shatner domiciles tells a tale of a career marked by dramatic ups and downs.

In May 1957, Shatner signed his first Hollywood movie contract, a two-year deal with MGM worth $100,000. With a young wife, Gloria Rand, and plans for a family, he naturally looked to purchase his first residence. The couple initially considered a palatial Hollywood spread with a pool, a barbecue pit, and a glass-enclosed living room. However, Shatner's agent convinced them this was not a good idea. "Don't mortgage yourself to Hollywood," he told the young actor. The Shatners ended up taking a one-bedroom apartment instead.

It proved to be good advice, as Shatner soon found himself bitten by the Broadway bug. With no movies upcoming under his MGM pact, in 1958 he and Gloria returned to Manhattan, where Shatner was slated to open in *The World of Suzie Wong* that October. In June 1959, the couple finally bought their first house, a fifty-year-old, eight-room Victorian country home in the idyllic community of Hastings-on-Hudson, about twelve miles north of Manhattan on the Hudson River. To avoid the cost of hiring laborers, they painted the place themselves.

Shatner and his brood take a dip in their Southern California pool in the mid-1960s.

When he landed the role of Captain Kirk on **Star Trek**, Shatner had to move back to the West Coast. The financial security of being the star of a network TV series no doubt influenced his choice, as he and Gloria opted for a home in the upscale Cheviot Hills section of Los Angeles, west of Beverly Hills and south of Century City.

One of Shatner's most interesting dwellings was the one that cost him the least. In 1969, following his divorce from Gloria Rand, Shatner scraped together enough money to make a down payment on a small home in Los Angeles. This was at the low point of Shatner's career (his so-called **lost years**), when work was scarce, and he found himself with only $300 left over for furniture. It was enough—barely. Shatner scoured downtown Los Angeles for used and irregular pieces, such as a bed with a torn mattress that had come out of a damaged crate. Then, to economize even further, he simply used the crates as tables. Fortunately, he did not have to live in the house for long. He spent most of those years on the road pursuing work, and moved out soon after marrying **Marcy Lafferty** in October 1973.

The newlyweds soon moved into a two-bedroom ranch in Los Angeles's Hillcrest section in Northern Glendale. It was an upgrade, if for no other reason than it had real furniture, but it also boasted a swimming pool. When Shatner's fortunes took an upswing in the 1980s, he and Marcy moved into a lavish mountaintop residence in Studio City in the San Fernando Valley, where he still resides today. Unsubstantiated rumors have long contended that the home's bathroom has been remodeled to replicate the USS *Enterprise* bridge, complete with a toilet bowl shaped like Captain Kirk's chair.

"HOW TO HANDLE A WOMAN"

Shatner performs this classic Lerner and Loewe song from the musical Camelot during a late 1970s appearance on Dinah Shore's TV chat show *Dinah!* Boldly going where such notable King Arthurs as Richard Burton, Richard Harris, and Laurence Harvey have gone before, Shatner delivers an impassioned spoken-word rendition from the comfort of a wooden stool. The performance is notable principally for the electric blue, butterfly-collared, faux satin shirt the actor is wearing. Opened invitingly at the chest in the true high '70s style, the garish blouse lends a creepy "after hours in the singles bar" vibe to what is supposed to be a whimsical rumination on love.

HUNTER, JEFFREY

Shatner replaced this stolid, handsome actor as commander of the starship *Enterprise* on **Star Trek**. A Twentieth Century Fox contract star in the 1950s, Hunter made his name playing Jesus Christ in

1961's *King of Kings*. Hunter was hired to portray Captain Christopher Pike on the initial **Star Trek** pilot, "The Cage," in 1964, but he passed on the show on the advice of his wife at the time, Joan Bartlett, who thought series television was beneath him. **Star Trek** creator Gene Roddenberry briefly considered future *Hawaii Five-O* star Jack Lord as Hunter's replacement, but finally settled on Shatner. Footage of Hunter as Pike was later excised from "The Cage" and used as flashback material in the classic two-part **Star Trek** episode "The Menagerie."

Ask Shat

Q: What is the meaning of life?

A: We all need some personal purpose, some goal, even if it's just learning to paint by numbers. I've tried to find challenges in my own life. My work is a daily challenge. I challenge myself with new skills, like motorcycling or tennis. The big challenge is to become a success as an actor.

"HE'S DEAD, CAPTAIN JANUARY!"

In making the transition from **Hunter** to Shatner, **Gene Roddenberry** also had to come up with a new name for his starship commander. Here is a list of the ones he considered, before settling on Kirk:

Boone	*Hamilton*	*Patrick*
Christopher	*Hudson*	*Raintree*
Drake	*January*	*Richard*
Flagg	*Neville*	*Thorpe*
Hannibal	*North*	*Timber*

"I AM CANADIAN"

Shatner delivered this declaration of national pride during an on-stage appearance at the *Just for Laughs* comedy festival in Montreal in July 2000. A parody of a popular Molson beer commercial—in which an anonymous flannel-clad Canuck repudiates a litany of Canadian stereotypes before avowing his national identity—Shatner's rendition included mocking references to Trekkies, green-skinned **alien sex** partners, and **Priceline.com**.

IDIC MEDAL

In a protest against the commercialization of **Star Trek**, Shatner refused to wear this medallion, designed by the show's creator **Gene Roddenberry**, and offered for sale through his marketing company, Lincoln Enterprises. A variety of earrings, keychains, and charms bearing the IDIC insignia were also made available. IDIC stands for "Infinite Diversity in Infinite Combinations."

In 1968, Roddenberry wrote a scene into the **Star Trek** episode "Is There in Truth No Beauty?" in which Captain Kirk presents one of the medallions to an *Enterprise* crewmember. Shatner refused to take part, claiming it demeaned the show to have its characters functioning as shills for the executive producer's products. In the end, **Leonard Nimoy** agreed to perform the scene instead. A few years later, Shatner chose to become a shill for a less benign product, **Promise margarine**, in a series of famous **television** commercials with his second wife, **Marcy Lafferty**.

IMPULSE   ✳

"Tawdry" doesn't begin to describe this 1974 feature, also known by the more exploitative title *Want a Ride, Little Girl?* Shatner plays Matt Stone, a charismatic gigolo who drifts into the lives of a rich widow and her nosy preteen daughter. Unknown to them (but instantly recognizable to the audience, who've been primed with twenty minutes of exposition), Stone is also a homicidal maniac. He preys on the widow and murders her best friend, a wealthy dowager played by Ruth Roman. Harold Sakata, the hulking Japanese wrestler who plays Odd Job in *Goldfinger*, has a small role as Karate Pete, a rival con man who runs afoul of Shatner's character. Also lending support is Shatner's wife, **Marcy Lafferty**, as a horny motel clerk who gives in to Stone's advances.

Filmed on the cheap in Poland Springs, Florida, *Impulse* is one of the lowlights of Shatner's **lost years**. He gives a curiously distracted performance, almost as if he's marking time between *$20,000 Pyramid* appearances. Outfitted in one of his worst **toupee**s

A beleaguered Shatner hits rock bottom with the unsavory 1974 exploitation feature *Impulse*.

and a succession of ghastly '70s sport jackets, he telegraphs his character's psychosis by portentously puffing on Tiparillos and sticking his pinkie in his mouth à la Dr. Evil in *Austin Powers*. The entire film has a tacky, unpleasant quality reminiscent of a porno movie. Fittingly, the climactic sequence takes place in a funeral home. Shatner has disavowed the project in subsequent interviews.

> "I've forgotten why I was in it. I probably needed the money. It was a very bad time for me. I hope they burn it."
>
> —*Shatner, on* Impulse, *aka* Want a Ride, Little Girl?

INCIDENT ON A DARK STREET ✳ ✳

His status diminished following the cancellation of **Star Trek** and the onset of his **lost years**; by 1973, Shatner was taking any part he could get. That explains his relatively small role in this **television** movie, which served as the pilot for an abortive series about the inner workings of a U.S. Attorney's office. The plot concerns the murder of a low-level hood who is about to testify against an organized crime syndicate. Shatner plays Deaver Wallace, a U.S. Justice Department official investigating the situation.

INCUBUS ✳

This incredibly odd 1965 horror movie was performed entirely in Esperanto, an "international" language developed by Polish eye doctor L. L. Zamenhof in 1887. Set in the mythical land of Nomen Tuum, the atmospheric black-and-white shocker was the brainchild of **Outer Limits** creator Leslie Stevens. Shatner, in his final pre-**Star Trek** role, plays Marc, a virtuous woodsman set upon by a pack of ravishing succubi who try to corrupt his unblemished soul. The beautiful blonde demons all look like extras from an Ingmar Bergman movie. In fact, the Esperanto dialogue sounds a bit like Swedish. English subtitles are provided for those who opted for Spanish instead of Esperanto in high school.

Incubus had a rough passage into cinema history. Director Stevens desperately wanted to secure studio backing for the project, but couldn't convince anyone of the commercial viability of an Esperanto language film. Millions of people worldwide speak Esperanto, he once told Desilu production chief Herbert Solow, who had recently tapped Shatner for the lead role on **Star Trek**. Yes, Solow conceded, "There are 300 in Chicago, 100 in Spokane, 400 in London, 17 in Bakersfield—but not enough in any one city to even partially fill any one theater more than any one night." Needless to say, *Incubus* was completed without Desilu backing. It premiered to great hoopla in the U.S. at the 1966 San Francisco Film Festival, but remained largely unseen for almost 40 years. The original print was thought to have been destroyed in a fire (tossed, no doubt, by someone who had watched it). In 2001, for reasons unknown, the Sci-Fi Channel funded a restoration of the only surviving print and released it on DVD. Unfortunately, *Incubus* proved more interesting as a long-lost curiosity than an actual film.

One final side note: For years, rumors abounded about an *Incubus* curse. Several of the film's stars died violently shortly after production, and Director Leslie Stevens went bankrupt. If there was a curse, it bypassed Shatner entirely. He achieved his greatest success immediately after putting this ill-conceived linguistic experiment behind him.

"Why would anyone make a feature film in Esperanto?"
—*television executive Herbert F. Solow, on* Incubus

INDICT AND CONVICT ✳ ✳

On January 6, 1974, a mere three weeks after Shatner's previous TV movie, **Pioneer Woman**, ABC aired his next offering, a courtroom drama starring George Grizzard, Eli Wallach, and Harry Guardino. Shatner appears as Sam Belden, a deputy district attorney working on a murder case. Wallach plays a flamboyant defense lawyer. Critics found little to like outside of courtroom verisimilitude.

SIX DEGREES OF *STAR TREK*

Arlene Martel (Ann Lansing in **Indict and Convict**) plays T'Pring, Spock's betrothed, in the classic **Star Trek** episode "Amok Time."

INTERRACIAL KISS

Shatner and **Nichelle Nichols** shared network **television**'s first interracial kiss on November 22, 1968. In the **Star Trek** episode "Plato's Stepchildren," Kirk and his crew come under the dominion of the Platonians, a community of intergalactic Plato devotees with telekinetic powers. In one hilarious scene after another, the faux Greeks force the **Star Trek** regulars—not to mention dwarf actor Michael Dunn—to perform degrading acts of musical comedy for their amusement. The torture session ends with Nurse Chapel (Majel Barrett) and Lieutenant Uhura (Nichelle Nichols) compelled to lock lips with Spock and Kirk, respectively.

Not surprisingly, given the nature of network politics, the scene did not come off easily. The original script called for Spock to kiss Uhura, but Shatner protested—vehemently, according to some accounts. "If anybody's going to get to kiss Uhura, it's going to be me —I mean, Captain Kirk," he railed. Typically, Shatner took credit for the whole concept. "I thought that it would be a good idea that Kirk, who was—who liked a lot of women—would be attracted to an obviously attractive woman, but also would hide it under the professional exterior of doing his job."

To inoculate themselves against a feared racist backlash, **Star Trek**'s writers made it crystal clear that both parties were being forced against their will to kiss each other. They even filmed the scene two ways: once with Kirk refusing to give in to the Platonians' power, and once with him succumbing. However, Shatner played the non-kissing version of the scene with deliberately crossed eyes and such a comically tortured delivery that the footage could not be used. Eventually, **blooper reel**s surfaced with this take, as well as a loop of Shatner and Nichelle Nichols kissing over and over again.

Shatner and his kissing cousin Nichelle Nichols smile for the cameras in 2006.

"We did try some variations," Shatner said later. "There could have been a whole different story, if anybody had wanted to emphasize an interracial love story. But in fact, that wouldn't have made the point as effectively. Kirk and Uhura wouldn't even think of a kiss or a love story as interracial. That would be the last thing they would think about. If we did any good with that kiss or anything we did on **Star Trek**, it was to push in the direction of not having to think about that."

In the end, NBC's jitters proved unfounded. "Plato's Stepchildren" inspired an unprecedented flood of positive fan mail. The network received all of one complaining letter about the scene, from a self-described opponent of "race-mixing" from the South. However, even he conceded that "any time a red-blooded American boy like Captain Kirk gets a beautiful dame in his arms that looks like Uhura, he ain't gonna fight it."

INTRUDER, THE   ✳ ✳ ✳

This black-and-white feature is one of two socially relevant melodramas Shatner made in 1961. (The other is **The Explosive Generation**.) Adapted for the screen by Charles Beaumont from his 1959 novel, it's also the first of two films he made for legendary producer/director Roger Corman. (The other is 1974's **Big Bad Mama**.)

As Adam Cramer, a racist rabble rouser who whips the inhabitants of a small southern town into an anti-integrationist frenzy, Shatner gives one of his best, most assured performances. He delivers a number of long, fiery speeches in front of frothing mobs, which give him ample opportunity to use every trick in his **acting** arsenal. If you ever wanted to see Shatner light a burning cross, cavort with Ku Klux Klansmen, or spew out lines like "Do you know where N***** Town is?" this is the film for you.

Like most Corman films, *The Intruder* was made on the cheap, in this case on location in East Prairie and Charleston, Missouri.

Townsfolk were kept in the dark about the film's anti-segregation message, and they did not take kindly to being depicted as race-baiting cracker trash. They refused to allow the crew to shoot in certain locations and repeatedly intimidated the cast. At one point, the state militia had to be called in to safeguard the production.

Undaunted, Shatner gave his all to a movie whose message he clearly believed in, for a salary reported to be about $200 above his expenses. He was rewarded with a Best Actor Award at the 1962 International Peace Festival. The *Los Angeles Times* called *The Intruder* "the boldest, most realistic depiction of racial injustice ever shown in American films." Unfortunately, the movie's controversial subject matter scared away many potential distributors. It was the first Roger Corman film to lose money at the box office. Later in the decade, it played under more sensational titles like *I Hate Your Guts!* and *Shame*, sometimes on a double bill with 1967's *Poor White Trash*.

SIX DEGREES OF *STAR TREK*
Veteran TV fantasist George Clayton Johnson (who plays Phil West in **The Intruder**) went on to write the first-season **Star Trek** episode "The Man Trap."

INVASION IOWA ✳ ✳

Shatner scams the entire town of Riverside, Iowa, in this reality TV miniseries, which aired over four nights on Spike TV in March/April 2005. After announcing that he would be filming a new sci-fi movie in the town of 930 people (best known as the future birthplace of **James T. Kirk**), Shatner showed up with a fake entourage made up of improv actors and began surreptitiously filming the unwitting locals. As a special thank you to the townspeople for allowing themselves to be played for suckers on national **television**, Shatner presented town officials with a check for $100,000. That didn't assuage the

Shatner eats some hot lead as a racist demagogue in Roger Corman's 1961 potboiler *The Intruder*.

fury of some Riverside residents, many of whom found the elaborate hoax mean-spirited and exploitative.

IRON CHEF USA ✳

Shatner plays the chairman of a fictional "Gourmet Academy" on this short-lived UPN cooking competition show, modeled on a similarly titled Japanese program with a sizable stateside cult following. It's still unclear why Shatner was selected for hosting duties, since he has little or no culinary expertise. The program, which pitted professional chefs against one another in a timed cook-off centered on a theme ingredient, was lambasted by critics and ignored by audiences. The reviewer for the *San Francisco Chronicle* called it "an abomination." Canceled after only two episodes, the show resurfaced three years later on the Food Network, with a different format and—mercifully—a different host, as *Iron Chef America*.

IT DIDN'T HAVE TO HAPPEN: DRINKING AND DRIVING ✳ ✳

In full **Rescue 911** mode, Shatner narrates this gory 1994 educational documentary, aimed at teenage motorists. Graphic recreations of fatal traffic accidents hammer home its alarmist message about the inadvisability of drinking and driving.

"IT WAS A VERY GOOD YEAR" ✳ ✳ ✳

Shatner covers this Ervin Drake song, made famous by Frank Sinatra, on his 1968 album **The Transformed Man**. A meditation on the splendors of love by an aging man now "in the autumn of the year," the elegiac number seemed like an odd fit for Shatner, who was only 37 at the time. Nevertheless, his spoken-word rendition is one of the highlights of the LP. He must have thought so too, as he chose to perform the song on *The Mike Douglas Show* to promote

"Allez cuisine!" Shatner presides over dueling culinary masters as the host of TV's *Iron Chef USA*.

the record. While this live version is somewhat restrained, especially in comparison with his later televised musical performances, it does exert a weirdly hypnotic effect on the viewer. Shatner gives an entirely new interpretation to the song during his appearance as **Lucifer** on Comedy Central's *Last Laugh '05*.

JANEK: THE SILENT BETRAYAL ✶✶

Richard Crenna stars as gruff New York City police detective Frank Janek in this 1994 TV movie, with Shatner, Helen Shaver, and a young Liev Schreiber in support. Shatner plays Bodosh, a martini-sipping Broadway producer who owns an apartment building where six gruesome murders have taken place. "Shatner's histrionics give the film a shot of much-needed energy," gushed *Entertainment Weekly*. Ironically, Shatner's first scene requires him to make a 911 call—something he was intimately familiar with from his stint as host of the TV reality series **Rescue 911**.

JUDGMENT AT NUREMBERG ✶ ✶ ✶

Shatner is part of an all-star ensemble in this 1961 feature about the Nuremberg war crime trials. He plays Captain Harrison Byers, a military lawyer who assists the presiding judge, played by screen legend Spencer Tracy. Shatner retells a story about the day he complimented Tracy on his ability to memorize page upon page of dialogue. Tracy, who was sixty at the time, took the remark as a sarcastic comment about his age and refused to talk to Shatner for the duration of the shooting.

Burt Lancaster, Maximilian Schell, Richard Widmark, Judy Garland, Marlene Dietrich, and Montgomery Clift also appear in the Stanley Kramer production, which won Academy Awards for Best Actor (Schell) and Best Adapted Screenplay (Abby Mann) and was nominated for nine others.

KARATE

This ancient Asian art of self-defense teaches practitioners how to disable an attacker by using crippling hard, fast kicks and punches. Shatner first began to study karate in 1966, under the tutelage of Hollywood screenwriter and black belt Terry Bleecker, who was impressed with the work habits of his star pupil. "His discipline as an actor and his gift for total recall make him a prime student of karate," Bleecker remarked.

Despite such high praise, Shatner has always downplayed his skill at self-defense. "I want to be very clear about the karate," he said in 1979. "I'm not good at all . . . my ability in karate has been greatly exaggerated." To excel at karate, he conceded, "requires a fanaticism which I just don't have the time to do [sic]."

For a while, anyway, Shatner's interest in karate did border on

The 1961 classic *Judgment at Nuremberg* gave a young Shatner a chance to break into big-budget Hollywood features.

the fanatical. In the mid-1970s he became fascinated with martial arts movies, convinced that by studying them he could make his own onscreen **fight** scenes more believable. He drove his second wife **Marcy Lafferty** to distraction by dragging her to see low-budget Hong Kong action slugfests.

"KEEP IT GAY"
Shatner performs a spirited rendition of this Perry Como song during an early 1970s appearance on *The Mike Douglas Show*. It's one

of the few recorded instances when the actor actually tries to sing, as opposed to recite a song's lyrics. Added novelty is provided by Shatner's addition of a dance component to the number—although his feet remain strangely glued to the floor throughout. Not until the infamous **"Rocket Man"** freak-out several years later would rump-shaking once again be a featured element of a televised Shatner musical performance. Also of note: This is one of the actor's rare duets. About halfway through, he exhorts the host to join him on the chorus with a jaunty "Come on, Mike!"

KELLEY, DEFOREST

This veteran American character actor played the gruff but lovable Dr. Leonard "Bones" McCoy on *Star Trek*. A fixture in Hollywood Westerns since the late 1940s, Kelley at first seemed an odd choice to serve as the starship *Enterprise*'s intergalactic medicine man. However, **Gene Roddenberry**'s casting hunch paid off. "Dee," as he was known around the set, brought a wry irascibility to the McCoy character that perfectly complemented the hot and cold styles of his costars. That "lukewarm water" approach extended behind the scenes as well. "Kelley was very savvy in the ways of Hollywood," explained *Star Trek* bit player David L. Ross. "He went way back . . . Kelley had experienced the ups and downs of the business and banked his money. He was very careful and always gracious. He never took sides with either Shatner or [Leonard] Nimoy."

Dee Kelley may have bit his tongue when it came to criticizing Shatner, but that didn't stop Shatner from teasing Kelley mercilessly about his advancing age—or from making him the butt of countless **practical jokes**. In one oft-told tale from the *Star Trek V* set, a mischievous Shatner repeatedly removed Kelley's English muffin from the craft services toaster when his back was turned, to make him think he was losing his mind. On another occasion, a callous Shatner broke down in stitches upon learning that Kelley's beloved chihuahua had died that morning. "I laughed. . . . He didn't talk to me for two years," Shatner reported.

MY CAREER'S DEAD, JIM

It sure seems like Shatner's *Star Trek* costars do a lot of yakking about his **ego**, doesn't it? Well, like your mom always said, consider the source. Other than **Leonard Nimoy**, Shatner's supporting players didn't exactly enjoy stellar careers in the decades after *Star Trek* beamed out of existence—which may explain why they enjoyed taking hacks at their more successful counterpart. Here are the lowlights of the post-*Trek* careers of some of Shatner's erstwhile costars:

DEFOREST KELLEY appeared in the 1972 "giant rabbits" horror show *Night of the Lepus*.

JAMES DOOHAN lasted one season on the Saturday morning sci-fi embarrassment *Jason of Star Command*, 1979.

WALTER KOENIG starred in the execrable deep space turkey *Moontrap*, 1989.

NICHELLE NICHOLS released unlistenable album *Uhura Sings*, 1986.

GEORGE TAKEI spent the 1990s designing Los Angeles' abortive subway system.

KENTUCKY DREAM

This saddlebred horse, owned by Shatner, won the 1986 National Horse Show. Kentucky Dream was originally named Sinatra, but Shatner suggested a name change. "Kentucky Dream is just such a nice name," he told the *New York Times* in 1986. "It was an executive decision of mine, though I know everybody still calls him Sinatra behind my back." Shatner himself rode Kentucky Dream around the ring at Madison Square Garden in Manhattan the night he won the prestigious national prize. As is his preference, the actor wore traditional English-style riding apparel, including a bowler hat.

KHAMBATTA, PERSIS

This beautiful actress, model, and former Miss India plays Lieutenant Ilia, the bald-headed Deltan navigator, in **Star Trek: The Motion Picture**. While Shatner reportedly flirted with her mercilessly during production, he once called Khambatta a "stunningly bad actress," and gleefully retold a story about her needing nineteen takes to speak the single line, "No." Khambatta's Hollywood career sputtered thereafter. Her post–**Star Trek** credits include the expensive bombs *Megaforce* and *Warrior of the Lost World*. She died of a heart attack in August 1998.

KIDD, NERINE

"She meant everything to me. Her laughter, her tears, and her joy will remain with me the rest of my life." So said Shatner of his third wife, Nerine Kidd, whom he wed in 1997, and who died tragically in a swimming pool accident at the couple's Studio City, California, home on August 9, 1999. A statuesque ex-model, Kidd was thirty years younger and several inches taller than Shatner. She battled drug and alcohol addiction throughout their brief, doomed **marriage**. The couple met in 1993 while Shatner was still married to his second wife, **Marcy Lafferty**. Their courtship included romantic trips to Europe and several canceled wedding ceremonies, reportedly because of Shatner's unwillingness to tie the knot without a prenuptial agreement. (He was fleeced for a reported $26 million in his previous divorce case.) Over the course of 1997, however, Kidd wore down Shatner's resistance on this point and the two set a November 15 wedding date at the posh Winterbourne Mansion in Pasadena, California. More than one hundred guests turned out for the affair, including **Leonard Nimoy**, who served as best man. Actors **Kevin Pollak** and Greg "**Jake Cardigan**" Evigan were also in attendance. Pouring rain forced the celebrants underneath an immense white tent, decorated in a fairy tale motif. There Judge Jack Tanner performed the ceremony, with wedding vows composed by the couple. The bride wore a sleeveless ivory satin gown, while Shatner donned a black tuxedo. The five-course menu included caviar, prawns, stuffed mushrooms, Lobster Newburg, and Dom Perignon champagne. Shatner refused to accept gifts, urging his guests to give the money to charitable causes instead. He did not place any such limitation on himself, however, as he presented his ecstatic bride with a gorgeous Tennessee walking horse as a token of his fealty. The freshly minted couple cut into the three-tiered white wedding cake, then cut it up on the dance floor to the soulful strains of Leroy and the Do Got Band. Leaving their guests to revel without them, Shatner and Kidd then climbed into his black Mercedes and headed off to his estate in the Hollywood hills for the first stop on their honeymoon.

Unfortunately, the elaborate wedding ceremony was to be the high point of the couple's **marriage**. Almost immediately, rumors began to circulate that there was trouble in paradise, largely due to Kidd's alcohol and drug habits. According to Shatner, Kidd stashed bottles of vodka throughout their home. He twice convinced her to enter a rehab facility, including one stint at the famed Betty Ford Clinic, to no avail. "I fought and fought to save my wife from the serpent of alcoholism—but I failed," Shatner later admitted. The couple separated and filed a motion for divorce in October 1998, but later reconciled. They were still trying to make a go of it ten months later, when Shatner returned from a business meeting to find Kidd face down at the bottom of their swimming pool. A frantic 911 call ensued, attempts at CPR proved futile, and Kidd was pronounced dead at the scene. An autopsy revealed that her blood-alcohol level was 0.27—three times the legal limit in California—and that she had Valium in her system at the time of her death. Her death was ruled an accidental drowning, with alcohol and drugs cited as contributing factors. In 2001, in Kidd's memory, Shatner established the Nerine Shatner Friendly House, a "sober living" facility for **women** recovering from alcohol and substance abuse.

KIDNAPPING OF THE PRESIDENT, THE ✳ ✳ ✳

Shatner enjoys one of his most heroic roles in this 1980 feature, based on Charles Templeton's novel. President Hal Holbrook is snatched by South American terrorists while visiting Toronto, and Shatner's intrepid Secret Service agent Jerry O'Connor must find a way to rescue him from their armored car hideaway. Van Johnson plays the feckless vice president. Production values are low, but still a step up from the kind of drek Shatner was getting in the late '70s. A gruesome opening sequence featuring dismemberment in an Argentine jungle seems to bear no relation to the rest of the film.

Shatner amps up the macho as a Secret Service man in the 1980 film *The Kidnapping of the President*.

Electronic **music** was provided by someone—or something—called Nash the Slash.

KIDNEY STONE

In January 2006, Shatner sold a kidney stone he had passed the previous fall to the online casino website GoldenPalace.com for $25,000. The enormous ball of calcium was so big, according to the actor, "You'd want to wear it on your finger. . . . If you subjected it to extreme heat, it might turn out to be a diamond." The lucky winners of Shatner's calcium deposit also received the surgical stint and string used to facilitate passage of the stone.

Shatner hit upon the idea of auctioning off the stone during a November 2005 appearance on *Jimmy Kimmel Live*, in which the host declared it "the ultimate *Star Trek* collectible." GoldenPalace.com originally offered Shatner $15,000 for the bauble, but he turned them down, claiming to have **Star Trek** tunics that sold for more than that. When the casino site upped its offer, he relented. Proceeds from the sale were donated to the housing charity Habitat for Humanity. "I retain visitation rights," quipped Shatner.

> "This takes organ donors to a new height, to a new low, maybe.
> How much is a piece of me worth?"
> —*Shatner, on his $25,000 kidney stone*

KING

This is Captain Kirk's designation in Paramount's twenty-fifth anniversary **Star Trek** chess set, released in 1991. Dubbed "the chess set that transcends time and space," the novelty game board pits the

Enterprise crew against a dream team of Klingons, Romulans, and assorted anti-Federation villains. "The battlefield is outer space," declared an ad that appeared in major magazines. The pieces were solid pewter. Kirk's opposing king is "Space Seed" ubermensch Khan Noonian Singh. **Fans** who ordered the chess set were billed by the piece at $29.50 per month, for a total of thirty-two pieces, which comes to $944. The chessboard was thrown in for free. What a deal!

Ask Shat

Q: What did you do to prepare for your role as a thinly veiled version of yourself in *Showtime*?

A: I read my biography. I learned I can't stand the guy. I made it to chapter five and put it down!

SHATNER'S WORLD OF PAIN

Does Shatner ever get the impression his directors don't like him? It wouldn't be surprising, considering how much agony they've put his characters through. Here are just some of the tribulations Shatner has had to endure on screen:

Burned at the stake by angry Puritans in ***The Devil's Rain***
Riddled with bullets during police ambush in ***Big Bad Mama***
Crucified by Ernest Borgnine in ***The Devil's Rain***
Overrun by voracious tarantulas in ***Kingdom of the Spiders***
Melted in Satanic rainstorm in ***The Devil's Rain***
Impaled on a sword by a 12-year-old girl in ***Impulse***
Kicked off a catwalk by Malcolm McDowell in ***Star Trek: Generations***

KINGDOM OF THE SPIDERS ✳

One of the undisputed lowlights of Shatner's **lost years**, this 1977 horror film depicts the gruesome consequences of indiscriminate pesticide use. Ten thousand hungry tarantulas descend on an Arizona town after their food supply is destroyed by spraying.

Shatner plays Dr. Robert "Rack" Hansen, a horny veterinarian who investigates the phenomenon—when he's not wasting time hitting on a beautiful female entomologist, played by '70s drive-in diva Tiffany Bolling. Shatner's second wife, **Marcy Lafferty**, also appears.

In 1989, Shatner signed a deal to direct and star in a sequel, but after the failure of **Star Trek V** the new spiders project never materialized. This film is not to be confused with the inferior and Shatnerless insect horror movie *Empire of the Ants*, also released in 1977.

KIRK, JAMES TIBERIUS

The role that made Shatner's career, the brash, dauntless captain of the starship *Enterprise* was modeled—not surprisingly—on the actor himself. "I utilize aspects I know about myself in portraying Kirk," he once said, "and sometimes I discover things about myself through Kirk." In 1968, during his second season on **Star Trek**, Shatner went into more detail about the many similarities between himself and his most famous creation. "I have a quickness to anger," he said. "I am alternately cursed and blessed with this quality which Kirk has also. I strive mightily to control it, as does he. . . . Kirk has to control his feelings being in charge of 435 people. I, too, have found that I have to disguise my emotions involving my private life on the set."

At first, Shatner did not realize the immense worldwide impact his portrayal would have. Over the course of the 1970s, however, he began to notice the strange reverence with which he was

KINGDOM OF THE SPIDERS

abc

STARRING
WILLIAM SHATNER
ABC FRIDAY NIGHT MOVIE

Shatner's decade-long descent into hell continues with 1977's voracious arachnid epic *Kingdom of the Spiders*.

held by those who grew up watching *Star Trek*. On one occasion late in the decade, Shatner saw a young woman wearing a Captain Kirk T-shirt. "It's a bizarre feeling," he joked, "to see your face on somebody's chest. Jiggling." By the time he made *Star Trek II* in 1982, Shatner was completely at ease with his big-screen alter **ego**. He even seemed to relish the opportunity to don the captain's ill-fitting tunic once again. "When I shave my sideburns to a point the first time I feel as if I'm drawing my sword from its scabbard," he said shortly after the sequel's release.

Unlike **Leonard Nimoy**, who once titled an autobiography *I Am Not Spock*, Shatner has never run away from his *Star Trek* character. "No matter how I felt about playing Kirk in the past, it was impos-

Shortly after this publicity still was taken, Shatner set aside his suit and donned a captain's tunic as commander of the starship *Enterprise*.

sible not to feel sad," he said on the occasion of Kirk's on-camera death in 1994's *Star Trek: Generations*. "So much fuss has been made over *Star Trek* and Kirk over the years that it felt funny to realize I'd never be playing him again."

In 1994, Shatner offered perhaps his most succinct epitaph for the intrepid starship commander. "Captain Kirk lived pretty much the way I wanted him to live. He was a distillation of all that I would like to be: heroic and romantic, forceful in battle and gentle in love, wise and profound. The ideal soldier/philosopher."

Ask Shat

Q: What do you say to fellow actors who claim that you're an egomaniac?

A: I love them all. They can't be angry at me, because I love them. So how can you be angry with someone who loves you?

SHATNER VS. KIRK: THE TALE OF THE TAPE

	SHATNER	KIRK
BIRTHDATE	March 22, 1931	March 26, 2229
SIGN	Aries	Aries
PLACE OF BIRTH	Montreal, Quebec	Riverside, Iowa
CITIZENSHIP	Canadian	Terran
OCCUPATION	Actor, writer, director, musician	Starship captain
HEIGHT	5'9" (wears lifts)	6'
WEIGHT	Varies	159 lbs.
HAIR	Fake	Light brown
EYES	Brown	Hazel

KOENIG, WALTER

This personable actor/writer played Ensign Pavel Chekov on **Star Trek** from 1967 to 1969. Koenig (pronounced KAY-nig) was a largely unknown quantity when **Gene Roddenberry** plucked him out of obscurity and cast him as the *Enterprise*'s new navigator—largely on the basis of his resemblance to diminutive Monkee Davy Jones.

Koenig was then asked to adopt a Russian accent to give the *Enterprise* crew more of an international flavor. Equipped with an ill-fitting Beatle wig, he was positioned to appeal to the emerging youth audience.

The other cast members were initially upset at the newcomer's popularity, but they eventually accepted him as part of the **Star Trek** family. Even Shatner was kind to Koenig, who in his early days on the show rarely followed his costars' lead in bashing the star. "He's a gentleman and a gentle man," Koenig once said of Shatner. "He tells very cool jokes and keeps everyone relaxed during the tensions of the day. It was Bill who helped me to develop the character of Chekov."

By the time of Star Trek II, however, Koenig had felt the full sting of Shatner's efforts to hog screen time and dominate the on-camera action. "Bill has a very strong sense of his value to Star Trek," Koenig told *Starlog* magazine, in what seemed like a calculated understatement, "and he explores and exploits it to its zenith. He will do whatever he can to make the picture better in terms of his performance. On the one hand, that's meritorious, but on the other hand, it may be at the sacrifice of the other performers." Like his fellow seven dwarfs, however, Koenig was loath to put his money where his mouth was. "At some juncture it was our responsibility to stand up [to Shatner]," he told *TV Guide* in 1998. "The fear was that we'd have our legs chopped off and find ourselves unemployed. But we never tested that." On the set of Star Trek: Generations in 1994, Koenig summed up his relationship with his "kyep-tin" this way: "He's not my pal, and there's no love lost between us. But he's not a monster." Not exactly a ringing endorsement.

After the **Star Trek** series wound down, Koenig resurfaced in another sci-fi **television** series, the syndicated *Babylon 5*, in the recurring role of a mind-reading officer in Earth's "Psi Corp" Intelligence Service.

"I feel affronted. I feel that I've been assailed by some of them."
—*Shatner*

"I have no feeling of animosity. I never did feel or understand what I read is their distaste for me."
—*Shatner, in the same interview, reflecting on the animosity of his* Star Trek *costars*

KOKO THE GORILLA

This world-famous mountain gorilla learned sign language from her keepers. Ever the daredevil, and always keen for publicity, Shatner got the chance to share a cage with the garrulous ape in 1988—and nearly paid the ultimate price. "I got scared. The only thing I could think of was to say to Koko 'I love you, Koko.' Because I knew that if I said 'I love you' then I would start to feel 'I love you.' It's a simple actor's trick." Looking deep into Koko's eyes, Shatner began repeating this amorous mantra to the fearsome simian, whose body language seemed gradually to soften. Then, he told an interviewer, "She put her hand out . . . and grabbed me by the balls!" Koko has kept mum about the encounter.

"Koko and I talked. We touched hands and we touched minds.
Feeling her powerful hand on the back of my neck was unlike any
other experience I've known."

—Shatner, on his 1988 "conversation" with Koko the Gorilla

LAFFERTY, MARCY

Shatner's second wife married him in 1973, and divorced him in 1994. The daughter of **television** producer Perry Lafferty and **radio** performer Mary Frances Carden, Lafferty studied ballet in New York. She abandoned dance for an acting career when her family moved to Los Angeles.

Lafferty first met Shatner in 1970, on the set of ***The Andersonville Trial***, where she was working as director George C. Scott's assistant. "I was down on my luck," Lafferty remembered, "and George wanted a female—it was an all-male cast—to run lines with the actors. And Bill was the only one who wanted to run lines with me because his part was bigger than *Hamlet*. And I fell in lust with him."

At first, this lust went unrequited. Lafferty spent weeks ogling Shatner while he recited his lines, but had trouble grabbing his attention. "Then one day he started looking a little more," she explained. Or as Shatner put it, "I gave her my look: And I reached out and kissed her." Various reports have Lafferty's knees buckling under the pressure of his smoldering manhood. Two weeks after filming completed, Shatner called to ask her out on a date. At the time, she had never seen a single ***Star Trek*** episode.

The relationship quickly turned sexual, and Shatner resisted commitment at first. "Bill had just been through a terrible divorce and a folded series," she recalled later. "He didn't want to get involved." But the leggy, dark-haired beauty wore down his resistance. Shatner surprised Lafferty by proposing to her in July 1973. They were married on October 20. At twenty-seven years old, she was fifteen years his junior.

The **marriage** ceremony was marked by a curious incident. "I heard a sob coming from someplace," Shatner reported. "I turned around—'who is that sobbing?' And it was me. I was sobbing." Perhaps he was envisioning the enormity of the eventual divorce settlement.

Lafferty supported Shatner through the most difficult period of his personal and professional life, the **lost years**. While the period

Shatner and second wife, Marcy Lafferty, smile for the cameras in the mid-1970s. Years later, she would sue him over improperly delivered horse semen.

was difficult, Lafferty never gave up on her man. "I didn't stay because I knew I'd get the brass ring if I stayed," she said. "I stayed because I loved him—and it was just more good than not good."

Elsewhere, Lafferty described her role in the **marriage**: "I make his life run as smoothly as possible, so he is free as an artist." Unfortunately, Shatner used that freedom to green light such stinkers as ***Big Bad Mama***, ***Impulse***, and ***The Devil's Rain***. The first featured three notorious **nude scenes** with Angie Dickinson, which Marcy claimed not to be bothered by at the time.

Marcy's tune began to change, however, when Shatner's real-life love affairs became increasingly public. Two **palimony** suits were filed against him in the early 1990s, by Shatner's former personal assistant **Eva Marie Friedrick**, and by Mexican actress **Vira Montes**. Both lawsuits were settled out of court, but the sting of infidelity hit Marcy hard. She acceded to Shatner's requests for reconciliation at first, but when he began seeing future third wife **Nerine Kidd** in 1993, the **marriage** was over.

"Life took us apart and it was time to move on," was how Lafferty assessed their marital breakup. "We both share the highest regard for one another and our loved ones." In fact, Lafferty had such high regard for Shatner that she socked it to him in the subsequent divorce settlement to the tune of $8 million. Though bitter over this financial misadventure, Shatner took much of the blame for the **marriage**'s failure. He wasn't so conciliatory the next time Lafferty sued him, in 2003, after a much-publicized dispute over **horse semen**.

> "She is essentially good, whereas I am not. Her essence is good, but I can be evil."
>
> —Shatner, on second wife, *Marcy Lafferty*

LAND OF NO RETURN, THE ✳

This low-budget 1978 disaster movie features Shatner and singer Mel Tormé. The "Velvet Fog" actually has a bigger role than Shatner, which gives you some idea of how Shatner's career was going at this point. The story concerns a circus plane that crash-lands in the snowbound wilderness of Utah. As Curt Benell, Shatner must battle captive animals unleashed by the crash and then rescue the crash survivors. Also known as *Snowman* and *Challenge to Survive*, *The Land of No Return* was filmed in 1975 and lay on the shelf marinating for three years before its unremarkable release.

LAWLER, JERRY "THE KING"

On March 31, 2007, Shatner helped induct this professional wrestling icon into the WWE Hall of Fame. Twelve years earlier, the two had met on less cordial terms. In 1995, Shatner dropped by Lawler's TV show *King's Court* to hype his then-upcoming TV movie **TekWar**. Just as he had with comedian Andy Kaufman several years earlier, Lawler began to taunt Shatner about his privileged Hollywood lifestyle. A physical confrontation ensued, during which Shatner subdued "the King" with a perfectly executed back body drop.

"I will boldly send you where no one's ever been
—courtesy of my fist!"

*—Jerry "the King" Lawler, taunting Shatner on
his wrestling show,* King's Court.

LIL' PIMP ✳

Shatner supplies the voice of Mayor Tony "Big Daddy" Gold in this 2005 animated film, the first feature to be made entirely with Flash animation. A lowbrow comedy set in a suburban town overrun by prostitutes and their procurers, the film relies heavily on crude **racial stereotypes** and scatological gags, to negligible effect. As the venal chief executive looking to subjugate the town's "hos" for his own nefarious purposes, Shatner gets to do a lot of off-camera moustache twirling while delivering lines like "Now that those pimps are behind bars, their stable of funky street skank will be working for Big Daddy Gold!" Despite the presence of such reliable B-list stars as Bernie Mac, David Spade, and Jennifer Tilly, *Lil' Pimp* sat on the shelf for two years after a calamitous test screening at which half the audience reportedly walked out in disgust. It went straight to video upon release.

LINE COUNTING

The practice of counting up one's lines of dialogue in a script is usually used to compare one's total to the number of lines given to other actors in the project. Reportedly, Shatner was a notorious line counter on the set of *Star Trek*. He was principally concerned that costar **Leonard Nimoy** not receive more lines than he did. In his 1996 account of the tortured birth of his 1966 teleplay "The City on the Edge of Forever," writer **Harlan Ellison** talks about Shatner line counting the script in his Hollywood home, then lobbying for rewrites when he discovered that Spock had more lines than Kirk. (A corollary anecdote about Shatner's **toupee** falling off upon his arrival at Ellison's house has been relegated only for *Star Trek* convention audiences.)

Shatner's efforts to maximize his own screen time on the series often affected the other cast members. For example, in her

1994 memoir *Beyond Uhura*, **Nichelle Nichols** explains how Shatner interrupted shooting of a scene in which her character had a significant part. "Later, when I scanned the revised script, my lines had been cut to 'I have Starfleet Command, sir,' before he and Spock took over." Nichols says she was furious over the incident, but it wasn't the first time she was a victim of Shatner's power plays. Even the performers' attempts to improvise fell under the star's domineering purview. As **George Takei** has explained, "Even if I tried to ad lib an entirely appropriate 'Aye, sir' to a command, he would nix it, claiming it would take away from the rhythm of the scene. This despite the fact that some of us had precious little to do in many of the scripts. Bill seemed totally immune to the sensitivities or the efforts of those he worked with."

Shatner claims to have remained oblivious to these complaints for many years. "I've always felt that the cast had a typical actor's sense of competition," he remarked to biographers in 1979. "We weren't saints, and we had actor's needs. But it was a good, healthy sense of competition, mostly focused on doing a good job, mostly good for the show."

Shatner's dialogue tabulating antics continued on the set of ***Star Trek: The Motion Picture*** in 1979. He even refused to feed lines off-camera to the other actors as they were being filmed for their closeups. "Bill was the reminder to me that coming back to *Star Trek* also meant coming back to nettlesome irritation," Takei observed in his autobiography *To the Stars!*

LIQUOR

Denny Crane may like to relax at the end of the day with a nice glass of Scotch, but his portrayer never touches the stuff. An avowed teetotaler, Shatner nonetheless served as his fellow actors' official taster during his days as a struggling performer in Ontario, **Canada**.

The actors were so poor they tried to make their own spirits, which Shatner then sampled to determine their degree of potency. "When I keeled over from the mixture, they knew it was ready for imbibing," Shatner recalled years later.

LITTLE WOMEN   ✷ ✷

This lavish four-hour 1978 TV movie retold the Louisa May Alcott classic about three loving sisters growing up in the shadow of the Civil War. Shatner is on hand, accent and all, as Professor Frederick Bhaer, the husband of Jo March (Susan Dey), the central character. Dorothy McGuire, Greer Garson, Robert Young, Meredith Baxter Birney, Ann Dusenberry, and Eve Plumb (Jan Brady of TV's *The Brady Bunch*) also star. In the short-lived *Little Women* TV series that followed, David Ackroyd assumed Shatner's role.

SIX DEGREES OF *STAR TREK*

William Schallert (Reverend March in **Little Women**) played Nilz Barris in "The Trouble with Tribbles." John DeLancie (Frank Vaughn in **Little Women**) went on to play the mischievous Q Entity on **Star Trek: The Next Generation**.

LIVE TELEVISION

Shatner enjoyed some of his finest moments as an actor in live performances during **television**'s "Golden Age" in New York City. Among his memorable portrayals were the leader of a lynch mob in the 1958 Playhouse 90 production *A Town Has Turned to Dust* and a virtuous western lawman in the 1958 U.S. Steel Hour playlet "Old Marshals Never Die." "Live television is exciting, a true art form," Shatner once observed. "You are performing for an audience, an audience of one, the director."

There are many pitfalls in live television that keep an actor up at night worrying. Among these is the fear of freezing up under the hot lights and the enormity of the proceedings. This happened to Shatner once, during the performance of the Studio One live drama "No Deadly Medicine" with Lee J. Cobb in 1957. Shatner was nonchalantly crossing the **stage** when, suddenly, it hit him: "My mind went, my God, there are 30 million people watching me walk," Shatner admitted to *Playboy* in 1989. For a brief moment, he found he could not move his limbs and had lost control of all motor functions. "I was asking 30 million people to suspend disbelief and assume that I was this person walking across the room." Luckily for him, he recovered quickly and went on with the show.

There is one actor's nightmare to which Shatner has never fallen prey: Forgetting his lines on live TV. He credits this to his uncanny ability to memorize dialogue. "I suppose I'm a quick study," he has said. "I think memorizing lines is a matter of confidence." To illustrate this point, Shatner told a story about Bert Lahr, the comedic actor best known for his portrayal of the Cowardly Lion in *The Wizard of Oz*. Shatner worked with Lahr on the live TV production of Jean Baptiste Moliere's classic *The School for Wives* in 1956. "He came to the first rehearsal with all his lines memorized, while the rest of us had barely cracked the book. But as rehearsals went on he began forgetting lines and by the last rehearsal he had to carry the script around with him. He had just choked up about the show." A lack of courage, perhaps?

LOCKLEAR, HEATHER

Locklear played Officer Stacy Sheridan from 1982 to 1986 on Shatner's police drama series *T. J. Hooker*. Shatner once dubbed her "The ultimate pinup." He went on to catalog the actor's physical attributes. "Her skin, eyes, teeth, all exude health. She's the criterion by which the clean, sexy, athletic California blonde is measured."

Locklear did not hold Shatner in nearly so high esteem. "I think it's chauvinistic," she declared of the macho cop series after *People* magazine named it one of the ten worst shows for Women in 1984. "But that's probably because William Shatner's on it." Locklear admitted to feeling intimidated by her world-famous costar, whose monopoly on derring-do left little for her character to do. "When it's your show, you can't be wrong," said Locklear. "You wouldn't see Captain

Shatner and his crew look for some lowlife punks to blow away in this publicity still from TV's *T. J. Hooker*.

Kirk—I mean *T. J. Hooker*—doing something wrong. It kind of frustrates me, because I'm always wrong. He's supposed to be a hero, and heroes can't do anything wrong. Right? I always had at least one line, but I was so nervous I couldn't always get it out. I would get really nervous when Bill Shatner would talk to me."

At the same time she was filming ***T. J. Hooker***, Locklear was playing the vixen Sammy Jo Dean on the hit nighttime drama *Dynasty*. That series role helped make her an international **sex** symbol—something Shatner says he could see coming all along. "Heather never had any sense that she was beautiful," he noted in 1995. "She had no sense of her appeal. I think she knows she's desired by America now, though." In 2005, the two old LCPD partners reunited when Locklear made two guest appearances on Shatner's series ***Boston Legal***.

LOS ANGELES PET MEMORIAL PARK

This celebrity pet cemetery in Calabasas, California, serves as final resting place for Shatner's beloved **Doberman** pinscher, China, laid to rest in 1988. "The Beauty Girl" is the inscription on the grave marker, which bears the likeness of the seven-year-old canine. Shatner had the dog buried in a secluded spot behind some shrubbery because, as he put it, "China always liked to spread out under the shade of a tree." Soon after China's interment, overzealous ***Star Trek*** **fans** (is there any other kind?) began descending on the park looking for the grave of Captain Kirk's best friend. Officials at the cemetery did not aid them in their search. China's neighbors in eternal slumber include Tori Spelling's pet poodle, Angel; Tony Orlando's beloved Yorkshire terrier, Bambi; and the ashes of a family of cats belonging to **game show** host Bob Barker.

LOST YEARS

This is the commonly accepted term for the period of Shatner's career between the cancellation of **Star Trek** in 1969 and the premiere of **Star Trek: The Motion Picture** ten years later. The decade was characterized by a steep personal and professional decline marked by dreadful movie and TV appearances, broken relationships, and erratic personal behavior. Catalysts for this descent include the 1967 death of the actor's father, **Joseph Shatner**, the loss of steady work and income (which had been brought in by **Star Trek**), and the dissolution of his **marriage** to first wife **Gloria Rand**. Lowlights of this dark time include Shatner's nude love scenes with Angie Dickinson in **Big Bad Mama**, his somnambulant performance as a perverted psycho killer in **Impulse** (aka *Want a Ride, Little Girl?*), and his bizarre rendition of Elton John's **"Rocket Man"** at the 1978 Science Fiction Film Awards.

The absolute nadir of the lost years seems to have been the stretch from 1969 to 1973, spanning the demise of his first **marriage** until his second wedding day. "There's a five-year period that I really don't remember," Shatner says of this dead zone. "I'd meet people and have no recollection of their faces. There are women I knew and had abiding relationships with, who I have completely forgotten." During this desolate span, Shatner lived out of a camper shell hooked up to the back of a beat-up pickup truck. In the summer months, when TV work was scarce, he hit the open road to seek out and explore strange new worlds of regional **theater**. Once, while he was parked outside a friend's house in Millburn, New Jersey, a small boy knocked on the door of his camper and asked for a tour of his "spaceship." Shatner obliged, showing the tyke such high-tech features as the "transporter module" (shower stall) and the "control panel" (his stovetop).

What might have passed for romantic slumming at an earlier age was a living nightmare for the fortysomething Shatner. His meager income was quickly gobbled up by taxes, agents' fees, and alimony. At one point, he found he lacked the funds to cash a check for fifteen dollars. "I'd travel—two or three jobs in one day, if I could—just to make some money to get . . . [everything] together again," he confessed to biographers in 1979. "I became frantic, obsessed." By the end of the 1970s, he was reduced to appearing on TV **game shows** like *Tattletales*, *Celebrity Bowling*, and ***$10,000 Pyramid*** to supplement the paltry $40 in annual residuals he then received for his work on ***Star Trek***.

Ironically, it was Paramount Pictures—the company that had steadfastly declared ***Star Trek*** a money loser despite its enormous popularity in reruns—that returned Shatner to national consciousness. The 1979 release of ***Star Trek: The Motion Picture***, while an

Brooke Shields pulls her eyes away from Shatner's peculiar blouse long enough to say "cheese" in this 1980s publicity photo for *Circus of the Stars*.

artistic disaster, resuscitated Shatner's moribund career and allowed him to forego the Z-grade projects that had sustained him during this long, lean period.

> "I was insane the way an animal is insane, because I had lost my family, I'd lost everything, and I was scrambling, clawing to get everything back and put it together again."
>
> —*Shatner, on his state of mind during the lost years*

LUCIFER

Shatner appears as the Lord of the Air and Crown Prince of Hell in a brief but memorable appearance introducing Comedy Central's annual year-end wrap-up special, *Last Laugh '05*. Dressed in stereotypically Satanic garb—red suit, horns, and Fu Manchu moustache (not to mention an exceedingly long tail)—Devil Shatner declares, "I had one hell of a year" before launching into a specially rewritten version of his *Transformed Man* chestnut **"It Was a Very Good Year."** Filled with topical references to hot desert wars, hurricanes, and Shatner's own Emmy win, the number is enlivened by the appearance of a gaggle of scantily clad Satanic dancers.

"LUCY IN THE SKY WITH DIAMONDS" *

This 1967 Beatles classic is one of the highlights of Shatner's epochal 1968 album, *The Transformed Man*. Written and sung by John Lennon, and inspired by the works of Lewis Carroll (and, some say, Lennon's own experiences with LSD), the original track is a masterpiece of psychedelic rock. Shatner's cover, by contrast, is an unnecessarily turgid reworking that substitute's the actor's speedy, spoken-word bleatings for the Beatle's nasal, hallucinogenic drone.

In May 2003, a BBC viewers' poll voted Shatner's "Lucy" the worst Beatles cover of all time. (It edged out Jim Carrey's "I Am the Walrus," among other tracks, for that honor.) Appearing on the long-running BBC **radio** show *Desert Island Discs*, actor George Clooney cited "Lucy" as one of the indispensable records to bring you with you in case you get stranded on a desert island. "You need a reason to get off the island," Clooney said, "and if you play William Shatner singing 'Lucy in the Sky With Diamonds' then you will hollow out your own leg and make a canoe out of it to get off this island."

Ask Shat

Q: What did you do as a child growing up in Montreal?
A: We'd milk cows. The feeling of warm milk being squirted into my face postdated my mother's.

SING A SONG OF SHATNER

For a man whose musical performances seem to defy all logic and taste, Shatner has been a surprisingly bountiful font of inspiration for other musicians. Here are just a few of the songs that pay tribute to the **Transfomed Man**.

- "Shatner," a 1987 song by Britpop icons The Wedding Present, name-drops the actor in the midst of a bouncy tune about an abusive relationship.

- Spizzenergi's 1979 single "Where's Captain Kirk" places the punk band on board *Enterprise* with no commander.

- "Everyone's a Captain Kirk" wails Teutonic rocker Nena in the English-language version of her 1984 anti-nuclear hit "99 Red Balloons."

- Comedian Adam Sandler's 1996 novelty hit "The Chanukah Song" lists Shatner in its catalog of Jewish celebrities.

- "Oh, Canada," a 1997 track by the Denver based ska combo Five Iron Frenzy, lists the many pleasures of the Great White North, including "that William Shatner is a native citizen."

- "Tell me why I bid on Shatner's old toupee?" queries Weird Al Yancovic in his 2003 song "eBay," sung to the tune of "I Want It That Way" by the Backstreet Boys.

MARRIAGE

Shatner has been married four times: to **Gloria Rand** (née Rosenberg) from 1956 to 1969; to **Marcy Lafferty** from 1973 to 1994; to **Nerine Kidd** from 1997 until her death in 1999; and to current wife **Elizabeth Anderson Martin** since 2001. His first two unions ended in divorce, with charges of constructive abandonment and chronic philandering hurled Shatner's way. Nevertheless, he has remained committed to the ideal of a permanent, monogamous relationship.

Addressing a *Star Trek* convention audience in Great Britain, Shatner could have been speaking of any of his marriages when he said: "A husband and wife live in a balance between humor and anger, ease and dis-ease. As with any relationship, there can be more positive or more negative elements. In my marriage there is tension, anger, and dissatisfaction."

Shatner and first wife, Gloria Rand, look the perfect couple—but there were rocky shores ahead.

MARTIN, ELIZABETH ANDERSON

This blonde horse trainer is Shatner's fourth wife. A native of Hinsdale, Illinois, Martin began training and showing her family's Arabian and half-Arabian **horses** as a young girl. She became a professional horse trainer in 1980. Married for 14 years to fellow trainer Mike Martin, she lost her husband to cancer in 1997. Feelings of commiseration over the loss of a spouse prompted her to write to Shatner after the sudden death of his third wife, **Nerine Kidd**, in 1999. Charmed by the red calligraphy on the condolence note, Shatner soon contacted her and arranged a meeting. Before long, the two began dating, bound by their shared love of **horses** and a common experience of grief. They were wed in an understated private ceremony in Lebanon, Indiana, on February 13, 2001—a

The fourth time's a charm for Shatner, who married
horse trainer Elizabeth Anderson Martin in 2001.

far cry from the all-star nuptials Shatner and Kidd staged in 1997.
Shatner and Martin live in Los Angeles. Together they raise westerns and saddlebreds, compete at equestrian events, and cosponsor the annual Hollywood Charity Horse Show.

"We are just having a ball. We have come from a perspective that makes
us grateful for every good moment. We've come through the fire."

—*Elizabeth Anderson Martin, on her second chance at love with William Shatner*

Shatner's on-screen marriages have been every bit as unstable as his real-life relationships. In fact, divorce lawyers could have a field day with some of the problems that have bedeviled Shatner as a TV movie husband. Here are some of the more egregious examples of marital dysfunction:

WIFE	MOVIE	POSSIBLE CAUSE FOR DIVORCE ACTION
Patty Duke Astin	*Secrets of a Married Man*	Daughter tormented by psycho sitter
Susan Blakely	*The Babysitter*	Daughter joins hedonist cult
Julie Adams	*Broken Angel*	Daughter gets hooked on LSD at unchaperoned party
Michelle Phillips	*Go Ask Alice*	Cheats on wife with a succession of sleazy prostitutes

MATZO KNEIDLACH

Shatner submitted a recipe for these traditional Passover dumplings to *The Celebrity Kosher Cookbook* in 1975. Apparently inspired by his grandmother's "tightly packed, indestructible and delicious kneidel," Shatner's recipe requires two separated eggs, three table-spoons of chicken fat, half a cup of hot water, a quarter cup of matzo meal, salt, and two quarts of boiling broth or hot, salted water. The egg yolks are beaten with the chicken fat until well blend-ed and thick, and then poured over the hot broth (or hot water) and then well heated. Matzo meal with salt is added next and folded into the egg whites. The resultant concoction is chilled for about thirty minutes. Then the mix is shaped into small balls, dropped (gently) into the two quarts of boiling broth (or salted water), and covered. The heat is reduced, and everything gets cooked gently for about twenty-five minutes. Shatner insists that the recipe should make about eighteen dumplings. A guaranteed crowd pleaser for your next celebrity seder!

> "To prevent rising beyond your station, [my grandmother] put a kneidel in your stomach. It made it very difficult to rise at all."
> —Shatner, on the addling effect of his grandmother's dumplings

MCGILL UNIVERSITY

Founded in 1821, Shatner's alma mater is the oldest university in Montreal. Shatner attended McGill's College of Commerce, majoring in business (not the long-rumored **dentistry**) from 1948 to 1952. His experience at McGill differed little from the typical collegian's. "I never attended classes. I took notes from other people's notes, went to exams and barely passed exams," he once confessed. Despite his abysmal academic record, the university saw fit in 1995 to rename the Student Union the **Shatner Building** in his honor.

Shatner did excel at one thing—**acting**. He put in long days on campus in pursuit of what was becoming his overriding passion. He wrote, produced, and directed college musicals, including his magnum opus, 1952's *The Red, White, and Blue Review*, which received media coverage across **Canada**. In those days before the widespread availability of television, Shatner also served as president of the university's **radio** club, experience he used to land paying gigs acting on **radio** in Montreal.

A beefy Shatner hams it up as a kidnapped beauty
pageant host in 2000's *Miss Congeniality*.

MISS CONGENIALITY ✳ ✳

Shatner plays smarmy beauty pageant emcee Stan Fields in this 2000
Sandra Bullock comedy, about an FBI agent who goes undercover at
a Miss America–type contest. The film was a box office hit and an
important step in Shatner's long climb out of D-list Hell. The *New York
Times* reviewer even lamented his relative lack of screen time. Costars
included his future **Boston Legal** sparring partner Candice Bergen.
Shatner reprised his role as Fields in the less successful 2005 sequel,
Miss Congeniality 2: Armed and Fabulous.

MONTES, VIRA

This Mexican actress filed a $6 million **palimony** suit against
Shatner following a six-year love affair. Shatner met Montes (best
known for playing Esperanza in the 1992 feature *American Me*) in
1984 when she appeared on an episode of his TV series **T. J.
Hooker** (1982–86). He quickly began courting the raven-haired,

twenty-five-year-old beauty, employing an unusual, but effective "mating" ritual: his customary tactic of rubbing his body up against hers during filming (a technique he used to less effect with *T. J. Hooker* costar **Heather Locklear**). According to Montes, a series of lunch and dinner dates followed, though Shatner was married at the time to **Marcy Lafferty**. Before long, Shatner and Montes were enjoying a torrid romance. Montes claimed the then married actor made her pretend to be his niece when traveling so they wouldn't arouse suspicion.

"I cannot believe what a fantastic lover he is," Montes once said of Shatner. "He makes me feel like no other man has made me feel. He is like no other man in my life, and nobody has ever had that effect on me. No one has ever handled me like Bill." By the end of the '80s, however, Vira was hands-off; the relationship had soured, and the lovers were headed for litigation.

"We were in close quarters a lot, and strangely, Bill just kept bumping into me. He especially kept making sure our chests kept rubbing together. I was very attracted to him, and who wouldn't be?"

—*Vira Montes, explaining how Shatner won her heart with frottage on the set of* T. J. Hooker.

MOTORCYCLES

Cycling in the Southern California desert became a way to blow off steam for Shatner during his years on *Star Trek*. "He would go off on weekends and come back bruised and slashed," costar **Leonard Nimoy** remembered. "He was forever running into tree branches and bramble bushes and God knows what else."

Shatner's companion on many of these outings was *Star Trek* bit

"Man down!" Shatner takes a spill on his hog in the mid-1960s.

player David L. Ross, a Kato Kaelin-like character who happened to excel at many of the dangerous activities at which Shatner longed to prove his own mettle. "He was really a man's man," Ross said of his famous friend, "the kind of guy who does the macho thing for the pleasure of it—not to tell *Variety* all the time: 'Look what I did.'" Ross was present for Shatner's first scuba diving excursion, and for one of his more embarrassing motorcycle moments. The two men were out riding in the desert with actor Gary Lockwood, who played the glowing-eyed villain Gary Mitchell in the second **Star Trek** pilot, "Where No Man Has Gone Before," when Shatner wiped out and landed backside-down on a cactus. His two friends had to pull the thorns from his bare rump, including one so big it had to be removed with pliers.

"William Shatner was much more macho than Steve McQueen ever was, but it was never publicized."

—*David L. Ross, Shatner's motorcycling companion, on their manly adventures in the desert*

MOUNTAIN PLAYHOUSE

Shatner began working at this Montreal summer stock **theater** in 1952 as the theater's business manager, but he quickly proved incompetent in that position. He repeatedly mislaid receipts and lost tickets while incessantly lobbying for auditions with the theater company. Eventually, the owners acquiesced, providing Shatner with his first break as an actor. He later relied on a professional reference from the Mountain Playhouse to secure a place with the **Canadian National Repertory Theatre**.

"MR. TAMBOURINE MAN"   ✳

Along with **"Lucy in the Sky with Diamonds,"** this Bob Dylan cover is one of the most popular tracks on Shatner's groundbreaking 1968 album *The Transformed Man*. Originally recorded for the album *Bringing It All Back Home* in 1965, Dylan's version of the song is regularly included on lists of the greatest rock songs of all time. In Shatner's hands, however, it becomes an undisputed camp classic. His confused, constipated phrasing climaxes in a guttural scream of the song's title that sounds as if it should be punctuated by gunfire; it robs Dylan's mellow acid dream of all its hypnotic power, leaving only bad vibes in its place. One wonders if Charles Manson's interior monologue sounded something like this. Unsurprisingly, Shatner thinks his rendition is utterly brilliant, though he's reconciled himself to the fact that his musical genius is misunderstood. "In the beginning it bothered me that people singled it out and poked fun at it," he told *Newsweek* magazine in 2004. "They didn't know what I was doing. The album *The Transformed Man* is much more extensive than that song. But since people only heard that song, I went along with the joke."

MUSIC

Second only to **acting**, music has been the touchstone of Shatner's creative life for more than 40 years. "I've been entranced with music for the longest time and the bane of my life is I really can't sing," he has admitted, "but I found that to move an audience and move myself, it's accomplished so much more easily and effectively with music."

Shatner's love affair with music began in the late '60s, when he first became enamored with the idea of reinventing himself as a rock star. "The rock world today is where it's happening," he told an interviewer at the time. "Rock is expanding the horizons of our ability to entertain. Rock stars are dynamites of creativity and energy, and we have nothing but to learn from them." A quick study, Shatner channeled the fruits of his education into **The Transformed Man**, his 1968 album of dramatic monologues and spoken-word renditions of pop songs.

In the 1970s, he again followed the trend with a series of **one-man shows** on college campuses. Borrowing from such super groups as Led Zeppelin and Pink Floyd, he employed synthesizers and a complex laser light show as accompaniment to his rants about space travel. Veteran rocker Mark Goldenberg, a member of the Al Stewart Group, played guitar at some of Shatner's performances. A 1977 double album from Lemli Records, **William Shatner Live!**, replete with gatefold cover and rock star glam shots, commemorated the events on vinyl.

After wisely electing to sit out the '80s (the thought of a beefy, bewigged Shatner popping and locking to a synthesized beat is almost too horrific to bear), Shatner re-inflated his musical muse in the 1990s. He rapped in iambic pentameter in the 1998 film **Free Enterprise** and recorded extensively with pop hitmaker **Ben Folds**. Their 2004 collaboration, **Has Been**, is one of Shatner's finest musical achievements.

> "I'm doing word jazz—expressing in jazz form words that
> come from my soul."
>
> *—Shatner, encapsulating his musical experiments from*
> The Transformed Man *to* Has Been

"MY WAY"

Accompanied by a chorus line of dancing imperial stormtroopers, Shatner croons a personalized comedic rendition of this Frank Sinatra classic to honoree George Lucas at the American Film Institute's 2005 tribute to the *Star Wars* impresario.

MYSTERIES OF THE GODS ✳

Carl Sagan had nothing to fear from Shatner, if this tedious 1977 documentary about "ancient astronauts" and the origin of life on Earth is any indication. As the on-camera narrator, Shatner promises "a searching and scientific look into the future," but the film dwells almost entirely in the past, as it examines the possibility of extraterrestrial visitations in Earth's primordial infancy.

Loosely based on the writings of Erich von Daniken, *Mysteries of the Gods* relies on interviews with scientists, UFOlogists, and clairvoyants to assess the "alien astronaut" theory of human religions, which purports to explain mankind's most sacred yearnings as the byproduct of a close encounter between cavemen and spacemen way back in prehistory. (Shatner himself subscribed to this crackpot theory at the time.) The general level of the film's credibility is indicated by the presence of celebrity telepsychic Jeane Dixon among the interviewees.

Helping Shatner coordinate scientific interviews for the film was **Jesco von Puttkamer**, the NASA official who served as a technical adviser on ***Star Trek: The Motion Picture***. In fact, Shatner prepared for **Mysteries of the Gods** while filming **Star Trek: The Motion Picture** and performing his **one-man show** "Star Traveler." It was a truly brutal schedule. Explained **von Puttkamer**, "He learned the lines in three days, while we made the film. And he would joke, laugh, carry on a serious conversation, plan how to handle the interviews of scientists for the film—all at the same time."

Shatner tried to break the tension during what must have been a grueling period for him professionally by resorting to his old **Star Trek** standby—**practical jokes**. Von Puttkamer tells of one time when Shatner was interviewing him on camera about extraterrestrial life: "You have to be very tight, you know, for the interview, for the close-ups—very close together—nose to nose. We had been working on it and I was not used to it. I was a little stiff or something. He wanted to loosen me up. All of a sudden Bill leaned forward and he kissed me!" The ensuing hysterics helped both men get through the scene more easily. If only there were a way to help the audience get through this film more easily. Oh wait—the fast forward button.

NAKED CITY
See **Burmese Sailor**.

NATIONAL LAMPOON'S LOADED WEAPON I ⭒
Thankfully, Shatner has a small role in this painfully unfunny 1993 spoof of the *Lethal Weapon* series. He plays a deranged military man named General Mortars. That name alone telegraphs the prevailing level of humor in this lowbrow big-screen farce. Emilio Estevez and Samuel L. Jackson are the unfortunate leads. **James Doohan** of **Star Trek** fame has an embarrassing cameo as an espresso machine repairman. "William Shatner is allowed to ham it up disturbingly," wrote *Daily Variety*. Perhaps the reviewer was thinking of the scene in which Shatner sticks his face into an aquarium and pulls out a fish with his teeth.

NEAR DEATH EXPERIENCE

Shatner had one while driving from Montreal to Toronto during his early days as an actor in the 1950s. A truck sideswiped his car, propelling it into a deep canal and leaving him struggling to escape as the vehicle filled with water. As his life flashed before his eyes, Shatner heard Macbeth's speech on the futility of life echoing in his head: "It is a tale, told by an idiot, signifying nothing." Just then the truck driver appeared and freed the drowning actor from his sinking automobile. A shaken Shatner decided on the basis of this experience to redouble his efforts to do something meaningful with his life.

NICHOLS, NICHELLE

This leggy, beguiling African-American actor played Lt. Nyota Uhura on **Star Trek**. An accomplished singer and dancer before she broke into **television**, Nichols brought to **Star Trek** a versatility that was not always fully utilized by the show's creators or acknowledged by her costars. Her most memorable contribution to the series was one she shared with Shatner, providing **television**'s first **interracial kiss** in the episode "Plato's Stepchildren" on November 22, 1968.

Over the years, Nichols' relationship with Shatner has occasionally been strained. In her 1994 memoir *Beyond Uhura*, she accused him of cutting her lines and general boorishness on the set. The two were also embroiled in a minor media controversy when Shatner used off-the-record discussions and out-of-context quotations as grist for his own book, *Star Trek Memories*. Despite these clashes, however, Nichols was never as unrelentingly critical of

Shatner as, say, **Jimmy Doohan**, and she has had nice things to say about him in interviews through the years. Nichols was one of only two *Star Trek* cast mates to join Shatner on **stage** for Comedy Central's *Roast of William Shatner* in 2006.

"Don't you want to hear how much we hated you?"

—*Nichelle Nichols, wrapping up her interview with Shatner for his book,* Star Trek Memories

NIMOY, LEONARD

This cerebral, saturnine actor, poet, and photographer won an enormous worldwide cult following with his portrayal of the half-Vulcan science officer Spock on *Star Trek*. The son of Ukrainian Jews who fled Europe during the Russian Revolution, Nimoy built his reputation playing Indians in low-budget westerns before joining the starship *Enterprise* crew in 1966. His misguided "rock" albums and collections of mawkish poetry—including 1983's ghastly *Warmed by Love*—rival Shatner's extracurricular pursuits for spectacular awfulness. In recent years, he has become an accomplished director, with the third and fourth *Star Trek* features and the comedy hit *Three Men and a Baby* to his credit, and has lately devoted much of his time to still photography.

Shatner and Nimoy first met while filming an episode of *The Man from U.N.C.L.E.* in 1964. Nimoy remembers his first impressions of Shatner as being "extremely professional, extremely talented, extremely energetic, extremely communicative." When Shatner signed on to do *Star Trek*, "I was very pleased because he had a very fine reputation as an actor and I felt that was a healthy sign about the possibilities [for the series]."

Despite their mutual respect, the two actors occasionally clashed on the set. "We were extremely energetic and extremely aggressive about expressing our ideas and sometimes there was a conflict," Nimoy has said. Reportedly, Shatner resented the media coverage and sacks of fan mail Nimoy received once his Spock character caught on with viewers.

One day, that envy exploded into anger. A *Life* magazine camera crew had set up around Nimoy's makeup chair to photograph every step of the star's pointed-ear application process. Unluckily, Shatner was in the next chair having his hairpiece applied. ("The top of his head was a lot of skin and a few little odd tufts of hair," costar **Jimmy**

Erstwhile rivals Shatner and Leonard Nimoy have become close friends in recent years.

Doohan later recalled. "The mirrors on the makeup room walls were arranged so that we could all see the laying on of his rug.") A simmering Shatner, dismayed that the secret of his **toupee** was being revealed to a national magazine audience, leapt from his chair, demanding that all future makeup sessions be held in his trailer.

"Bill Shatner's problem," *Star Trek* scriptwriter Norman Spinrad once observed, "was that he wasn't given as interesting a character to play as Nimoy was." Eventually, both men were dueling each other for lines, screen time, and character development on the series. The writers' attempts to mollify both actors' **ego**s proved awkward and insufficient. The conflict reached its nadir midway through the first season, when a despondent **Gene Roddenberry** turned to science fiction wise man Isaac Asimov for advice. Asimov suggested that Roddenberry accentuate the closeness of the relationship between the two lead characters, making their byplay less argumentative and more believable. In the end, the show's costars settled into an uneasy truce. They even negotiated their contracts in concert with one another, including a so-called "favored nations" clause ensuring that no benefit enjoyed by one would be denied to the other.

On a personal level, Shatner and Nimoy have little in common, outside of a shared love of fried egg sandwiches on rye bread. "I try to be diplomatic, but Leonard tends to be more forthright," says Shatner. "He's a very passionate guy," observes the taciturn Nimoy. "He plunges into stuff. . . . I like to tease him: 'Bill, why don't you do something with your life?'" In 1992, the two men took their Alphonse and Gaston act on the road for a series of joint appearances to commemorate *Star Trek*'s twenty-fifth anniversary. The eleven-city **Twenty-Five Year Mission Tour** featured stories and anecdotes from their days on the TV and movie series and played to sellout houses across America. Nine years later, they used the same concept as the basis for *Mind Meld*, a conversation about the **Star Trek** phenomenon filmed at Nimoy's Beverly Hills home and released on DVD.

NORTH BEACH AND RAWHIDE   ✳ ✳

In this 1985 TV movie, Shatner plays Rawhide McGregor, a Father Flanagan-type figure who operates a correctional ranch for wayward urban boys. Tate Donovan plays North Beach, a teen troublemaker whom Rawhide endeavors to rehabilitate. Chris and Leo Penn (Sean's younger brother and his actor/director dad, respectively) and Ron "Superfly" O'Neal round out the cast.

Shatner was not the original choice for Rawhide, the one-time convict turned do-gooder. However, when journeyman actor Frederic Forrest bowed out at the last minute, the dedicated equestrian leapt at the chance to act alongside so many beautiful **horses**. "We filmed in northern Los Angeles," Shatner told the *New York Daily News*. "It was a rare experience galloping across the land and sharing a unique experience with my horse, so unfettered and away from everybody. I love to ride!"

NUDE SCENES

Shatner has done a number of nude scenes over the course of his **acting** career. When he played Tom, a swinging tennis instructor, in the 1971 play "Remote Asylum," he had to simulate **sex** with Anne Francis live on **stage**. "I had to reach an orgasm at the Ahmanson Theatre in Los Angeles, in front of 2,200 people, every night for six weeks. That was tough. Because how much do you reveal? Are you a screamer or aren't you?"

He had no such trepidation when it came to his most famous movie nude scenes opposite Angie Dickinson in the 1974 feature **Big Bad Mama**. "Angie is beautiful. She is luscious, sensuous, intelligent," Shatner enthused to *Playboy* in 1989. The pair appeared naked on three separate occasions in the low-budget action yarn. Dickinson, who at the time was a national **sex** symbol for her role as TV's *Police Woman*, quickly overcame her fears of being filmed in the buff with the esteemed Captain Kirk. "Angie started the movie about two weeks before I did," Shatner reported. "When I came in, the first scene, of course, was the nude scene. So I got my body make-up on and wore my shorts under a kimono on the set. Angie was already there, in her dressing gown on the bed. I awkwardly took

A vigorous *Star Trek*-era Shatner during the time when he eagerly took his shirt off for the camera.

off my slippers and stepped out of my shorts and kept my robe clutched around me. That's when I noticed that her robe had spilled open a little and she wasn't wearing any shorts." Shatner's pubic hair is briefly visible in one of the scenes, photos from which were later published in adult men's magazines.

Thereafter, time was not kind to either performer. Dickinson employed a body double for her nude scenes in the 1987 sequel *Big Bad Mama II*, while Shatner had bloated so much by 1991 that he demanded that technicians airbrush his gargantuan behind in **Star Trek VI: The Undiscovered Country**.

See **butt tightening**.

NUKES IN SPACE: THE RAINBOW BOMBS ✳ ✳

Shatner narrates this 1999 documentary about the lingering effects of nuclear tests conducted by the United States and the Soviet Union in near space and the upper atmosphere over a 35-year period. His cadence is restrained throughout, befitting the gravity of the subject. The soundtrack is by the Moscow Symphony Orchestra.

ONE-MAN SHOWS

Shatner mounted a series of one-man **stage** performances in the 1970s under a variety of titles. Common elements of the events included live readings from great literature, laser light shows, and a space travel theme. Occasionally, Shatner incorporated some of his own prose and poetry into the ambitious proceedings. He described one such early production as "a history of the imagination and how it's been limited by various forces like religion and sciences."

The early one-man shows were popular on college campuses and helped alert Shatner to the mushrooming phenomenon of **Star Trek** fandom. By the end of the 1970s, thanks largely to the interest generated by the as-yet-unreleased **Star Trek: The Motion Picture**,

Shatner's **stage** "evenings" had developed into multimillion dollar coliseum productions featuring the latest in laser-concert technology.

The 1976 national tour of *An Evening with William Shatner* featured recitations from the works of Shakespeare, Bertolt Brecht, Edmund Rostand, and H. G. Wells. It played at forty-five college campuses to audiences totaling more than 100,000 people. In 1978, Shatner took to the **stage** again with *Symphony of the Stars: Music from the Galaxies and Beyond*, this time with musical accompaniment from local philharmonic orchestras. In 1977, he reworked the material from this trek and performed it under the title *Star Traveler*. An album compiling material from Shatner's one-man shows was released in 1978 under the title ***William Shatner: Live***.

OPERATION LAZARUS

A code name for a covert military operation into Laos led by American soldiers in 1983, this shady sortie was partially funded by Shatner. The unsuccessful mission to rescue American prisoners-of-war caused an international incident and resulted in the deaths of three Laotian guerrillas. The tangled web of intrigue began, of all places, on the set of ***T. J. Hooker***. There Shatner met **Bo Gritz**, a self-promoting former Green Beret and itinerant mercenary. Shatner reportedly became fascinated by Gritz's life story and paid him $10,000 to develop a TV movie about himself for Paramount Pictures. "What he was going to do with the money was none of my business," Shatner said after the incident became public.

What **Gritz** did was violate the U.S. Neutrality Act. Using an additional $35,000 from other sources, including actor/director Clint Eastwood, he assembled a high-tech strike force and invaded Laos through neighboring Thailand. Hoping to free American servicemen who, he was convinced, were being held in a cave near the Mekong Delta, Gritz instead found himself ambushed, captured, and charged with illegal entry and arms possession. Bankrolling such an illegal operation could have earned Shatner a three-year jail term. However, he repeatedly denied all knowledge of Gritz's activities and was never charged with wrongdoing.

OSMOSIS JONES   ＊＊

Shatner supplies the voice of Mayor Phleggming, the corpulent burgermeister of a "city" located inside the body of a disheveled zookeeper, in this 2001 comedy feature starring Bill Murray and Chris Rock. A strange melange of live action and animation, *Osmosis Jones* was a major box office disaster that helped drive a stake through the heart of the venerable Warner Bros. animation department. Oddly enough, this is the first of two films within a four-year period in which Shatner provides the voice for a cartoon mayor. The other is 2005's execrable **Lil' Pimp**.

OUTER LIMITS, THE   ＊＊

In one of his final **television** appearances prior to signing on as Captain Kirk on **Star Trek**, Shatner played a beleaguered astronaut on the September 26, 1964 installment of this science fiction anthology series. "Cold Hands, Warm Heart" spins the tale of Col. Jeff Barton, a space traveler who returns from a mission to Venus only to find himself mutating into a creature with scaly forearms, webbed fingers, and a low body temperature. The slow-moving script is not among the series' finest, but Shatner's intense portrayal makes the episode somewhat entertaining.

SIX DEGREES OF STAR TREK

Malachi Throne, later Commodore Mendez in "The Menagerie," plays a doctor in **The Outer Limits**; extra Larry Montaigne would go on to play Decius in "Balance of Terror" and Stonn in "Amok Time."

Take a look at these hands!" Space is not kind to spaceman Shatner in a 1964 episode of *The Outer Limits*.

OUTRAGE, THE ✶✶

Paul Newman joins Shatner in this ill-conceived western remake of Akira Kurosawa's classic film *Rashomon*. Shatner is woefully miscast as a timid, disillusioned clergyman. The *New York Times* found his performance "callow and unsure." Newman is even worse as a boisterous, drunken Mexican bandit. Actors Laurence Harvey, Claire Bloom, and Edward G. Robinson round out the cast.

> ### SIX DEGREES OF *STAR TREK*
> Paul Fix, who plays an Indian in *The Outrage*, went on to play Dr. Mark Piper in the second *Star Trek* pilot "Where No Man Has Gone Before."

OVER THE HEDGE ✶✶✶

Shatner supplies the voice of Ozzie the Opossum in this 2006 animated children's feature. As an over-the-top Shakespearean ham who wows woodland audiences with his ability to play dead, Shatner

Shatner plays possum in the 2006 animated children's feature *Over the Hedge*.

gets a chance to mock his own signature **acting** style. He also appears on the movie's soundtrack, as an aggrieved homeowner on a remake of **Ben Folds**' song "Rockin' the Suburbs."

OWEN MARSHALL, COUNSELOR AT LAW ✴ ✴

Arthur Hill has the title role in this 1971 TV movie, with Shatner, Vera Miles, Dana Wynters, and Tim Matheson in support. Dubbed "Marcus Welby with torts" by *Variety* magazine, the film served as the pilot for a successful weekly series. The plot involves a hippie (Bruce Davison) falsely accused of murdering a well-to-do house-wife. Shatner plays Dave Blankenship, the district attorney who prosecutes the case. Shatner had also played a prosecutor the previous year in *The Andersonville Trial*.

PAINTBALL

In his 70s, Shatner became a passionate devotee of this popular weekend wargame, in which competitors battle one another in simulated combat scenarios using guns that shoot bladders filled with dye. Recruited to take part in a charity event by his friend J. J. Brookshire of the Society of Paintball Players and Teams (SPPLAT), Shatner soon caught the paintball bug big time. "Once he started, we had to make him stop playing," Brookshire has said. Shatner now regularly takes part in charity paintball tournaments around the United States, most famously as the team captain of the "Federation" in the *Star Trek*-themed pay-per-view extravaganza *William Shatner's Spplat Attack*.

> "The essence of paintball is the fact that when you get hit by a ball full of paint, it hurts just enough to say, 'Ow, I gotta get out of the way,' but not enough to say, 'I quit.'"
>
> —*Shatner, on one of his favorite weekend pursuits, paintball*

PALIMONY

Shatner has been the subject of two multimillion-dollar palimony suits. The first, filed in December of 1989 by his one-time personal assistant, **Eva Marie Friedrick**, sought $2 million in compensation based on promises of jobs and **acting** roles that Shatner made to her while they were having an affair. Friedrick claimed that Shatner dismissed her and disavowed their relationship following her injury in an October 1988 car accident. "I was fired when he got tired of me," an incensed Friedrick later confided to a friend. While she was recovering from her injuries, Shatner reportedly had all of her personal belongings taken out of his Paramount studio trailer and left on its roof for her to retrieve.

A second palimony suit, filed in January 1990 by Mexican actress **Vira Montes**, sought a total of $6 million in damages from Shatner. The twenty-eight-year-old Montes, whom Shatner met and romanced on the set of *T. J. Hooker* in 1984, claimed she was suddenly rejected by the actor after a six-year affair. During the relationship, Montes claimed she routinely had to pretend to be Shatner's niece while she accompanied him on ski weekends in **Canada**. Shatner even purchased a house in the San Fernando Valley for the aspiring starlet. For six years, Montes alleged, Shatner had been "materializing in her bed and then beaming back up to his wife."

Both palimony suits were settled out of court in 1992 for sums not disclosed to the public.

PANTY HOSE

Shatner wore panty hose on the set of *Star Trek: Generations* in 1994—and encouraged **Patrick Stewart** to do the same. The tight leggings helped ease the chafing caused by long days spent filming scenes on horseback. Ever the sensualist, Shatner prefers sheer panty hose, with a seam in the middle, for their aesthetic qualities.

PEOPLE, THE ✶✶

Francis Ford Coppola served as executive producer for this 1972 TV movie starring Shatner, along with actors Kim Darby, Dan O'Herlihy, and Diane Varsi. Based on Zenna Henderson's sci-fi novel *Pilgrimage: The Book of the People*, the supernatural tale concerns a community where parents and their children possess superhuman powers. Shatner is Dr. Curtis, the town physician. Composer Carmine Coppola, the great director's father and an Oscar-winner that year for *The Godfather*, provided the score.

SIX DEGREES OF *STAR TREK*

Kim Darby (Melodyne Amerson in **The People**) previously worked with Shatner in the first-season **Star Trek** episode "Miri."

PERILOUS VOYAGE ✶✶

This 1976 TV movie, filmed in 1968, features Shatner as a passenger on a hijacked cruise liner. As Steve Monroe, a high-living playboy, Shatner gets to act drunk for the first half of the hastily assembled picture, which also stars Michael Parks, Lee Grant, Frank Silvera, Victor Jory, and Charles McGraw. The plot involves the takeover of the luxury ship by South American revolutionaries. (In an odd side note, Shatner endured his own "perilous voyage" during filming, when the small boat he was riding in got lost at sea for several hours in a dense fog.)

Tired of deep space, Shatner embarked on a high seas adventure in the 1968 TV movie *Perilous Voyage*.

The lackluster film remained in steerage for eight years before a reluctant NBC finally aired it on July 29, 1976. Its original title was *The Revolution of Antonio DeLeon*. Viva la revolución!

PETTYJOHN, ANGELIQUE

This American actress and ecdysiast played Shahna, Kirk's "drill thrall" in the memorable ***Star Trek*** episode "The Gamesters of Triskelion." The pair shared a torrid love scene on screen, and for years they were romantically linked off camera as well. However, Shatner apparently had trouble picking her out from among the many genetic oddities he seduced on camera during the series' three-year network run. "Was she the big-busted girl with the hair?" he queried *Playboy* in 1989. "I remember her." Pettyjohn—who also acted under the names Angel St. John, Roxanne Rolls, and Heaven St. John—later screen-tested for the role of Nova in the 1968 feature *Planet of the Apes*, coming perilously close to experiencing the rare privilege of costarring with both Shatner and Charlton Heston in the same lifetime.

PHONE CONTROVERSY

Like the **high chair controversy**, the phone controversy was a "my perk is bigger than your perk" battle that broke out on the set of ***Star Trek*** in the late '60s. A competitive situation developed when directors complained about the amount of time Shatner spent monopolizing the one and only soundstage telephone. It wasn't entirely his fault; after all, he was in almost every scene, and he needed some nearby place to conduct his personal business during working hours. A second phone was installed on the set, but Shatner found it convenient to keep this line open for his incoming calls. When executive producer **Gene Roddenberry** issued an edict banning all personal calls from the set, an enraged Shatner demanded that a phone be put in his dressing room. At that point, Herb Solow, the executive in charge of production for Desilu Studios, exploded.

"No!" Solow commanded. "If Bill Shatner gets a phone, then Leonard wants a phone, De wants a phone, Nichelle wants a phone, Jimmy wants a phone, George wants a phone, Walter wants a phone, and Majel probably wants a phone." Solow went on to speculate about how Shatner's phone demand might impact other Desilu productions, such as *Mannix* and *Mission: Impossible*. "The only Desilu actor on the lot who ever had a dressing room phone is Lucille Ball. And she owns the place!" In the end, Shatner abandoned his campaign for a dressing room phone. However, he stopped speaking to **Gene Roddenberry** and continued to use the stage phones to everyone's consternation.

PIONEER WOMAN ✳ ✳

Joanna Pettet plays the title trailblazer in this 1973 TV movie set in the Wyoming Territory of 1867. Sporting a comically bad costume-store moustache, Shatner is John Sergeant, Pettet's ne'er-do-well husband, who uproots his family, brings them into the godforsaken frontier country, and then conveniently drops dead off camera. The film represented ABC's attempt to tap into the frontier mojo exhibited by the CBS hit *The Waltons*. Shatner's on-camera daughter is played by Helen Hunt, later the star of TV's *Mad About You*. Filmed on location in Alberta, Manitoba, **Canada**, this was Shatner's fourth and final TV movie of 1973, his most prolific year in that medium.

POETRY HALL OF FAME COLLECTION

Shatner recites two poems—"Gone" by Carl Sandburg and an excerpt from "The Hill" by Edgar Lee Masters—on this educational video featuring readings of great poems by 1970s film and TV personalities. Also on hand are "Grampa Walton" (Will Geer), Henry Fonda, and a pre–*Star Trek: The Next Generation* LeVar Burton. The video was officially released in 1993, but the readings, including Shatner's, seem to have been filmed much earlier. (For one thing, in 1993 both Fonda and Geer had been dead for over a decade.) Shatner recites one of his selections while strolling through a graveyard.

POLICEMEN

Shatner has long been fascinated by policemen. He played one on **T. J. Hooker**, narrated their exploits on **Rescue 911,** and invented the cop of the future in **Jake Cardigan**, the gumshoe hero of his **Tek** book series. Shatner has even likened his most famous creation, Captain James T. Kirk, to an intergalactic gendarme.

Shatner's regard for cops may be reflected in his own high-energy, risk-taking lifestyle. "I think they're adrenaline junkies," he has said of society's "new centurions." "Very macho. I think a policeman has an overabundance of testosterone." His impressions then tend to drift off into a litany of "me Tarzan" ramblings of the kind inspired by his reading of anthropological theorist **Robert Ardrey**. "They're the hunters," Shatner observed. "You know, bop the prey on the head and drag it home for you to eat."

POLLAK, KEVIN

This diminutive actor and stand-up comic is best-known for his work in *A Few Good Men* and *The Usual Suspects*; but he's also famous for his dead-on Shatner impression, which he has parlayed into a personal friendship with the actor. Pollak attended Shatner's 1999 wedding to **Nerine Kidd** and was one of the interview subjects for Shatner's memoir *Get a Life*. Reportedly, Pollak even convinced Shatner that his trademark **acting** style originated as a brilliant attempt at "lifting the drama" during **stage** performances early in his career—an explanation Pollak later admitted he had concocted on the way over to Shatner's house. Pollak was one of the celebrity roasters at Comedy Central's *Roast of William Shatner* in 2007.

PRACTICAL JOKES

Shatner has always been an inveterate prankster. As a child, he loved to show up unexpectedly at his sisters' birthday parties, turn off the lights, and tell ghost stories. On Halloween, he had two standard tricks. In one, he put a coin at the end of a string and left it on a person's doorstep. After ringing the bell, he waited in the bushes for the poor pigeon to emerge. When the person bent down to pick up the coin, Shatner pulled the string, luring his quarry away from the door. An accomplice would then dump a bucket of water on top of the unsuspecting homeowner. In another less creative gag, Shatner would simply shoot pellets of red paint at his victims, causing them to think they had been shot.

Shatner's passion for practical jokes continued on the set of **Star Trek**. Perhaps his most famous prank involved costar **Leonard Nimoy**'s red bicycle. The contemplative actor had acquired the bike to pedal back and forth to the Desilu studio commissary during breaks in shooting. Before long, Shatner became obsessed with it, bent on taking it, hiding it, suspending it from the ceiling, doing whatever he could to keep it out of Nimoy's hands. At one point, Shatner had the bicycle hidden in his trailer, with Morgan, one of his legion of **Dobermans**, standing guard over it. An exasperated Nimoy eventually had to lock the bike in his Buick to keep it away from his costar. But even that couldn't stop Shatner, who simply had Nimoy's car towed.

Nimoy soon realized his only recourse was to sink to Shatner's childish level. One day, he put a bucket containing Shatner's body makeup into a refrigerator. Applying the frigid ablution later in the day, Shatner howled in pain. Revenge, it seems, is a dish best served cold.

PRACTICE, THE

✶✶✶✶

In 2004, Shatner finally landed a role to rival Captain Kirk in the public imagination, when producer David E. Kelley created the brilliant, pompous attorney **Denny Crane** for this ABC legal drama.

Shatner only appeared on *The Practice* five times, but his portrayal earned him his first Emmy Award, for Outstanding Guest Actor in a Drama Series. He would reprise the role on Kelley's next series, **Boston Legal**, to even more critical accolades, securing a second Emmy in the process. For more details, see entries for **Boston Legal** and **Denny Crane**.

James Spader and Shatner gaze lovingly into each other's eyes in a scene from *The Practice*.

PRAY FOR THE WILDCATS

Shatner is a harried advertising executive in thrall to tyrannical client-from-Hell Andy Griffith in this 1974 TV movie. The testosterone flows freely as Griffith orders Shatner and fellow ad men Robert "Mike Brady" Reed and Marjoe Gortner to accompany him on a wild **motorcycle** ride through the Mexican Baja. To no one's surprise, the trip takes a deadly turn. There's lots of motorcycling footage set to groovy '70s **music**. Angie Dickinson is on hand to add **sex** appeal to the whole enterprise. She and Shatner manage to keep their clothes on throughout. They weren't so fortunate in that same year's theatrical feature *Big Bad Mama*.

PRICELINE.COM

Shatner has been the principal celebrity spokesman for this web-based purveyor of discount travel services since 1998. "We were looking for a figure who was trustworthy, known for having futuristic ideas, and instantly identifiable across multiple generations," explained Priceline's Chief Marketing Officer Brett Keller. "Bill met those criteria."

Shatner's early TV spots for the company played off his spoken-word musical career. The campaign, dubbed "Troubadour," depicted the actor as a lounge singer belting out misbegotten renditions of '70s **radio** hits like "Jive Talking" and "Convoy." In a prescient move, Shatner agreed to waive his fee for appearing in the ads in exchange for Priceline stock. That paid off handsomely, as shares reached a high of well over $100 during the dot-com boom. Shatner sold them, earning a hefty profit just months before the bubble burst and the price plummeted into penny stock territory. Apparently it helps to have the Guardian of Forever as your financial advisor.

In late 2000, rumors began to circulate that Priceline was looking to jettison Shatner as its spokesman. Company executives were said to be peeved because Shatner had admitted in interviews that he never actually used the "name your own price" service. *Sex and the City* star Sarah Jessica Parker briefly replaced Shatner as spokesperson. By February 2002, the troubadour was back in the fold. In an act of contrition worthy of St. Augustine, Shatner renounced his past transgressions: "Over the years, my relationship with priceline.com has broadened, from a celebrity spokesman to a customer who has enjoyed the significant savings benefits of price-line.com," the once and future pitchman confessed in a prepared statement. New ads were cut featuring Shatner interacting with a fictitious Priceline "supercomputer" programmed to search for low-cost airline tickets. "Given the futuristic side of William Shatner, the new campaign is a natural," gushed Priceline's Keller.

When five years later that approach had run its course, Priceline retooled Shatner as "The Negotiator," a James Bond-like figure driven to secure the best deals on behalf of Priceline customers. More iterations were likely to follow. As the creative director for Priceline's ad agency observed: "Most celebrity spokesperson campaigns are short-lived, either because the celebrity has lost audience appeal or the ad treatment has gotten stale. Neither has occurred here. Bill's popularity is growing and priceline.com continues to find fresh ways to present its message."

PRISONER OF ZENDA, INC. ✳ ✳

This 1996 **television** film is loosely based on the classic adventure novel *The Prisoner of Zenda* by Anthony Hope, with more than a passing nod to Mark Twain's *The Prince and the Pauper*. In this updated version Shatner plays Michael Gatewick, an evil executive seeking control of a computer firm. He kidnaps his own nephew and replaces him with a perfect lookalike, a visiting high school baseball champ. Later released to video under the title *Double Play*, the fanciful film took a pasting from critics, though Shatner was credited with providing some much-needed camp value. "The plump Shatner mesmerizes," observed a reviewer for *Entertainment Weekly*, adding that Shatner's bushy false mustache made him look like Teddy Roosevelt. "Too bad the only double he has is a chin."

PRODUCING

Repeatedly frustrated in his ability to win meaningful parts in quality projects, Shatner has at times tried to take matters into his own hands and produce his own work. In the mid-1960s, he formed Lemli Productions (named after his daughters **Leslie**, **Melanie**, and **Lisabeth**) in hopes of attracting socially relevant screenplays in which he could star. However, while he had no trouble finding screenwriters willing to sell him their moldering scripts, Shatner found himself stonewalled by the major studios when he requested money to bankroll those projects.

During his days on **Star Trek**, Shatner used his popularity to attract attention to a number of pet projects, including *Where I Stand: The Record of a Reckless Man*, the life story of newspaper mogul Hank Greenspun; and "The Twisted Night," a screenplay by veteran fantasist Jerry Sohl. Shatner even tried to get a green light for a script about the Vietnam War, but he was told by studio executives that the subject was box-office poison.

"Half the job of producing a picture is getting the property and its ingredients," Shatner once observed. "From then on, it's a matter of coagulating the elements." The victim of the monetary equivalent of a blood clot, Shatner eventually threw up his hands and quit the producing business entirely. It was only after he returned to prominence as a result of the success of the **Star Trek** film series in the 1980s that he found himself able to coagulate—er, produce—successfully. "There were three companies vying for

TekWar," he said of the 1994 cable TV series based on his science fiction novels. "That had never happened [before]. . . . I had spent a lifetime trying to get a project of my own going."

By the turn of the twenty-first century, Shatner was on a roll as a producer—thanks to positive mojo generated by his role on **Boston Legal**. *Mind Meld*, **William Shatner's Splat Attack**, and **Invasion Iowa** are just a few of the projects that bear his imprimatur. Not bad progress for a guy who couldn't cash a $15 check in the early 1970s.

PROMISE MARGARINE

Shatner and his then-wife **Marcy Lafferty** hawked this oleaginous breakfast spread in a series of **television** commercials in the late 1970s. In an interview for NBC's *Today Show*, host Jane Pauley asked Shatner whether it was demeaning for Captain Kirk to be shilling butter substitutes. "For Captain Kirk, maybe, but for William Shatner it was perfectly feasible," replied the obviously irritated actor.

SHAT THE SHILL

On the *Today Show* in 1980, Shatner tartly reprimanded host Jane Pauley for casting aspersions on his endorsement with **Promise margarine**. Little did Pauley know that her interviewee was about to embark on a three-decade odyssey of televised product pitching. Here's a decade-by-decade rundown of some of the products and services Shatner has hawked in recent years:

1980s Wishbone Salad Dressing, **Commodore** Computers, the 1980 Olympics, Western Airlines, the U.S. Open Tennis Tournament, and Oldsmobile (with daughter **Melanie**)

1990s The Sierra Club, Guide Dogs for the Blind, MCI Friends and Family (with **Star Trek** costars), a Public Service Announcement promoting AIDS Awareness, the Tournament of Roses Parade on KTLA-TV in Los Angeles, the 1994 Winter Olympics, the NFL on Fox, AT&T, and **Priceline.com**

2000s Molson Beer, **Priceline.com**, Crest White Effects Toothpaste, Wendy's, DirecTV, Kellogg's All-Bran, Blockbuster Video, and the Law Offices of Joe Bornstein

PUBERTY

A unique specimen in all respects, Shatner (not surprisingly) claims to have had a most atypical puberty. "I never went through that off-putness, that adolescent, awkward puberty," he once told biographers. Shatner also claims he never suffered from acne, but the he had trouble attracting the opposite **sex**. "I never fulfilled that adolescent dream," he has said. A dream, one assumes, of the soil-the-sheets variety. "I think there must be inside me a sense of unworthiness that brings me up short, many times, so that whatever physical attributes people think I have, I don't see."

QUEST FOR TOMORROW　✦✦

This series of five science fiction novels, penned by Shatner with the assistance of writer Bill Quick, chronicles the adventures of Jim Endicott, a teenager who carries in his DNA the secret of transforming the human race into a powerful organic supercomputer. Titles in the *Quest for Tomorrow* series comprise, in order: *Delta Search* (1997), *In Alien Hands* (1997), *Step into Chaos* (1999), *Beyond the Stars* (2000), and *Shadow Planet* (2002).

RACIAL STEREOTYPES

Like many actors who got their start in the 1950s, Shatner has played his share of racial caricatures. His gallery of offensive portrayals includes a half-breed Comanche in the 1968 feature **White Comanche** and a **Burmese sailor** in a notorious episode of **The Naked City**. Unlike many performers, who outgrew the "slanted eyes and pidgin English" approach by the mid-1960s, Shatner persisted in his heavy-handed manner of portraying ethnic characters well into the politically correct 1990s. It is especially apparent in his reading of an abridged book-on-tape version of his 1991 novel *TekLords*. As Keith DeCandido observed in his review of the tape in *Library Journal*, "Shatner's range of voices is limited: his female voices are unconvincing, his rendering of Japanese characters borders on the offensive, he uses a third-rate Speedy Gonzalez voice for Cardigan's partner, Sid Gomez. This abridgement . . . is actively awful."

> "I love to see the variations in people and things. I love the variations in skin tone and characteristics, and the slant of the eye and the color of the skin. Diversity is the magic of the world."
>
> —*Shatner, on the manifold variety of humanity*

RADIO

Shatner has done occasional parts on radio shows over the years. In fact, one of his first regular **acting** gigs was with the Montreal Radio Fairytale Theatre, for which he started performing at the tender age of ten in 1941. For three years, Shatner voiced famous fairy tale heroes like Prince Charming for the Canadian Broadcasting Corporation (CBC).

During his college days at **McGill University**, Shatner worked as a radio announcer for the CBC. He not only gained valuable experience, he also earned enough to pay for his college books and fees.

In November of 1997, Shatner made a return to radio when he played the part of the Martian **king** in a televised live reading of H. G. Wells's *First Men in the Moon*, featuring an all–*Star Trek* cast.

RALKE, DON

This prolific composer and record producer arranged and produced Shatner's 1968 album *The Transformed Man*. Known for working with celebrity singers, Ralke was a veteran of the Hollywood studio system with a twenty-five-year background in films, **television**, and pop recordings. He convinced Shatner to eschew singing in favor of talking song lyrics over a musical background, much like Rex Harrison did on **stage** for his role in the musical *My Fair Lady*. Ralke's other "golden throat" credits include 1964's *Ringo*, the lone album from *Bonanza* patriarch Lorne Greene.

RAND, GLORIA

Shatner's first wife, a Canadian actress, was born Gloria Rosenberg. The couple was married from 1956 until 1969 and produced three daughters: **Leslie Carol** in 1958, **Lisabeth Mary** in 1961, and **Melanie Ann** in 1964.

Shatner met Rand in January 1956 while he was appearing on Broadway in *Tamburlaine the Great*. At the time, Rand was struggling to find work as an actress. Smitten with the pretty blonde, Shatner arranged for her to join him in Toronto on the set of *Dreams*, a CBC **television** drama he had written and in which he was starring. Romance blossomed, and they were married on August 12, 1956. The newlyweds honeymooned in Scotland, where Shatner was appearing in the Edinburgh Festival's production of *Shakespeare's Henry V*.

Curiously, while Rand went out of her way to accompany her new husband wherever his budding career took him, he did not return the favor. Late in 1956, Rand secured a featured role as the Player Queen in the Stratford (Ontario) Shakespeare Festival production of *Hamlet*. However, she gave up what may have been her big break when Shatner chose to move to New York to pursue TV and **stage** roles. "I'm the breadwinner," Shatner later reasoned about such matters. "And it's just perforce that [my wife] must come with me if I go on location."

By 1967, however, Shatner did not want the company. He flew to Spain without his family and spent three months filming the cheesy western **White Comanche**. Gloria never forgave him and they separated shortly after his return to the United States. Several attempts at reconciliation failed, and they split for good in March 1969. In the divorce proceeding, Rand cited Shatner for keeping irregular hours and spending too much time away from home. In the ensuing settlement, she received their home, alimony, child support, and half of their other assets. The breakup hit Shatner hard. "Working as I did," he admitted to *TV Guide*, "not a day off in three years, I never realized how dependent I was on my wife and children. It brought on a whole new sense of aloneness."

REHEARSAL TABLE

This command center was established by Shatner for emergency rewrites and script conferences on the set of TV's **Star Trek**. Located outside his dressing room, the rehearsal table served more often than not as the cemetery where the lines of supporting cast members were laid to rest. "Every time you would hear 'Cut. Print' you'd have these guys under Bill's command rushing over to the table to work on the next scene," recalled director Joe Pevney. Shatner used these conferences to maximize his own dialogue at the expense of the rest of the cast. It got to be such an infringement on the director's discretion that Pevney refused to work on the show. "When you're doing television in five or six days," Pevney complained, "there's no time for this constant rehearsal—with pencils in hand making changes. . . . It destroys the disciplinary control of the director."

RESCUE 911

Shatner presided over this reality-based rescue program from 1989 to 1992. *Rescue 911* featured actual recordings of emergency phone calls and film of real-life police, paramedics, and rescue workers in action.

Shatner claims he was attracted to the concept because of its potential for drama. "It has two things going for it," he told the *New York Post* in 1989. "It rips your head off with excitement. You hear the real telephone call, see the news footage and watch the harrowing things that are happening in front of you. And it serves a purpose by showing what a 911 call does. It's useful information."

Shatner prepared for his portentous voice-over narration by visiting a real-life 911 dispatch center. "I am fascinated by the whole machinery of civilization taking care of itself," he told the *Washington Post* in 1991. "I've learned how it all works, from the time somebody in dire need calls up. Policemen in their hours of boredom and their moments of terror, or firemen and doctors for that matter, intrigue me."

Shatner described his work on *Rescue 911* as "something I'm extremely proud of." And why not? It helped revive his flagging **television** career. In the 1990s, as a result of *Rescue 911*'s success, Shatner became something of an itinerant spokesperson for safety and first aid. His face appeared on the cover of the *National Safety Council's First Aid Handbook*, and he landed hosting gigs on such alarmist educational videos as **Ultimate Survivors** and **It Didn't Have To Happen: Drinking and Driving**.

Shatner mans the barricades as America's guardian of public safety on TV's *Rescue 911*.

"Rescue 911 is to me the best show on television. It makes me laugh and cry more than any other show on the air."

—Shatner, on his reality television program Rescue 911

RIEL ✶✶

This 1979 Canadian Broadcasting Corporation TV movie tells the tale of Louis Riel, the nineteenth century rebel leader known as the father of Manitoba province. The lumbering historical drama follows Riel as he battles against the Canadian federal government. Shatner has a supporting role as a Canadian army officer who tracks down Riel. *Variety* panned the effort as "half-baked, clogged with an abundance of declamatory speeches, passed off as normal conversation." Shown in two ninety-minute segments on the CBC in May 1979, the film was later edited into a 150-minute version for home video.

SIX DEGREES OF *STAR TREK*

Christopher Plummer (Prime Minister John A. Macdonald) went on to play Chang, the Shakespeare-quoting Klingon, in *Star Trek VI: The Undiscovered Country*.

"ROCKET MAN" ✶✶✶✶

In one of his most memorable musical performances, Shatner "sang" this Elton John hit at the 1978 Science Fiction Film Awards, which was televised live in Los Angeles on January 21, 1978, on KTLA and syndicated stations. The surreal performance defies description and must be seen to be believed. Nevertheless, here is one man's attempt at synopsis.

After an introduction by Elton John's lyricist Bernie Taupin, a pensive, tuxedoed Shatner appears, seated on a stool, clutching a cigarette in the European manner. Slowly, he begins to speak the song's lyrics. Before long, a wailing synthesizer joins him, its other-worldly tones adding to the prevailing mood of alienation. After the first chorus, the brooding "Shatner One" is joined, via video trickery, by his alter **ego**, a clear-eyed, puffed-chest version full of false bravado. About halfway through the number, these two are joined by a third incarnation: a shimmying, presumably inebriated figure with his tie and cummerbund undone. Shatner, playing each of the three characters with a commitment that would be admirable if it weren't so hilarious, never quite crosses the line between reciting and singing. The performance is marked by the actor's trademark staccato delivery, inexplicable pauses, and idiosyncratic line readings ("I'm a rocket, man" he intones at one point; at another he's a "rock-it man.")

Word of mouth made this amazing clip legendary. Bootleg video copies of the hard-to-find performance circulated among Shatner aficionados for decades, until the advent of YouTube and other online video sites gave it wide exposure. In interviews, Shatner has tread a fine line between embracing and disavowing the bizarre performance. "I feel badly about it," he told his daughter **Lisabeth** in an interview on his Shatnervision website, "because I never intended this song . . . to see the light of day. It was in the nature of experimentation. It would be like sketching something before you make the painting, and then you throw the sketch away, but somebody saves the sketch."

"He couldn't sing. He was smoking, so he would talk the lyrics between puffs. It was horrible and hilarious at the same time."
—*actress Susan Tyrell, on Shatner's performance of "Rocket Man"*

Can't get enough of singing, dancing Shatner? Downloading **"Rocket Man"** is only the beginning. Here are three other musical clips no discerning Shatnerphile should be without:

In the **Star Trek** episode "Plato's Stepchildren," at the behest of their telekinetic captors, Kirk and Spock perform a rousing duet called "I'm Tweedledee, he's Tweedledum." The lyrics convey but a taste of the hilarity as the singers verbalize about their happy-go-lucky adventures in outer space.

In the 1975 variety special *Mitzi and a Hundred Guys*, Shatner joins host Mitzi Gaynor and a 25-man chorus that includes **Leonard Nimoy**, Tom Bosley, and Monty Hall. Unfortunately for his **fans**, Shatner's voice is submerged beneath the general din.

The 1985 all-star cabaret *Night of 100 Stars II* once again finds Shatner high-stepping and belting as part of a kickline of celebrities. In the rousing finale, the stars release 100 helium balloons, hoping their careers won't follow suit and disappear into the air above them.

RODDENBERRY, GENE

Star Trek's burly creator cast Shatner in his most famous role, as **James Tiberius Kirk**, commander of the starship *Enterprise*.

Roddenberry's first impressions of his new star were less than favorable. "He came in and said, 'I have a few comments about the script' and I thought 'Oh no,'" Roddenberry told *TV Guide* in 1966.

A control freak who prided himself on dominating every aspect of **Star Trek**'s production, Roddenberry soon came to chafe at Shatner's input. There were long stretches during filming when he and his leading man simply did not speak to each other. In his 1993 memoir *Star Trek Memories*, Shatner claimed to have regretted the "cool working relationship" he shared with Roddenberry over the years. "There was never anything said," Shatner explained. "It's just that working with somebody for years, you'd think that there'd be more warmth in the relationship and there never was."

SATURDAY NIGHT LIVE ✳ ✳ ✳ ✳

Shatner hosted the December 20, 1986, edition of the popular comedy sketch show. The highlight of the program was a sketch set at a **Star Trek** convention, in which Shatner lambasted the loyal Spock-eared throngs with his withering admonition to "get a life." The pointed skit became notorious in the world of science fiction fandom, and Shatner was regularly heckled during subsequent convention appearances. In other sketches, Shatner sent up **T. J. Hooker** and essayed the part of a pompous actor.

SECRETS OF A MARRIED MAN ✳

"Straight sex. Sixty dollars." If you've ever dreamed of hearing Shatner utter those words to you, then rent this trashy 1984 TV movie and prepare to wear out the rewind button on your DVD player. Shatner dominates the action as Chris Jordan, an aeronautical engineer who inexplicably grows bored with his gorgeous wife (Michelle Phillips) and starts visiting a succession of skanky prostitutes. Cybill Sheperd plays a high-priced call girl who almost destroys his **marriage**. Glynn Turman plays the town pimp. Highlights include watching a beefy, bewigged Shatner cruise up and down the streets of the red-light district, ogling hookers to

Cybill Shepherd tugs on Shatner's tie, and ruins his marriage, in the tawdry 1984 TV movie *Secrets of a Married Man*.

the strains of a Chopin waltz. Working titles for the venture, filmed entirely in Vancouver, British Columbia, included *Trick Eyes* and *Portrait of a John*.

Ask Shat

Q: What's it like being a television icon?

A: Being an icon is overblown. Remember, an icon is moved by a mouse.

SEVEN DWARFS

This epithet became Shatner's derisive term for the supporting play-ers in the *Star Trek* cast—each of whom at one time or another fell victim to Shatner's penchant for trimming the dialogue given to his fellow performers. For obvious reasons, they kept their objections largely to themselves. "Other than Leonard [Nimoy], Bill could have had any of them fired," bit player David L. Ross once remarked. Several of the "dwarfs" later used their published memoirs as a forum to punch back at their tyrannical leading man.

> "From the beginning, Bill believed the credits—that there were three actors above the title and the rest of us below. The rest of us were not significant, not only as actors, but as people."
>
> —*Walter Koenig, on Shatner's attitude toward the seven dwarfs*

SEX

"Anything done supremely well is an act of sex," Shatner once opined—and by all accounts he knew whereof he spoke. Shatner admits to having no sexual inhibitions or taboos. Such frankness has led some observers to speculate about his sexual preferences. The testimony of Iggy Pop guitarist **Ron Asheton** has fueled persistent rumors that, at the very least, Shatner went through an "experimen-tal" phase in the 1970s. If that were true, of course, he would be no different from countless other celebrities, including John Lennon, Mick Jagger, and David Bowie.

Like many actors, Shatner sees a sexual component in his relationship with his audiences. He has spoken candidly about "making love to a whole audience, making them my lover, and I theirs." Shatner's musings on sexuality have even extended outside the realm of terra firma. In a wide-ranging *Playboy* interview in 1989, he expounded on extraterrestrial erotic technique: "First of all, you take off your boots. Then you have to find the erogenous zones. They differ on every alien. An alien erogenous zone can lead you down some strange paths—some of which I can tell you and some of which I can't. Let's just say that when you scratch your head, you may be fulfilling the sexual fantasies of some alien."

His alien conquests may beg to differ, but Shatner seems to have done his most prolific work as a heterosexual here on Planet Earth. "I'm so content being a man that I would miss the clanging of my balls," he told *Playboy*. His roster of reputed conquests over the years includes Angie Dickinson, Joan Collins, and Yvette Mimieux. "If I'm Hollywood's number one love machine—in terms of quantity and quality—it certainly is a distinction," Shatner informed the *National Enquirer* in 1995.

> "Sex should be a template for your day. You need to start slow and end completely."
>
> —*Shatner, outlining his approach to life*

SEX EDUCATION, SHATNER STYLE

Sigmund Freud is famous for reading a sexual subtext into our perception of everyday objects. But Herr Doktor may have met his match in William Shatner, for whom a cigar is never just a cigar. Here is a partial list of things and activities that get Shatner's sap a-rising:

ARCHERY "The arrow and the bow as you draw it taut, gathering the tension—your strength, your thrust, and then the release—like an ejaculation, thrusting the arrow forward to impale the target. The arrow arcs up and flies straight home and penetrates the center of the bullseye."

FLYING "You have this stick between your legs and you're turning, and the centrifugal force is forcing the blood down. . . . I mean, it's all sexual."

HORSEBACK RIDING "There's a real connection between love and riding a horse well. You've got to use your body, you've got to use your hands, you've got to make love to the horse, and she's a neat lady."

ROCK MUSIC "A real sexual thrill takes place hearing the hot beat of a rock number."

SHATNER, ANNA GARMAISE

Shatner's mother brought forth not only William but also his two sisters, Joy Shatner Ruttenberg and Farla Shatner Cohen. While the Montreal diction teacher never took to the **stage** herself, she provided the early impetus for her son to become an actor. "It's genetic," reported Shatner's sister Farla. "My mother was a bit of a clown. She never really pursued her acting in a professional way, but she had talent." "She dreamed that her son would be a star one day," added Shatner's close friend Hilliard Jason. Anne Shatner's other legacy to her only son includes, according to him, his sense of humor. "My mother is an amusing person," Shatner once remarked. "My mother is probably the source of the humor. I think she probably provided me the impetus of trying to be amusing."

Whoa, Nellie! Horseman Shatner controls an unruly mount.

SHATNER BUILDING

The Student Union Building at **McGill University** in Montreal was renamed in 1995 to honor its most famous graduate. Dubbed The William Shatner University Centre, the five-story brick and poured concrete structure houses student activities and administrative offices, as well as a cafeteria. It is notable for a long staircase which winds up the center of the building. McGill officials estimate that 2,000 students navigate their way through Shatner Centre on a daily basis.

Controversy has dogged the building since the renaming. Some objected to the very idea of Shatner Centre, asking why a living person should be so honored. "He's the only student to captain a starship within fifteen years of graduation," quipped McGill's dean. In fact, the impetus for the Shatner tribute came at the acclamation of the student body, not the administration, which demanded a donation from the actor in return for the renaming. Shatner refused to pay up, and as a result some McGill officials still refuse to recognize the new name. In 1997, the Shatner Building came under fire from the Office for Students with Disabilities for being inaccessible to persons with physical impairments. An audit was conducted in which the Shatner edifice was cited for its high elevator keyholes, heavy bathroom doors, and a lack of room numbers printed in Braille. As a result, explained disabilities activist Eleanor Girt in the McGill *Tribune*, "Students with disabilities are not using Shatner at all."

SHATNER, JOSEPH

Shatner's father was the son of Jewish immigrants who moved to Montreal in the early 1900s. Joseph and William Shatner shared a stormy relationship, often arguing over the younger man's career choice. The elder Shatner headed Admiration Clothes, a successful clothing manufacturing company in Montreal. Joseph hoped his only son would follow him into the family business. When William decided to pursue a show business career instead, Joseph cut him off from all financial support.

"For five years I lived in cheap rooms and starved," Shatner told *People* magazine in 1982, "which didn't make my father happy. It's a terrifying decision for a parent to take away a child's support." Joseph Shatner asked his son to return home, but William refused. Joseph eventually gave up his dream of handing over the family business and hired a young assistant to take the place of his son.

Joseph Shatner died of a heart attack on a Florida golf course in 1967. Shatner received the news on the set of the **Star Trek** episode "The Devil in the Dark." Overcome by grief, he nevertheless insisted on completing the day's shooting. An almost numb Shatner had trouble remembering his lines but managed to struggle through the scene in which Kirk directs his men to search for the deadly Horta. "We quit around five or six o'clock and I went home," Shatner said later. "And everybody was crying when we made that scene."

On the flight home to Montreal with his father's body, Shatner experienced an epiphany. "I remember banking over the city and looking out the window. But what I was really doing was looking into myself. What I saw was an empty pit—and it terrified me." The death of Joseph Shatner is widely believed to be a contributing factor in William Shatner's long personal and professional descent, known as the **lost years**.

SHATNER, LESLIE CAROL

The firstborn child of Shatner and **Gloria Rand**, Leslie Shatner was born on August 13, 1958. The character of Lieutenant Leslie, played by Eddie Paskey on **Star Trek**, was named after her.

SHATNER, LISABETH MARY

The second daughter of Shatner and **Gloria Rand** was born

June 6, 1961. When she was only five, Lisabeth felt the sting of abandonment as Shatner left the house to begin work on **Star Trek** in 1966. "I stood on the front porch, begging him not to go. He appeared only once or twice a week after that to see me and my sisters."

Despite the pain caused by her parents' divorce in 1969, Lisabeth later reconciled with her father. She has collaborated with him on numerous projects, including the Shatnervision and williamshatner.com websites and the book *Captain's Log: William Shatner's Personal Account of the Making of Star Trek V*.

SHATNER, MELANIE ANN

The third daughter of Shatner and **Gloria Rand** was born on August 4, 1964. Following in her father's footsteps, she has pursued an **acting** career, mainly in low-budget science fiction films.

"Do something else!" Shatner thundered when Melanie told him she was going into show business. But Melanie found the lure of the bright lights too strong. She attended Beverly Hills High School, majored in **theater** at the University of Colorado, and won parts in *The First Power*, *Cthulhu Mansion*, *Bloodstone: Subspecies II*, and other features, as well as a small role as a yeoman in *Star Trek V*. She also appeared with her father in a series of Oldsmobile commercials in the 1980s.

SHIRTLESSNESS

Early in his **acting** career, Shatner was never shy about removing his shirt on screen. Over time, it became one of his trademarks. The origins of his inclination to disrobe go back to his earliest days on **television**. "I was doing a scene in a judo costume," he explained, "and it was subtly agreed it would look better to leave the long outside coat off." From that moment on, Shatner knew his muscular figure was his meal ticket. He worked out with weights for a year prior to filming

As astonished bathers look on in the background, Shatner leads the cheers for his own sculpted physique

Alexander the Great in 1963 "so I could take off my shirt and look like a hero."

"Part of what you're buying when you watch an actor perform is appearance," Shatner once explained. "People in Hollywood are expected to be beautiful. Viewers want to see a perfect specimen. They want you bigger than life." Bigger than life is exactly what Shatner was during much of his time on **Star Trek**, when he was bedeviled by a persistent and very visible **weight** problem. When he started working on the series in 1966, he would walk around the Desilu soundstage with twenty-pound weights strapped to his waist, ankles, and wrists to keep in top shape "so I can take my shirt off on camera." As any dedicated Trekkie knows, he did so often and enthusiastically. In the earliest episodes, scenes of Kirk working out in his quarters or being examined by Dr. McCoy were inserted for no discernible dramatic purpose. To prepare for these "money shots," Shatner kept a small gym in his dressing room to rein in his ballooning figure.

SHOT IN THE DARK, A

Shatner played Paul Sevigne, the diligent examining magistrate, in the Broadway production of Harry Kurnitz's French farce from October 1961 to February 1963. The comedic mystery revolves around complications that follow the murder of a Parisian chauffeur. Julie Harris and Walter Matthau joined Shatner in the production, which ran for 389 performances and earned Matthau a Tony Award.

Adapted from the French comedy *L'Idiote* by Marcel Archard, *A Shot in the Dark* was distilled into a 1964 movie comedy starring Peter Sellers, Elke Sommer, and Herbert Lom. The role played by Shatner was somewhat rejiggered to accommodate Sellers' bumbling Inspector Clouseau persona, which he had originated in 1963's *The Pink Panther*.

SHOW ME THE MONEY ✳

This short-lived ABC TV **game show**, apparently inspired by Cuba Gooding Jr.'s catch phrase from the movie *Jerry Maguire*, aired for five weeks in November and December of 2006. Shatner served as host. A curious amalgam of *Deal or No Deal* and *Who Wants To Be a Millionaire*, the loud, busy trivia contest featured scantily-clad female dancers, dramatically unfurled scrolls, and cash prizes in an ever-escalating sequence of dollar amounts that bewildered viewers and players alike. Promos depicted Shatner—billed in press materi-

Howie Mandel gets all the glory, but Shatner blazed the trail as the ringmaster of the raucous high-tech game show *Show Me the Money*.

als as "the audacious master of ceremonies"—boogeying shame-lessly with the assembled beauties. Predictably, this spectacle failed to produce the longed-for ratings bonanza. The ill-conceived monstrosity was cancelled with two shows still left in the can. For reasons unknown, it is now available on DVD.

> "I don't want to think that people turned it off because of me, so I'll blame the game."
>
> —*Shatner, on the failure of* Show Me the Money *to catch fire with viewers*

SOLE SURVIVOR ✶ ✶

Ghosts from a crashed World War II bomber return to haunt a surviving crew member, 25 years later, in this 1970 TV movie starring Shatner, Vince Edwards, Richard Basehart, Brad Davis, and Patrick Wayne. Shatner plays Lt. Col. Joe Gronke, the spooked crewman's assistant. The film plays like a mediocre *Twilight Zone* episode—hardly surprising, since the plot is directly lifted from an episode of that series.

SIX DEGREES OF *STAR TREK*
Lou Antonio (Tony in *Sole Survivor*) played Lokai, the black-white guy, in the *Star Trek* episode "Let That Be Your Last Battlefield."

SPADER, JAMES

Recently, Shatner's *Boston Legal* costar has entered his small circle of actor friends, an exclusive club that includes **Leonard Nimoy**, **Jason Alexander**, and **Kevin Pollak**. "I'm actually in love with James Spader," Shatner declared to an interviewer in 2005. "He's a wonderful actor, wonderful guy."

Best known for his portrayals of skeevy, creep-inducing characters in films like *Sex, Lies, and Videotape* and *Less Than Zero*, Spader fit the character of Alan Shore like a glove and provided the ideal Laurel to Shatner's overbearing Hardy. He won Emmys for his performance in 2004, 2005, and 2007 and has become somewhat fixed in the public mind as Shatner's thinner, more nebbishy alter **ego**.

The bond between the two actors was formed in their early days on **Boston Legal**, after they filmed a scene in which Alan Shore and **Denny Crane** spend an evening in bed together. "After we finished the scene, he sort of was dealing with me in a very different way than he had before," Spader reported. "He spoke in a different tone, a sort of closer tone—pillow talk." Shatner's distinctive musklike scent, in particular, seemed to impress the younger actor. "You can tell a lot about a person by that first impression, that first smell. He had a very sort of, a strangely very attractive sort of pungent sort of gamey, sort of a venison or a lamb sausage . . . and a little bit of rosemary with a touch of ranch dressing."

Unsurprisingly, a whole category of homoerotic "slash" fiction detailing Crane/Shore sexual encounters now exists online. Google at your own peril.

STAGE

Shatner began his career on stage and has never lost his love for the **theater**. The classical experience he received with the **Stratford Shakespeare Festival** in **Canada** clearly influenced his mature **acting** style. Early in his career, theatrical acting seemed to be Shatner's priority. He even backed out of a lucrative Hollywood movie deal in order to play the lead in **The World of Suzie Wong** on Broadway. For many years, he maintained his Canadian citizenship in case he wished to move to England and join that country's thriving theatrical community. However, the lure of big money in America kept him from exercising that option.

Though he achieved success on Broadway, in the 1950s Shatner found **live television** an adequate substitute for the proving ground of stage performance. "American television in the early days gave an actor this kind of training," he later recalled. "There were so many dramatic productions at that time that an actor had a chance to try his hand at many roles. Nowadays, there's very little, and a young actor is hard put to find this kind of theatrical groundwork."

Most of Shatner's significant stage credits—**The World of Suzie Wong** (1958) and **A Shot in the Dark** (1961)—came before his days on **Star Trek**. However, he has maintained his ties to the theatrical community and worked regularly in that medium throughout his lengthy career. During his **lost years**, Shatner took to the road to seek out parts in regional summer stock productions. His credits during this period included *There's a Girl in My Soup* (1969), *Remote Asylum* (1970–71), and *Arsenic and Old Lace* (1973). In 1981, Shatner fused his love of **theater** with his passion for **directing** when he put then-wife **Marcy Lafferty** through her paces as Maggie the Cat in a Los Angeles production of **Cat on a Hot Tin Roof**.

Ultimately, Shatner likes stage work for the same reason he loves **dual roles**: there's more room available for him to dominate the action. "It takes about a minute to overcome the image of Kirk on stage," he told the *New York Daily News* in 1982. "What I like about it is that the evening's entertainment is on my shoulders." Shatner performed the ultimate feat of solo gratification with his series of **one-man shows** on stage in the 1970s.

STALKING SANTA   ✴ ✴

In a send-up of his occasional role as the portentous host/narrator of earnest documentaries (see **It Didn't Have To Happen: Drinking and Driving**, **Mysteries of the Gods**, **Nukes in Space**, and **The Vegetarian**

World), Shatner supplies faux-pompous voice-over narration for this 2006 holiday-themed mockumentary about a self-proclaimed "Santologist" who sets out to prove the existence of Jolly Saint Nick.

STAR TREK (ORIGINAL SERIES) * * * *

Shatner made his bones—and created an immortal TV icon—playing Captain **James Tiberius Kirk** of the USS *Enterprise* from 1966 to 1969. His heroics provided the show with a solid action/adventure footing, from which its more philosophical pretensions could take flight.

The brainchild of writer/producer **Gene Roddenberry**, *Star Trek* was conceived as an attempt to bring the conventions of the western genre to an outer space setting. Earlier science fiction TV shows like *Captain Video*, *Tom Corbett*, *Space Cadet*, and *Space Patrol* had explored similar dramatic terrain. However, these primitive futuristic series were often childish in approach and amateurish in execution. Roddenberry's innovation was to bring humanistic values, sophisticated themes, and high production values to the science fiction genre.

Shatner was 35 when he took on the role of Captain Kirk. He considered it his last, best chance at success in show business. If the new series failed, he told friends, he planned to give up **acting** entirely and try his hand "selling ties at Macy's." Despite his anxiety, his confidence as a performer was at an all-time high. As he told interviewers in 1967, "I feel at the height of my powers at this moment, like a finely tuned racing machine."

The superfueled Shatner was able to hit a number of high personal notes with his early work on *Star Trek*. He gives fine, subtle performances in such classic first season episodes as "The Enemy Within," "The Naked Time," and "The City on the Edge of Forever." As the series progressed, however, he grew anxious about the expanded role of **Leonard Nimoy**, and he began to lobby producers for more rock-'em sock-'em Kirk-centric action. Toward the end of the first season, rumors abounded that Shatner would abandon the show, which was suffering from low ratings. Somewhere in all of this an accommodation was reached, and the program began to focus almost exclusively on the "Big Three" of Kirk, Spock, and McCoy—with Kirk the undisputed godhead of the trinity. The supporting players suffered the most from this subtle shift, as their already small number of lines dwindled appreciably.

In the show's second season, violence and action became the order of the day, as subtlety flew out the window. *Enterprise* crewmembers engaged in gladiatorial combat in two separate episodes, a sure sign of creeping creative sclerosis. An increasing number of installments adopted the high concept "*Star Trek* Meets . . . " formula, with Kirk and his crew encountering the Romans ("Bread and Circuses"), the Nazis ("Patterns of Force"), and the very thinly veiled Vietnamese ("The Omega Glory"). Shatner himself seemed to be reveling in the change of direction. He got to take his shirt off a lot more (see **Shirtlessness**), he got a lot more play from the ladies, and he even got to read the U.S. Constitution, tortuously, in "The Omega Glory." The giant sucking sound viewers heard was the show's artistic integrity flying out the window.

By *Star Trek*'s third and final season, artistic integrity was the punchline to a dirty joke. With a dramatically reduced budget and a time slot from hell on Friday nights at 10 pm, new producer Fred Freiberger didn't even try to find good scripts anymore. Wind out of the ass of a simpleton could have served as a better shooting script than Shatner and his cohorts were saddled with in "Spock's Brain," "The Lights of Zetar," and the grotesque "hippies in space" monstrosity "The Way to Eden." Episodes like "That Which Survives" and "The Empath" were filmed on minimalist sets, not for artistic reasons, but merely because the show could no longer afford even the papier-maché rocks that served as backdrops in previous seasons. By the time Abraham Lincoln appeared flying through space in a stovepipe hat, it was clearly time to close up the shop. The show creaked to a halt on June 3, 1969, with one final Shatner showstopper: the gender-bending "Turnabout Intruder," one of the campy gems of the series.

Star Trek seemed destined to pass into obscurity alongside Lost in Space and other failed sci-fi series. But the show's **fans** simply would not let it die. While Paramount always cited Star Trek as a loss in its official financial filings (and denied Shatner and his costars any residuals or merchandising royalties for much of the decade), in the 1970s Star Trek became a syndicated rerun juggernaut. Its earthling fan base exploded by 77 percent between 1977 and 1979 alone. Buoyed by these numbers, and by the success of Star Wars in 1977, Paramount launched the Star Trek movie series in 1979 with Star Trek: The Motion Picture. Six features starring the original cast were produced between 1979 and 1991. Shatner returned for a seventh in 1994.

"It sounds a little presumptuous, but I think that Star Trek provides a mythology for people in a culture that has no mythology."
—Shatner, on the reasons for Star Trek's success

Ask Shat

Q: How do you deal with overzealous Trekkies?

A: I take karate lessons and walk around with mace. They can be very violent people if you challenge their belief system.

1. **"THE PARADISE SYNDROME"**

   PLOT: Kirk gets bonked on the noggin and thinks he's the chief of an alien Indian tribe.

   WHY IT'S GREAT: delusions of godhood, sex with a beautiful squaw, shirtless hand-to-hand combat, and a juicy dual role as Kirk and Big Chief "Kirok." This is the ultimate Shatner showcase.

2. **"THE OMEGA GLORY"**

   PLOT: Kirk intervenes in a planetary conflict eerily similar to the Vietnam War.

   WHY IT'S GREAT: This episode is a tedious slog right up until its brilliant conclusion: Kirk reads the preamble to the United States Constitution, aloud, in high Shatnerian style. This scene should be shown in every acting class everywhere, at all times.

3. **"TURNABOUT INTRUDER"**

   PLOT: Kirk's resentful old flame, Janice Lester, uses an alien machine to place her mind in Kirk's body, and vice versa.

   WHY IT'S GREAT: In a profound setback for the women's movement, Shatner plays a female as a dithering, nail-biting shrew prone to unprovoked rages. Exhibit A in the case for *Star Trek*'s immediate cancellation.

4. **"PLATO'S STEPCHILDREN"**

   PLOT: Telekinetic Greeks in space force Kirk and his crew to hit one another and perform musical comedy.

   WHY IT'S GREAT: Forget the kiss with Uhura. The real taboo being violated here is the Biblical injunction against embarrassing yourself on national television. Witness Shatner and Nimoy's duet on "I'm Tweedledee, He's Tweedledum."

5. **"THE ENEMY WITHIN"**
PLOT: A transporter malfunction splits Kirk into two people: "Good" Kirk is kind and gentle; "Bad" Kirk is rude, boorish, and he steals McCoy's brandy.
WHY IT'S GREAT: Shatner's done some of his best work in dual roles—and this is no exception. As the growling, uninhibited, lecherous Dark Kirk, he gets to show a side of himself normally seen only by his female costars.

6. **"MIRROR, MIRROR"**
PLOT: Yet another transporter malfunction deposits an *Enterprise* away team in an alternate universe where Spock has a cool-looking goatee.
WHY IT'S GREAT: Granted, this one's more of a Spock showcase, but the concept of evil quantum universe Kirk having a secret device in his cabin that can zap people out of existence is pure gold. If Shatner could have used this on Jimmy Doohan, he would have.

7. **"CITY ON THE EDGE OF FOREVER"**
PLOT: While trapped on Earth in the 1930s, Kirk falls in love with a doomed social worker, played by *Dynasty* diva Joan Collins.
WHY IT'S GREAT: It's so rare for Shatner to deliver an understated performance that it's almost jarring. Plus, DeForest Kelley gets to play the bug-eyed loon in this one.

8. **"MIRI"**

   PLOT: Kirk and his crew encounter a group of ragamuffins who have a strange disease that kills them at puberty.

   WHY IT'S GREAT: Four words: "Bonk bonk on the head." When you watch it, you'll know what I'm talking about.

9. **"THE NAKED TIME"**

   PLOT: A strange disease infects the *Enterprise*, bringing out the emotional insecurities of the crewmembers.

   WHY IT'S GREAT: The "space madness" plot device gives Shatner a perfect excuse to melt down on camera. His blubbering take on Kirk's emotional attachment to the *Enterprise* is outdone only by George Takei's sword-wielding samurai histrionics.

10. **"THE GAMESTERS OF TRISKELION"**

    PLOT: Kirk, Uhura, and Chekov are forced to engage in gladiatorial combat by a race of oozy, brain-like beings.

    WHY IT'S GREAT: Fans of Shirtless Shatner, this is your *Citizen Kane*. Kirk spends most of the episode clad in a revealing leather harness, and the mind-numbing scenes of hand-to-hand brawling (set to the pulsating *Trek* "fight theme") make this the perfect episode to bring to your next Fire Island cookout weekend.

STAR TREK (ANIMATED SERIES)

Production on an animated *Star Trek* TV series began in June 1973, after demographic studies convinced NBC executives of the show's continued appeal to young viewers. A desperate Shatner signed up to provide voice-overs, along with the rest of the original cast. With scripts from many of the original *Star Trek* writers and creative input from series creator **Gene Roddenberry**, the half-hour program had the potential to be respectable. However, the quality of the animation provided by Filmation Enterprises was execrable (a fact Shatner tacitly acknowledged by recording some of his voiceovers while sitting on the toilet). The principals wearily mailed in their vocal performances for two years before the axe of cancellation mercifully fell. Astonishingly, the program won an Emmy Award for Outstanding Entertainment Children's Series—proof of the sad state of animation in the 1970s.

STAR TREK (NOVELS)

Shatner has authored nine *Star Trek* novels in collaboration with veteran sci-fi authors Judith and Garfield Reeves-Stevens. Not surprisingly, Captain Kirk is the focal point of each one. In order of publication, they are:

The Ashes of Eden (1995)

The Return (1996)

Avenger (1997)

Spectre (1998)

Dark Victory (1999)

Preserver (2000)

Captain's Peril (2002)

Captain's Blood (2003)

Captain's Glory (2006)

STAR TREK: GENERATIONS ✳ ✳ ✳

The seventh entry in the *Star Trek* film cycle, this 1994 release is Shatner's last on-camera appearance to date as Captain **James T. Kirk**. He got to play a heroic death scene only after test audiences found the original ending unsatisfactory.

The feature film marked a passing of the torch from the original crew to the cast of *Star Trek: The Next Generation.* "We had gotten older," Shatner said of his original cast mates. "And the question, I guess, in Paramount's mind was how long would the audience pay to see elderly men trying to remember their lines?" Nevertheless, he was one "elderly man" who was invited back for a seventh go on the big screen.

"I really thought the sixth movie was the last for my character," Shatner said, curiously failing to mention that he had submitted a treatment for *Star Trek VII* that was rejected by Paramount. When Paramount decided to feature the *Next Generation* cast in the new project, it appeared the original series regulars had reached the end of the gravy train at last. However, executive producer Rick Berman decided on his own initiative to write some of the old characters into his story treatment. Overtures were made to all the actors. Most of them declined to participate, but Shatner, **Walter Koenig**, and **James Doohan** eagerly signed on. As the story process went on, the death of Captain Kirk became a centerpiece of the movie.

Word soon leaked to the press that this would be Shatner's swan song as Kirk. "I thought it was a good dramatic idea until I realized it would turn out to be my funeral," Shatner quipped. But the chance to bring his most famous character full circle held undeniable appeal for the actor, who received a $6 million salary for the project. "The whole idea of Kirk's death and my own seemed to combine," he said. "I wanted Kirk to die the way I would like to—at peace with himself and the life he had lived." Besides, killing off Kirk would make Shatner the focus of numerous national magazine and newspaper features, no small boost to his fledgling literary career.

Filming of *Star Trek: Generations* commenced in February 1994. For Shatner, the shoot had an empty feeling about it. He missed having his TV and movie series friends **Leonard Nimoy** and **DeForest Kelley** around. Equally alienating was the attitude of the younger *Next Generation* actors, several of whom found it hard to perform in the presence of their childhood heroes. "I felt like a guest on my own show," Shatner explained. "I could tell I no longer belonged, that my time had passed."

Adding to Shatner's vexation was the experience of sharing the lead with **Patrick Stewart**, *Next Generation*'s Captain Jean-Luc Picard. Rumors swirled that the two men despised each other, though both chose to downplay rumors of their feud for the sake of the ongoing franchise. Especially upsetting to Shatner was a scene in which his character says to Picard, "Who am I to argue with the captain of the *Enterprise*?" Shatner later admitted, "Those words stuck in my throat and I couldn't get the line out." "By the third take, people were starting to get annoyed. But I had trouble saying those words. It was a very sad time for me."

One actor who had a grand time on the project was British actor Malcolm McDowell, best remembered for his portrayal of Alex, the vicious, insolent hero of Stanley Kubrick's 1971 masterpiece *A Clockwork Orange*. As Soran, the heavy of the piece, he brought a special relish to the task of terminating Captain **James T. Kirk**. In the scene as originally shot, Soran blasts Kirk from behind with a phaser. "It felt lovely," McDowell cackled afterwards.

On September 14, 1994, the film was screened before a preview audience. The response was not exactly encouraging, especially where the ending was concerned. "The test audience told us a truth we should have known earlier," Shatner observed, namely that Kirk deserved better than to be shot in the back by a sneering Malcolm McDowell. The principals returned to the desert to reshoot the sequence, at an additional cost of $4 million. In the revised ending, Kirk dies heroically, crushed to death after slugging it out with Soran on a high catwalk.

A curse dictates that all odd-numbered *Star Trek* feature films fall flat with critics, and this one was no exception. *Star Trek: Generations* reached theaters on November 18, 1994, and was savaged in most major publications as a tedious, convoluted mess.

"The highly awaited time-travel teaming of Picard and Kirk," wrote *USA Today*, "isn't quite the clash of the follicle-impaired titans that it's meant to be." The talented *Next Generation* ensemble was given little to do, while Malcolm McDowell's most significant contribution to the film was a stylish haircut, apparently on loan from Sting. Nevertheless, Trekkies dutifully lined up to watch the unimaginable—their childhood hero dying. *Generations* grossed $23 million in its opening weekend and $75 million overall—about the same as *Star Trek VI* made in 1991. For the first film with the new cast, it was a respectable showing, paving the way for the far superior *Star Trek: First Contact* in 1996.

STAR TREK: THE MOTION PICTURE ✳

The first of the *Star Trek* big-screen features beamed into theaters on Pearl Harbor Day, 1979—an omen of bad tidings if there ever was one. The on-again, off-again project began as a $3 million TV movie, was redesigned as a pilot for a new TV series called *Star Trek: Phase II*, and ended up as a $44 million spectacle that was loathed by almost everyone who saw it. Shatner was on board every step of the way, astutely sensing that *Star Trek* was his only ticket out of TV **game show** and B-movie hell.

Veteran director Robert Wise of *Sound of Music* fame was signed on to helm the project, initially budgeted at $15 million. That figure would quickly swell, as special effects consumed almost two-thirds of all money spent on the project. The entire cast returned to play their original roles. Even **Leonard Nimoy** put aside bitterness over merchandising royalties to reprise his Spock character.

At a press conference announcing his participation in the upcoming theatrical feature, Shatner tried hard to conceal his glee at finally being given a lead in a big-budget theatrical feature. "I somehow always felt that we would be back together," he crowed.

"Regardless of what I was doing, or where my career was taking me at the moment, I knew Captain Kirk was not behind me."

As filming approached, Shatner saw an opportunity to bring a fresh perspective to his character. "Both Leonard and myself have changed over the years," he told reporters, "to a degree at any rate, and we will bring that degree of change inadvertently to the role we recreate." One of the changes Shatner had undergone was a twenty-five-pound **weight** gain that looked like forty-five pounds on camera. Convinced that William Ware Theiss' form-fitting pajama-style costumes would make him the butt (so to speak) of Hollywood jokes if he didn't do something quickly, Shatner embarked on a grueling diet and weight training regimen under the supervision of "nutritionist to the stars" **Dr. Ernst Wynder**. The results can be seen in the finished film, as Shatner, of all the cast members, appears to have aged the least. Tinseltown gossip suggested that Shatner had resorted to more radical measures, such as face lifts and liposuction, to achieve the desired effect.

The production was beset by problems from the start. As many as four different writers had their fingerprints on the script, one of whom, Dennis Clark, lasted only three months. Two of these months, he later declared, "I spent hiding from Nimoy and Shatner because [the producers] didn't want me to talk to them. I'd have to leave my office when they were on the lot, because actors want to tell you, 'This is how I perceive the character,' and Gene [Roddenberry] didn't want their input. He didn't even like Bob Wise's input."

The story everyone settled on, after countless rewrites, was ostensibly based on "In Thy Image," a **Gene Roddenberry** script for the abortive *Star Trek: Phase II* project. "In Thy Image," in turn, was a rehash of "Robot's Return," another unfilmed teleplay from Roddenberry's failed *Genesis II* series. The dirty little secret, however, which anyone who ever watched *Star Trek* could instantly perceive, was that *Star Trek: The Motion Picture* was a brazen copy of the original TV series episode "The Changeling." Expanded to almost three times the length and prettied up with special effects, yes, but still "The Changeling." Most galling of all, according to the show's rabid **fans**: "The Changeling" was actually better.

The film premiered in grand style at the Kennedy Center in Washington, D.C. However, in a portent of things to come, both Shatner and **Jimmy Doohan** fell asleep during the screening. Perhaps they were lulled into a stupor by one of the film's many interminable special effects sequences. A sure sign that the movie's mammoth effects budget had not been wisely allocated is an early sequence where Kirk and Scotty spend twenty minutes gazing out at the starship *Enterprise* as it sits in dry dock. Try staring at a parked car for that length of time and see if you don't get sleepy too.

Star Trek: The Motion Picture enjoyed a huge opening weekend, grossing $20 million—the second largest box-office splash to that point. However, it could not maintain that level of enthusiasm in the wake of a withering critical reception. The operative word was "soporific" as reviewer after reviewer lambasted the picture's plodding, deliberate pace. The promiscuous use of special effects enervated Richard Schickel of *Time*, who carped, "The spaceships take an unconscionable amount of time to get anywhere, and nothing of dramatic or human interest happens along the way."

In purely financial terms, *Star Trek: The Motion Picture* can be judged a success. It grossed over $175 million, almost four times its budget. However, it did serious damage to the series' credibility with the show's most rabid **fans**—many of whom sat through it more than once out of sheer loyalty to the *Star Trek* ideal. "It was embarrassing to watch the fans," explained original series writer David Gerrold, "because they were all apologists for this picture: 'Well, it's not that bad. It's a different kind of *Star Trek*.' Instead of really just acknowledging that it was a bad movie, they tried to explain that it was wonderful and you were an idiot for not understanding it."

Like a fart in a space station, the stench from *Star Trek: The Motion Picture* lingered in the air long after it departed theaters. It took almost three years for Paramount to green light another *Star Trek* project. To add insult to injury, one of the film's early script iterations, "The God Thing," about the *Enterprise*'s search for **God** at the end of the **universe**, would form the basis for the even more unwatchable *Star Trek V: The Final Frontier*. Still, for Shatner, the first movie was the beginning of a career renaissance. His credibility as a major star now restored, he largely gave up on the **game show** circuit and began to command more substantive parts. His bank account swelled, thanks to a contract granting him a generous percentage of *Star Trek* movie merchandising royalties. Also, he had the satisfaction of knowing that, standing next to **Jimmy Doohan**, he looked positively svelte.

"... curiously smooth-skinned and hairy."

—*Newsweek's appraisal of Shatner's appearance in* Star Trek: The Motion Picture

STAR TREK II: THE WRATH OF KHAN ✶ ✶ ✶ ✶

This second film in the *Star Trek* movie series was released in 1982. Directed by Nicholas Meyer, it returned the series to its action/adventure roots and won back the hearts of **fans** dispirited by *Star Trek: The Motion Picture*. Shatner had a particularly meaty part in the new installment. His epic verbal duels with costar Ricardo Montalban helped make *Star Trek II* a favorite among Trekkies and general audiences alike.

The movie owed its positive vibe to one particularly smart pre-production decision. To ensure the mistakes of *Star Trek: The Motion Picture* were not repeated, Paramount executives promoted **Gene Roddenberry** to the post of executive consultant. This took the increasingly meddlesome "Great Bird of the Galaxy" out of the story development process. Creative control over the project was given to Harve Bennett, a former **television** producer whom Shatner later called "the man who got *Star Trek* back on track."

Despite the streamlined **writing** process, Shatner had his apprehensions about the new big-screen project. "I was nervous about it, especially after the first film," he admitted. "The success of your performance rests in the words. As this script developed, I swung wildly from awful lows to exalted highs." By the time filming began, however, Shatner was stoked. "I knew *The Wrath of Khan* would be great," he said.

Boosting everyone's spirits on the *Star Trek II* set was director Nicholas Meyer. The scenarist behind two inventive high-concept movie hits, 1976's *The Seven-Per-Cent Solution* (Sherlock Holmes meets Sigmund Freud) and 1979's *Time After Time* (H. G. Wells meets Jack the Ripper) Meyer was relatively inexperienced as a director. Nevertheless, the cast and crew had full confidence in his abilities behind the camera. "Even though it was only the second picture he had directed, Shatner opined, "we felt that his imagination should be given full flower."

Production on *Star Trek II* got under way on November 9, 1981. The project went through several subtitle changes on its way to completion. Originally, it was to be called *Star Trek II: The Undiscovered Country*, after a line from Shakespeare's *Hamlet*. When that was scrapped as too erudite for mass audiences (though later revived as the subtitle of *Star Trek VI*) the producers switched to *Star Trek II: The Vengeance of Khan*. However, fears of competition from George Lucas' forthcoming third *Star Wars* movie—at that time called *Revenge of the Jedi*—forced Bennett, Meyer, and company to settle on the shorter, punchier *Wrath of Khan*. Also downsized was the film's budget, to around $11 million, about a fourth of what was spent on *Star Trek: The Motion Picture*. The belt-tightening approach helped give the final movie some of the charming "slapped together in a week-and-a-half" quality of the original series.

As befit its cash constraints, the plot of *Star Trek II: The Wrath of Khan* was stripped to the bare bones. A starship probing a distant sector of the galaxy stumbles upon ubermensch Khan Noonian Singh (Ricardo Montalban) and his cadre of genetic freaks stranded on the planet where Captain Kirk exiled them some fifteen years earlier (in the original series episode "Space Seed." The devious Khan hijacks the ship and steals the Genesis Device, an untested Federation innovation that creates life on barren planets. Kirk and the *Enterprise* crew (including a young, svelte **Kirstie Alley** as a Vulcan lieutenant) are dispatched to investigate. The ensuing violent confrontation claims the lives of Khan, his crew, and, in a moving climactic scene, Spock himself. All the regulars returned for another shift in space, although of all the subsidiary players only **Walter Koenig** is given anything substantive to do.

While *Star Trek II* is best remembered by audiences as the *Star Trek* movie where Spock dies, it is also arguably the most Shatner-centric of the six original-crew motion pictures. After seemingly sleepwalking through much of *Star Trek: The Motion Picture*, Shatner seems rejuvenated here. He has many chewy scenes and does not miss a beat in his attempts to dominate all the action. Throughout the film, Kirk must wrestle with a mid-life crisis triggered by his birthday and the appearance of his estranged son David, played by Merritt Buttrick of TV's *Square Pegs*. After vacuuming the lines off his face for the previous picture, Shatner finally accepts the realities of aging and change by donning granny glasses and ruing his misspent youth on screen.

Star Trek II was more than just Steel Magnolias in space, however. It was also a top-notch action romp in the tradition of old school episodes like "Arena" and "The Doomsday Machine." Shatner's byplay with costar Ricardo Montalban is particularly compelling. Squaring off exclusively via viewscreen (the chief flaw in the picture is their lack of a face-to-face confrontation) the two grand hams snarl and quote poetry to each other with a vigor that almost makes you forget what bad wigs they're both wearing. Especially efective is the scene where Shatner finds the crew of a science station massacred by Khan and his followers, then excoriates him via communicator. "Like a poor marksman, you KEEP . . . MISSING . . . the TARGET!" Shatner rants in perhaps his finest moment on the big screen. Then, his head seeming to expand like a basketball being filled with air, his red cheeks bulging, and he wails, "KHAAAAN! KHAAAAAAAAN!" with such a convulsive intensity that one might almost think a man's heart attack has been captured on camera. **Theater** and **television** audiences invariably erupt into fits of laughter when this scene is played, no matter how many times they've seen it before.

Viewers may have been laughing, but they were also paying. Star Trek: The Wrath of Khan grossed almost $80 million in the United States alone, easily earning back its relatively small budget. Critics were pleased with the scaled-down look and feel of the new series entry, which in the eyes of many played like a feature-length **television** episode. None were more pleased than Star Trek's dedicated **fans**, who finally had a Trek film for which they could proudly proclaim their affection after the debacle of Star Trek: The Motion Picture.

As for Shatner, he reveled in the return of the movie series to its Kirk-centric glory days. "I always knew there was a large audience that wanted to see me," he revealed to *People* magazine, before going on to designate himself as the fulcrum of *Star Trek*. Not so pleased with the functioning of their fulcrum were the other cast members, several of whom compared Shatner unfavorably with Ricardo Montalban. "It was great not having scenes reblocked by our leading man," **Walter Koenig** told *Starlog* magazine. "Montalban was always there for your close-up and always very giving. The two weeks I worked with Bill as the leading man weren't as much fun." There were the usual complaints among the cast about Shatner trimming their lines, even excising whole scenes designed to give their characters something more to do than stand around and say "Aye, sir." Also, Hollywood neophyte **Kirstie Alley** added her name to the list of actresses who reportedly have been the object of Shatner's romantic attentions off camera. For the record, she resisted his advances.

Walter Koenig explained the Shatner dilemma succinctly: "When you have one actor so dominating the proceedings in terms of participation, regardless of how good he is, I don't think it's possible for the other actors to feel totally comfortable about the situation. The sense of ensemble playing wasn't there. In most cases, Bill dominated every scene he was in, and that's the way it was photographed."

For better or worse, Shatner's aggressive scene-hogging made *Star Trek II* what it was. And in the eyes of Paramount executives, that was a hit. They would repeat the same formula, with slightly less spectacular results, in 1984's *Star Trek III: The Search for Spock*.

STAR TREK III: THE SEARCH FOR SPOCK ✳✳✳

The third entry in the *Star Trek* movie series was released in 1984. It was the feature film directorial debut of **Leonard Nimoy**, who appeared only briefly on screen as Spock, much of that in flashback to the previous installment. *Star Trek III* wrapped up loose plot ends from *Star Trek II* and returned Spock to the land of the living, much to the delight of *Star Trek*'s ardent **fans**.

Production began on August 15, 1983. At first, Shatner chafed at having his longtime rival behind the cameras. "It was more awkward in the beginning than any of the other two [films]," he reported, likening the experience of being directed by Nimoy to being ordered around by your brother. Elsewhere he placed their relationship in a marital context. "It's like your wife is suddenly earning more money than you. The relationship has changed and you have to make an adjustment. Once that adjustment is made, you might sit back and relax and enjoy it. Which is what I've begun to do."

Once the new power arrangements were sorted out, filming proceeded briskly. Principal photography was completed in only forty-nine days at a relatively tight budget of $16 million. All the usual suspects returned to keep their SAG cards valid for another few years, although a disgruntled **Kirstie Alley** was replaced by Robin Curtis. This time, the supporting cast even had a few scenes of their own to display their talents.

After dominating the action in *Star Trek II*, Shatner must have been salivating at the prospect of acting in a film in which Nimoy plays a corpse for most of the picture. However, while Kirk is given a few priceless scenes here, he does not command the same presence he did in the previous film. Shatner had even less to do in the original script, but quickly made his objections known to Nimoy and producer Harve Bennett. More screen time for Kirk was added—at the expense of the other actors, as usual.

In one of the more memorable scenes in this installment, Shatner gets the chance to do some method hamming when Kirk learns his son David has been executed by a Klingon war party. Director Nimoy even cleared the set to get his star in the appropriate emotional state for this key sequence. He left it up to Shatner to decide how far to go in showing Kirk's grief, and Shatner went quite far indeed. When given the news of David's death, Kirk stumbles backward and falls on his behind, croaking "You Klingon bastards, you've killed my son!" in a breakneck staccato. "He looks deeply hurt," Nimoy said of the performance, refusing to clarify whether he meant by the fall or the emotional blow. Shatner would later call it his finest piece of **acting** as Kirk.

Somehow, though, as a piece *Star Trek III* does not come off as well as it might have. It moves at a snail's pace. The funereal mood set in the opening moments lingers throughout, accentuated by the death of David and the gratuitous destruction of the *Enterprise*. Shatner himself acknowledged the gimmicky nature of these developments by summing up the screenwriters' dilemma as "What else can we kill?" The concluding scenes on Vulcan, obviously meant to be moving, are merely tedious. Even the action scenes fail to compel. The Klingon plot seems tacked on and perfunctory. Seriously damaging these sequences is Christopher Lloyd, who seems to be playing his **"Taxi"** role of Reverend Jim Ignatowski in Klingon makeup.

Despite the picture's flaws, audiences eager for more *Star Trek* gave this installment the thumbs-up. *Star Trek III* grossed more than $76 million. "Installment three falls somewhere ahead of the first feature and way behind the high-water mark of [*Star Trek*] *II*," observed the *New York Daily News*, capturing the general consensus of **fans** and critics. Moviegoers were especially cheered by the return of Spock to the *Enterprise* fold. Some of the more rabid Trekkies had threatened to boycott *Star Trek* films if the beloved Vulcan was not sprung from his space coffin. They had nothing to worry about. Spock and the rest of the crew would be back with full faculties engaged for 1986's *Star Trek IV: The Voyage Home*.

STAR TREK IV: THE VOYAGE HOME ✳ ✳ ✳ ✳

The fourth of the *Star Trek* feature films was released in 1986. A light-hearted time-travel romp with an environmentalist twist, it was a much-needed change of pace for the series and proved to be a colossal hit with the public. Again, **Leonard Nimoy** took the reins as director, with creative assistance from screenwriters Harve Bennett and Nicholas Meyer.

Now regarded as one of the best *Star Trek* movies, *The Voyage Home* almost did not get produced. Shatner played hardball with Paramount before signing on for another voyage as Captain Kirk. Securely ensconced in prime time as TV's ***T. J. Hooker***, at last he had the leverage to demand a sizable pay increase. Negotiations dragged on for months, and at one point Paramount was prepared to move without Shatner. Their contingency concept, a prequel called *Starfleet Academy*, was configured as a kind of "*Top Gun* in space," with young actors assuming the roles of the *Star Trek* regulars. To the relief of all concerned, that concept was scrapped when Shatner agreed to a $2 million contract.

Star Trek IV would prove to be quite a departure from the previous films. After the gloomy goings-on of *Star Trek III*, Leonard Nimoy and Harve Bennett had a simple story prescription for the next entry: Make 'em laugh. "We felt that we should lighten up," said Nimoy. "The picture should be fun in comparison to the previous three. The first movie had no comedy at all. That was intentional. It was intended to be a serious study of a problem. The second film had a little. The third film had a little. But there we were dealing with a lot of serious drama. There was a lot of life and death going on. . . . I just felt it was time to lighten up and have some fun."

Originally slated to provide that fun was comedy juggernaut Eddie Murphy, then fresh off his *Beverly Hills Cop* success. A longtime *Star Trek* fan, Murphy was to play a wacky college professor whose belief in UFOs is validated by the appearance of the *Enterprise* in modern-day San Francisco. However, Paramount grew skittish about inserting its major comedy star into its franchise science fiction series, so Murphy's part was rewritten as a touchy-feely marine biologist, played in the finished film by Catherine Hicks. Producers were also eager to provide Kirk with a love interest after letting his hormonal urges go largely unattended in the previous three pictures. In fact, two young screenwriters, Steve Meerson and Peter Krikes, were brought in to work on the project with explicit instructions to expand Shatner's screen role. "The approach we were told to take is that Kirk really had to be the one to lead everyone," Meerson recalled. "Not necessarily that he had to actually have the idea to do something, but it had to appear as if he has the idea. . . . We were told Bill had to be the leader at all times."

Star Trek IV went before the cameras in February of 1986. Shooting took fifty-three days at a still relatively restricted budget of $23 million. Using modern-day exteriors like San Francisco's Golden Gate Park and the Presidio helped keep costs under control, while the production itself was almost completely devoid of expensive science fiction trappings.

The absence of special effects wizardry, however, did not detract at all from *Star Trek IV*'s entertainment quotient. That was provided by some snappy patter, inventive situations, and a humanistic theme that recalled the very best original TV series episodes. *The Voyage Home* opens with a gigantic probe paralyzing twenty-third century Earth in a misguided attempt to communicate with some long-extinct humpback whales. The starship *Enterprise* must travel back in time to 1986 and bring back two of the keening leviathans to keep the **universe** from being destroyed. Along the way there are a lot of the usual "how do we explain Spock's ears?" shenanigans. All of it might have seemed dreadfully familiar in the hands of a different director and cast. But by this time the *Star Trek* players had learned the secret of not taking themselves too seriously. Instead they play to the nostalgia of their audience, letting them feel as if they are in on the joke from the first scene to the last.

Shatner called the approach "joie de vivre." "We discovered something in *Star Trek IV* that we hadn't pinpointed in any of the other movies," he said, "and it just shows how the obvious can escape you—that there is a texture to the best *Star Trek* hours that verges on tongue-in-cheek but isn't." True **fans** of *Star Trek*—and Shatner—have been grooving on this texture for years.

Star Trek IV: The Voyage Home reached theaters in time for Christmas of 1986. It was the most successful *Star Trek* big-screen excursion to date, grossing over $125 million, more than five times its budget. Critics lauded the movie's lighthearted tone and ensemble playing—particularly the Spock/McCoy byplay. "Nimoy and Kelley are at their most amusingly snippy," raved David Denby in *New York* magazine. "They appear to be playing two aging gays dishing at each other at a party while vying for the attention of William Shatner." Refreshingly, the names of supporting cast members like **Walter Koenig** and **George Takei** were cited by reviewers as often as the so-called "Big Three." The **seven dwarfs** were delirious. "For the first time I felt the dialogue was indigenous to my character," explained **Walter Koenig**, "that only Chekov could say these lines." Never one to give up an old saw, he then added tellingly, "And I had the opportunity to work away from Bill Shatner."

STAR TREK V: THE FINAL FRONTIER ✳

This fifth entry in the *Star Trek* film series is the only one directed by Shatner. "Things don't turn out exactly the way you want them to," were the words Shatner used to sum up his participation in the 1989 project, and the show's **fans** mostly agreed. *Star Trek V* remains a notable failure in the *Star Trek* cinematic cycle, with turgid and amateurish direction often cited among the litany of critical complaints.

The *Star Trek V* storyline germinated for almost ten years before taking root. It is loosely based on "The God Thing," an early script for 1979's *Star Trek: The Motion Picture.* That screenplay had the starship *Enterprise* encountering **God** at the far edges of the **universe**. It was rejected by Paramount as too pretentious, but Shatner found it fascinating. "It was a mind-boggling script," he gushed, "something along the lines of 2001. The dialogue was incredible. Spock was questioning the logic of a supreme being whose actions appeared questionable and inconsistent. It would have made a classic science fiction film."

In the final screenplay, cowritten by Shatner from his original story, Sybok, a renegade Vulcan holy man, commandeers the *Enterprise* go on a search for **God**. Along the way, the charismatic guru manages to convert a number of the ship's crew to his philosophy of spiritual healing. Complications ensue when a Klingon vessel attacks the *Enterprise* to exact vengeance against Kirk. The film's climax takes place at the Great Barrier at the center of the galaxy, where **God** is found to be a large holographic head with a flowing white beard—and, in reality, an evil alien projection. The film concludes with cosmic order restored and the star troika of Kirk, Spock, and McCoy warbling "Row, Row, Row Your Boat" around a campfire.

Shooting began on October 11, 1988. Anxious to bring his grand vision to fruition on time and under budget, Shatner was manic on the set, ordering people around in a nonsensical patter. "He thought that by talking fast it would speed up the schedule," observed Leonard Nimoy. "But you couldn't understand a word he was saying." Eventually, he got a hold of himself, but the production was doomed from the start. With a $30 million budget (a third of which went to special effects), the fledgling big-screen director Shatner was, understandably, like a kid in a candy store. And like any candy store, this one was plagued by petty thievery. In one instance, $60,000 worth of costumes was stolen from a trailer. Cost overruns, labor disputes, and shoddy planning also dogged the project. In the end, *Star Trek V* came in $3 million over budget, a striking departure from the tidy and economical production of the three previous films in the series. Shatner tried to write off the gaffes as the inevitable runoff of his boundless creative energy, but studio executives weren't buying it. "Directing multiple episodes of *T. J. Hooker* just did not prepare Bill Shatner for the wide screen's demands," opined Harve Bennett.

Following months of bad publicity, the film debuted in June 1989 to eager if apprehensive audiences. Before long, moviegoers' worst fears were confirmed. If *Star Trek V* had any redeeming moments, they surely must have ended up on the cutting room floor. Most longtime *Star Trek* **fans** found themselves wincing through the movie's many embarrassing scenes, including a staggering sequence in which an aging **Nichelle Nichols** performs an ostensibly sexy striptease for a group of ogling barbarians. The other supporting characters were likewise stripped of all dignity. "Chekov and Sulu were supposed to be the best navigator and helmsman in Starfleet," an angry **George Takei** pointed out. Shatner's script has them getting hopelessly lost in the forest. "Engineer Scott was supposed to know every inch of the *Enterprise* like 'the back of my hand.'" Yet Shatner depicts him bonking his head on a crossbeam. The humor, Takei concluded, "instead of being light and frolicsome, seemed only mean-spirited."

Shatner was apparently oblivious to these complaints. For him, *Star Trek V* represented a grand vision unrealized due to budget constraints, studio tinkering, and his own lack of experience as a director.

"What the final result was, was the final result," he observed nonsensically after the picture wrapped. "I have certain regrets but I feel in total that a lot of the vision was there. . . . I thought [the film] was flawed. I didn't manage my resources as well as I could have. I thought it was a meaningful attempt at a story and I thought it was a meaningful play. It carried a sense of importance about it."

Perhaps most damaging to *The Final Frontier* is its lackluster finale, in which the highly anticipated confrontation with **God** turns out to be nothing more than an encounter with a hologram of a head. In Shatner's original vision, Kirk is pursued by a legion of malevolent gargoyles let loose by the God creature. But cost restrictions forced him to scuttle this idea. Detractors blasted Shatner for coming up with grandiose sequences that were impossible to film. But Shatner defended his unorthodox approach. "A first-time director knows no boundaries," he said, "and it's not knowing them that you shatter them. Rather than accepting the status quo, I tried to break the boundaries and make the camera do things that it wasn't supposed to, not because I didn't know how, but I thought that by standing firm and being as adamant as possible it would happen. But there came a point where I had to compromise."

One problem that did not plague *Star Trek V* was conflict between the director and his costars—despite initial reservations among the supporting players. "To say that most of us were dreading standing before a camera with Bill on the other side of it would be an understatement," said **Nichelle Nichols**. "After twenty years of enduring his overbearing behavior on the set, our apprehensions about working on *Star Trek V* were not unfounded." Nevertheless, she found him to be "supportive, encouraging, [and] inspiring" as a director. **Leonard Nimoy** was equally effusive. "With us as actors, [Bill] was personable, charming, well-prepared, and boundlessly enthusiastic." Even that stalwart Shatner detractor, **James Doohan**, was won over. "The man's not half as bad as I thought he'd be," he cracked.

Alone among the original crew members, **George Takei** saw a darker motivation for Shatner's seeming change of heart. "It was not an unpleasant working experience to be directed by him," he remarked in his 1994 autobiography. "In fact, he was actually quite good at creating a positive environment on the set, marshalling his considerable reservoir of charm, loading into his weapon, and placing the setting at 'enchant' . . . His charm was intended, however, always to burnish his own star. I knew I was only watching another acting performance—this time, he was acting the role of a cheerfully earnest and helpful director."

Earnest and helpful, perhaps, but ultimately unsuccessful. Shatner's compromised vision didn't connect with *Star Trek* **fans**. After a solid opening weekend, *Star Trek V* bombed with audiences. During a summer when *Batman* was setting huge box-office records, its final box office take was only $52 million, down by half from the previous film. Given its bloated budget, the profit margin for an unhappy Paramount was even smaller. Today it is widely considered the worst of the *Star Trek* films. The lone dissenter? Why, Shatner himself, of course. "Regardless of where it tanked in anybody else's lexicon," he told the *Washington Post* in 1991, "*Star Trek V* was life-changing for me. . . . All the other films have special things about them. But *V* is very special to me."

"Oh my God. What are we going to do?"

—*George Takei, on learning that Shatner was to direct* Star Trek V

STAR TREK VI: THE UNDISCOVERED COUNTRY ✳ ✳ ✳

The sixth film in the *Star Trek* cinematic cycle is the final numbered installment. A story of intergalactic political intrigue inspired by the end of the Cold War, *Star Trek VI* was released in time for Christmas of 1991 and was a hit with **fans** and critics alike, helping to erase the bitter taste left behind by *Star Trek V*.

In *Star Trek VI: The Undiscovered Country* the near-geriatric *Enterprise* crew reunites for a diplomatic mission. It seems the Klingon high command has decided to seek peace with the Federation after years of galactic conflict. However, a renegade Klingon, General Chang (Christopher Plummer), hatches a plan to disrupt the peace conference by assassinating the Klingon High Chancellor. Captain Kirk and Dr. McCoy are framed for the crime and sentenced to hard labor on a frigid prison planet. After a bizarre interlude in which Kirk enjoys a roll in the snow with a shape-shifting alien (played by supermodel Iman), the action ends up back at the peace conference. There, with some help from the newly commissioned Captain Sulu, our heroes foil Chang's plans to assassinate a Federation delegate.

While not high on theatrics, *Star Trek VI* benefited from a sound, politically relevant storyline. "It's a really good idea," Shatner said. "It's a classic *Star Trek* idea in that the important issue of the day is incorporated into the story of *Star Trek*, and by doing so—and because we put it into the future—we're able to comment on it as though it has nothing to do with today, yet it makes a commentary."

The script was written by **Leonard Nimoy** and Dennis Martin Flinn, a newcomer to *Star Trek*. Initially, Shatner was disappointed when the director's nod went to Nicholas Meyer. "I felt a sense of loss that I couldn't be the problem solver," he groused. "I would have loved to have been immersed in those very same problems and bring to bear what I had learned on the previous film." Paramount, however, had no intention of turning the reins over to their quixotic star. The studio was in a cost-cutting mode; in fact, studio executives wrangled over tightening the picture's $26 million budget all through filming. The production could have been a rocky one—but somehow, it was just the opposite.

Anyone who thought that Shatner would be a pain in the neck on the set after being passed over for the director's assignment was soon disabused of that notion. In fact, production of *Star Trek VI* rolled along with nary a hitch. "It went a lot smoother than I thought," said new producer Ralph Winter. "I had a great time with Bill. He was terrific and he was a lot of fun." Canadian sexpot Kim Cattrall, who played a perfidious Vulcan crewmember, also had nothing but nice things to say about her leading man. "He was a gentleman with me and it doesn't matter how I feel about him personally," the future *Sex and the City* star reported. "We're both Canadians and I had a professional relationship. . . . I don't think anybody does better what he does. He is Captain Kirk and he's amazing in what he does."

Adding even more Canadian flava to the cast was Christopher Plummer, Shatner's longtime friend from their **Stratford Shakespeare Festival** days in Ontario. Plummer brings real classical heft to his performance as Chang, though his incessant, nonsensical quotations from *Hamlet* get a bit annoying after a while. His presence on the set obviously helped bring out the best in Shatner, who gives a delightfully chewy performance in this, his last go-round as a leading man in a *Star Trek* movie.

For the first time since *Star Trek II*, Shatner was actually prompted to think seriously about his character. "The portrayal of Kirk attempts to show a man who has spent a lifetime imbued with the idea that his mission in life is to subdue, subvert, and make the enemy submit to his nation's or his Federation's view," he said. "That's his whole training and that is the military training. He learns differently and that is the classic dilemma that *Star Trek* has sought to present in its most successful shows."

Critics and audiences alike found *Star Trek VI* very successful indeed. "The crew's hairpieces are worse than ever, the bags under their eyes could hold a week's worth of groceries," wrote the reviewer for *People* magazine, but, she conceded, "hardcore Trekkies will get their rockets off with *Star Trek VI*." In fact, Trekkies—hardcore and otherwise—poured out almost 150 million of their hard-earned dollars to watch the *Enterprise* crew beam off into the sunset. The movie's powerhouse performance helped convince Paramount to continue the film cycle with the characters from *Star Trek: The Next Generation*.

Star Trek VI ends with one final touching flourish. All the original series actors sign their names in the *Enterprise*'s last log book, while majestic orchestral **music** plays in the background. Guess who lobbied for top billing? "They reversed the order of the names so Shatner's is last, like an opera," revealed composer Cliff Eidelman. "It's a minute of signing off, which is real emotional music." A baton of sorts had been passed to the cast and crew of *Next Generation*, who would soldier on in 1994's *Star Trek: Generations*.

STEWART, PATRICK

This bald, lean, sharp-featured British actor, with a distinctive stentorian voice, played Captain Jean-Luc Picard on *Star Trek: The Next Generation* from 1987 to 1994. He also appeared with Shatner in the 1994 feature **Star Trek: Generations**.

A thinking man's captain who plays the recorder and sends his burly first officer out to do his fighting for him, Picard was the polar opposite of the brash, impulsive **James T. Kirk**. Yet Stewart brought an intelligence and dignity to the role that won him a substantial fan following in his own right. One man not charmed was Shatner, who saw his successor on the *Enterprise* bridge as a rival, not a friend. In interviews during the years when *Next Generation* was on the air, Shatner took every opportunity to compare Stewart unfavorably to himself—or damn him with faint praise. "Stewart is not the captain, he's just a wonderful actor," was a typical remark. At other times, like a fan arguing with his buddies, Shatner would take up the "my captain is better than your captain" argument. "Kirk was the better captain," he once told a TV interviewer, "because he was more three-dimensional." While he was aware of such comments, Stewart largely remained above the fray.

Sparks were expected to fly when the two men worked together on **Star Trek: Generations**. According to Shatner, however, "instant liking and respect transpired" when the duo first met at the ShoWest movie exhibitors' convention in Las Vegas. "Patrick told me that he felt very lost among all these people neither one of us knew, so we held hands and kind of clung together like two howler monkeys might." That evening, the two men shared a corporate jet back to Los Angeles.

Shatner denied rumors that he and Stewart fought on the set of **Generations**. In fact, he says they bonded over their mutual love of **horses.** Before long, Shatner was practically sharing his **panty hose** with the cerebral Shakespearean veteran. "We became very friendly," Shatner explained to *TV Guide*. The two captains have since teamed up to promote pre-paid phone cards together and have made numerous joint **Star Trek** convention appearances.

"If William Shatner ever calls you into the bathroom and asks you to see the 'Captain's Log,' say no! I fell for that nine times."
—*Patrick Stewart, on working with his predecessor as* Enterprise *captain*

STILLER, BEN

As a child, this popular actor/director, the son of comedians Jerry Stiller and Anne Meara, idolized Shatner. In 1975, Stiller got a chance to meet his hero. But like many such encounters, this one ended in disillusionment. Stiller had a guest spot on his mother's short-lived TV drama *Kate McShane* on the Paramount lot. Shatner was shooting his series **The Barbary Coast** on the next soundstage. "I thought it couldn't get any better," recalled Stiller, "one day I went up to him and yelled, 'Captain Kirk!' He turned around and had a handlebar mustache. I felt so gypped. It was an early lesson on the bitter disappointments of Hollywood."

STRATFORD SHAKESPEARE FESTIVAL

In 1953 Shatner joined this Ontario-based Shakespearean repertory company, founded by the renowned English director **Tyrone Guthrie**. For $80 a week, Shatner got to appear in 60 plays during his three-year stint with the festival, learning his trade alongside such established stars as James Mason, Alec Guinness, and Anthony Quayle. Shatner undertook nearly 100 parts at Stratford, including Lucentio in *The Taming of the Shrew*, Gratiano in *The Merchant of Venice*, and Lucius in *Julius Caesar*.

"TAXI"

Shatner warbles this classic Harry Chapin story-song during a 1975 appearance on *Dinah!* With host Dinah Shore and fellow guest Yul Brynner looking on in amazement, Shatner talk/sings his way through Chapin's melodramatic tale of a lonely, pot-smoking cab driver who picks up an old lover one rainy night in San Francisco. Obviously workshopping the weirdly overemotive style he would perfect three years later in his **"Rocket Man"** performance at the Science Fiction Film Awards, Shatner delivers a spoken-word tour de force that would reset

Shatner in makeup for his TV series *The Barbary Coast.* Could this be the moustache that frightened a youthful Ben Stiller?

the bar for his televised musical appearances. Sporting a dark blazer and a pink, butterfly-collared sport shirt, Shatner does not merely play Harry the melancholy hack, he becomes him, spitting out the lyrics to the song's bridge with a mesmerizing urgency.

Even the man himself was impressed with his performance. "I thought that was rather good," he recalled many years later in an interview posted on his Shatnervision website. Shatner went on to explain the appeal of his rendition of "Taxi" by putting himself in the mind of a viewer wondering "'What's that guy doing?' And you listen because it's interesting, and [to] find out what it is he's doing." More than 30 years after this clip first graced the airwaves, we're still searching for the answer.

> "The first premise is I can't sing. I can't sustain a note, so . . . I used the lyrics as though they were poetry."
> —*Shatner, on his rendition of Harry Chapin's "Taxi"*

3RD ROCK FROM THE SUN ✶ ✶

In 1999, Shatner received his first Emmy nomination for his recurring role as Big Giant Head on this popular 1990s sitcom about a "family" of extraterrestrials living in present-day Ohio. An officious **alien** overlord from an unnamed planet, Big Giant Head becomes a lascivious satyr when he assumes human form. He fathers a child with Jan Hooks' Vicki Dubcek character and is later revealed to be the father of Dick Solomon, played by John Lithgow. A broad comedy in the tradition of *ALF*, *3rd Rock* gave Shatner ample room to mug and preen, while playing off his sci-fi persona. The show was also notable for its occasional in-joke references to other Shatner projects. Several episodes made allusions to "Nightmare at 20,000 Feet," the classic

Twilight Zone episode in which Shatner starred and which Lithgow later reprised for 1982's *Twilight Zone: The Movie*.

T. J. HOOKER   ✴ ✴ ✴ ✴

Shatner played the title role in this prime-time **television** police drama from 1982 to 1986. The action-packed show centers around a gruff but lovable detective who relinquishes his gold shield for a job on uniformed patrol. One-time *Dance Fever* host **Adrian Zmed** plays Hooker's wisecracking partner, Officer Vince Romano, while **sex** symbol **Heather Locklear** makes her initial network splash as Officer Stacy Sheridan.

Originally, the series was to be called *The Protectors*, with Shatner portraying a hardnosed police academy instructor whose young cadets would see most of the chase-and-gun action. "*Dallas* with cops" was how executive producer Rick Husky framed the initial concept. When test audiences responded positively to the Hooker character, however, the cadets were expelled, and the series reconfigured around the stocky, bewigged Shatner. For the record, Hooker worked for the mythical Lake City Police Department (LCPD).

The series soon became renowned for its spectacular action sequences. In fact, the lasting image of *T. J. Hooker* in most viewers' minds—famously parodied by Shatner himself in a **Saturday Night Live** sketch—is of Hooker clinging on to the hood of a criminal's speeding getaway car. To prepare for the physically demanding role, Shatner worked out daily in his home and ran three to five miles a day. Typically, he lost so much **weight** that his police uniform had to be taken in at the start of each season—only to be let out again as he ballooned over the course of the year.

Shatner played Hooker as a tough but tender man squeezed by the constraints of the system, a man whose greatest fear, he once said, was "feeling too much for the victims." Unwilling to be part of just another TV cop show, Shatner consistently lobbied for

Old friend Leonard Nimoy plays a cop turned vigilante on an episode of *T. J. Hooker*.

more character development amidst the weekly mayhem. Over the course of the show's four-year run, Hooker lost a partner in the line of duty, dealt with relationship issues, and stared down the barrel of a different ethical crisis every week. The series gave Shatner a chance to play another complex hero—without falling prey to type-casting. "Viewers think of Hooker as the archetypal conservative cop fighting for justice," Shatner said of his creation, "which Kirk does, but on a higher plane. They are both universal characters doing what they can to preserve peace and justice. They share similar qualities, but there are differences, too. Kirk has a thoughtful, analytical approach to problems. Hooker is an angry man who reacts to stress with action. Actually, the core of each of them, of course, is within myself."

In addition to playing the lead, Shatner also directed ten episodes of *T. J. Hooker* during the course of its four-season run. His dominance of the show alienated some of his costars, particularly **Locklear**. Reportedly, she also resented Shatner's habit of rubbing himself up against her during rehearsals. Over the years, the Beach Boys, Jerry Lee Lewis, and **Leonard Nimoy** all had memorable guest-starring roles on the program. Shatner briefly reprised his role as Hooker in the 2002 comedy feature *Showtime* starring Robert De Niro and Eddie Murphy. Or did he? Although Shatner's TV cop show character is called T. J. Hooker in the credits, De Niro's character addresses him as "Bill," leading some to believe that Shatner is actually playing himself.

TAKEI, GEORGE

This bantam Japanese-American actor played navigator extraordinaire Hikaru Sulu on ***Star Trek***. Takei (pronounced Ta-KAY) endured four years in a Japanese-American internment camp during World War II before embarking on an acting career in the late 1950s. He brought to the role of Sulu an understated integrity and dry sense of humor. Around the set, Takei was known for his wickedly funny Shatner impersonation, which he invariably uncorked immediately after having his lines cut by the domineering star. He believed Shatner's ultimate dream was to play all the characters on the show, so rankled was the star at having to share dialogue with supporting players. "Shatner was the one who made life trying for all of us," Takei said, speaking on behalf of his fellow **seven dwarfs**.

Over the years, Takei has frequently chafed at Shatner's attempts to undercut him in small ways, such as sleepwalking through an important scene in ***Star Trek II***, in which Sulu receives his captain's commission. "When we shot the scene, Bill played it as he had rehearsed it, disinterested, murmuring some trivia about my captaincy, looking straight out into the void. There was no eye contact. No emotion. No relationship. Nothing. . . . I was not surprised when I later learned that the scene was cut."

For all of the tension between them, however, Takei has never regarded Shatner with the same strong, unrelenting resentment as, say, **James Doohan**. Takei has maintained a fairly clear-headed view of Shatner as a charmer, not an ogre. "He always managed to keep that smiling, charming facade up, as if nothing out of the ordinary had happened, joking, giggling, and bantering. And always that sunny, oblivious, rankling smile. That smile as bright, as hard, and as relentless as the headlights of an oncoming car. You just had to get out of its way."

> "Like any large family, you have that Uncle Bill that you just can't stand."
> —*George Takei, on the dysfunctional* Star Trek *clan*

TAMBURLAINE THE GREAT

Shatner made his Broadway debut in this classic Christopher Marlowe tragedy on January 19, 1956. The play follows the rise and fall of Tamburlaine, the **king** of Persia. Anthony Quayle played the title role in the drama, which had a short run of 21 performances, despite great critical acclaim, at the Winter Garden Theatre. As Usumcasane, one of Tamburlaine's faithful attendants, Shatner had little to do beyond lugging a sedan chair around the stage, but he apparently lugged it well. A Twentieth Century-Fox official who saw him perform offered Shatner a seven-year movie contract with the studio, but he rejected it, reportedly on the advice of a mysterious stranger. "I thought there was nothing to be gained from signing and everything to lose," he told *TV Guide* in 1966. "Mainly my youth."

TEK

This addictive brain stimulant serves as the focal point of Shatner's science fiction book cycle, later adapted for the small screen. *Tek* is Shatner's most popular series of novels to date. "I wrote them as the sort of books you could read on airplanes and throw away afterwards," Shatner commented to *Entertainment Weekly*, "but they've become this phenomenon."

Set in the 22nd Century, *Tek* chronicles the exploits of **Jake Cardigan**, a rough-and-tumble hero whom Shatner has likened to *T. J. Hooker*. Jake's future world is one of nefarious corporations, killer androids, and cryogenic prison chambers. Shatner originally envisioned *Tek* as the basis of a screenplay for a movie in which he could then star, but decided instead to expand the concept into a series of novels. His consultant for the project was veteran science fiction writer **Ron Goulart**. Titles in the *Tek* book series are as follows: *TekWar* (1989), *TekLords* (1991) *TekLab* (1991), *Tek Vengeance* (1992), *Tek Secret* (1993), *Tek Power* (1994), *Tek Money* (1995), *Tek Kill* (1996), and *Tek Net* (1997).

TEKWAR   ✴ ✴ ✴

TekWar is the name of both a 1994 TV movie and a 1995-1996 TV series based on Shatner's *Tek* book cycle. Shatner coproduced, directed, and costarred in the original telefilm, playing the role of Walter Bascom, one of the enigmatic mandarins of the *Tek* **universe**. Budgeted at a tidy $4 million, the movie stars Greg Evigan of *B. J. and the Bear* fame as futuristic sleuth **Jake Cardigan**. Scottish pop star Sheena Easton appears as Warbride, the leader of a band of radical environmentalists.

"It is all fairly lightweight, not to mention convoluted," wrote the reviewer for *Maclean's*. "Shatner manages to keep the plot flowing, and there are occasional flashes of a movie—odd camera effects and angles—lurking amid the TV truisms and idiot-box dialogue." The critic went on to laud the film for its top-notch special effects. "All its visual gewgaws, however, cannot mask the lack of a plausible script." The follow-up TV movies *TekLords*, *TekLab*, and *Tek Justice* followed in rapid succession in 1994.

In January of 1995, a *TekWar* TV series was launched, with Evigan again starring as **Jake Cardigan**. Shatner appeared frequently as Bascom, along with Eugene Clark as Sid Gomez, Maria Del Mar as Sam Houston, Leya Doig as Cowgirl, and Ernie Gruenworld as Spaz. "In retooling *TekWar* into one-hour form," wrote the *New York Daily News*, "the series has regained some energy and vitality, and relied much less on special effects 'stun gun' footage." Filmed in Toronto by Atlantis Films, Ltd., the action-filled *TekWar* series represented Shatner's attempt to draw on "a Canadian pool of talent . . . that is as good as the best I've ever worked with." The series lasted for eighteen episodes over a two-year span.

Shatner as Walter Bascomb, one of the enigmatic mandarins, of the *Tek* universe.

TELEVISION

From *Star Trek* to *Boston Legal*, Shatner's greatest successes have come on the small screen. Partly it stems from his ability to control the creative process on a series where all the action revolves around him. "I've gotten a great insight into the omnipotence of the series lead," he observed from his high chair of power on the *Star Trek* set in 1966. "Everybody does his best not to upset the star. It's an almost unique position few in the entertainment world achieve. . . . It's like absolute power."

The fact that the vast majority of his **acting** gigs have been in television has never stopped Shatner from criticizing the medium that Lilliputian science fiction author **Harlan Ellison** once called "the glass teat." "Television, by its nature, has to appeal to as many people as possible," Shatner has said. "Which means the lowest common denominator. Occasionally—and those are the occasions I watch TV for—television will do something extraordinary." Among

TV's "Mr. Kotter" Gabe Kaplan interviews a victorious Shatner after another successful appearance on *Battle of the Network Stars*.

the extraordinary TV shows Shatner has said he watches are "reality programming, *National Geographic* specials, sports, and CNN." The list of shows he doesn't watch includes **Star Trek** reruns, *Star Trek: The Next Generation*, or any of the other series offshoots. Shatner finds television useful mainly for its soporific effects. "It provides a rhythm that puts me to sleep," he once declared.

TENTH LEVEL, THE ✳ ✳

Shatner plays a psychologist who conducts mind control experiments on human subjects in this 1976 TV movie. (The title refers to a study in which over 90 percent of the participants would obey a researcher to the point of inflicting the tenth level of pain on another person.) Calling the film "repulsive and pointless," *Variety* recommended it only "for people who like to pull the wings off flies."

TESTIMONY OF TWO MEN ✳ ✳

This 1977 TV miniseries, adapted from the Taylor Caldwell novel, follows the lives of two surgeon siblings in post-Civil War Pennsylvania. Shatner has a supporting role as Adrian Ferrier, a relative of the two heroes. Shown in three parts, the sweeping six-hour costume drama was part of Operation Prime Time, a joint initiative by independent **television** stations to produce high-quality programming. Like the subsequent telefilm **The Bastard**, also starring Shatner, this one focuses more on **sex** than history. Others in the large eclectic cast include David Birney, Barbara Parkins, Ralph Bellamy, Theodore Bikel, Tom Bosley, Ray Milland, Margaret O'Brien, and Dan Dailey.

THEATER
See **Stage**.

THIRD WALKER, THE ✴ ✴

Set in Ireland, this 1978 film features Shatner as the trouble-plagued Munro Maclean. The murky, flashback-laden drama concerns twins who are mixed up at birth and raised by different mothers. Colleen Dewhurst plays Shatner's shrewish wife. The first-time director was Teri McLuhan, daughter of hip media philosopher Marshall McLuhan.

THIS WAS AMERICA ✴ ✴

Shatner is your host for this twelve-part 1981 historical documentary that uses early photographs to recreate the lives of Americans at the turn of the twentieth century. Historian and author Martin Sandler gathered the material for this offering, which was produced by the Boston-based BBI Communications group. The *Boston Herald American* called Shatner "the best documentary narrator since Basil Rathbone."

TINNITUS

This medical condition is characterized by a hissing or ringing in the ears. Shatner was diagnosed in the 1990s after he noticed hissing in his ears while walking on a Malibu beach with **Marcy Lafferty**. The condition, which is incurable, became so serious that it helped wreck Shatner's **marriage** and made him contemplate suicide.

"There was a time when I thought, 'I don't think I can deal with this anymore,'" Shatner said of the ssshhhhhh-like drone that constantly played in his head. "And I began to actively think of what means you could use that—that you could end your life."

Relief finally came in January 1996 in the form of hearing-aid-like devices prescribed by Dr. Pawel Jastreboff of the University of Maryland Tinnitus and Hyperacusis Center. The devices continuously feed white noise into Shatner's ear, drowning out the annoying drone. A relieved Shatner now serves as a spokesperson and fundraiser for the Baltimore-based center.

It wasn't until later that Shatner realized the cause of his condition. "Leonard Nimoy, who also has the problem, reminded me that there had been an explosion on the *Star Trek* movie set. We both got this ringing in the ears. My ringing is in my left ear, and his ringing is in his right ear." Other celebrities who suffer from tinnitus include David Letterman, Barbra Streisand, and Bono.

> "I wanted to run and escape the sound. And that only increased the panic because there was no place to run."
> —*Shatner, on his tinnitus*

TOUGHY

Shatner earned this scrappy nickname for his tenacity in fighting off anti-Semitic classmates at Montreal's **West Hill High School**. The sobriquet appeared beside his name in his high school yearbook. "But we know that Shatner isn't tough," the yearbook writers added, "he just thinks he's strong." The yearbook cut-ups apparently found Shatner's pugnacity quite amusing. They listed the actor/jock's pet aversion as "People who think they can beat him up" and his favorite expression as "You want to make something out of it?" For the record, Shatner's own yearbook quotation was "They always talk who never think."

TOUPEE

Speculation has long run rampant about the true nature of Shatner's impeccably coifed hair. While some deluded **fans** still maintain it is nothing but an expensive perm (and Shatner himself denies it is anything but 100 percent real), words like weave, plugs, and rug are more frequently used to account for the ever-changing shape and color of Shatner's mane over the decades.

Because his personal wigs were too ratty-looking, **Star Trek**'s producers had two custom hairpieces made for Shatner at the beginning of each **television** season in the late 1960s. That way, he could wear one while the other was being cleaned. Unfortunately, somewhere along the line the reserve hairpiece disappeared from the makeup department. A search was conducted, the usual inquiries were made, but the missing lid was never recovered. Suspicions began to turn toward Shatner himself, who, some allege, may have preferred the top-quality $200 workplace wig to the substandard ones in his own collection.

In the 1980s, Shatner opted for a fuller, wavier hairstyle that called even more attention to the issue. Reports had him spending as much as $2000 a month to maintain his weave. The curly monstrosity earned him recognition in a *National Enquirer* feature rating worst celebrity hairpieces. Together with the tight bodice that Shatner wore to restrain his distended belly, the toupee is one of Shatner's few concessions to vanity. "I don't like to see youth slipping away," he admitted to *Playboy* in 1989. "Seeing old photographs, buried in the attic someplace, that's one thing. But to see yourself walking around on a television screen in one instant and then to compare that with your present-day form in the next is tough."

In 1991, Shatner had to deal with more than just seeing his image reflected in old reruns, when placards featuring doctored photos of him—along with five other bewigged celebrities—began appearing on walls and lampposts around lower Manhattan. The posters were part of a baldness outing campaign conducted by writer Ed Leibowitz and graphic designer Lorraine Heffernan, whose stated purpose was to "wrest the toupees from the chrome domes of America's leading celebrities." For the record, the other cueballs exposed in the campaign were Charles Bronson, Ted Danson, Larry Hagman, Joe Namath, and John Wayne.

Why the public fascination with Shatner's hairpiece? The lure of the taboo, for one thing. Few have seen it—and fewer still lived to tell the tale. One of the few actors to speak openly about eyeballing Shatner's rug is Alan Tudyk, who costarred with him in 2004's **Dodgeball: A True Underdog Story**. Asked by an interviewer for his impressions of Shatner's piece, Tudyk reported: "It's beautiful. . . . [W]e also had Chuck Norris on that movie—his is nowhere near as good as Shatner's."

> "I don't wear a hairpiece. That's the stupidest question I ever heard."
>
> *—Shatner, to a radio DJ who asked about his toupee in 1994*

TOWN HAS TURNED TO DUST, A ✳ ✳ ✳

This **live television** play, starring Shatner and Rod Steiger, aired on CBS' *Playhouse 90* on June 19, 1958. Shatner plays the ringleader of a lynching party in the Rod Serling-penned drama, which earned rave reviews from critics. Jack Gould, writing in the *New York Times*, called Shatner "the embodiment of hate and blind physical passion," and termed his portrayal "[one] of the season's superlative performances."

TRANSFORMED MAN, THE ✳ ✳ ✳ ✳

The holy grail of Shatneriana, this album of **music** and monologues was unleashed upon an unworthy public in 1968. The phrase "a collection of songs and dramatic readings set to music" does not begin to describe the contents of this bizarre, visionary recording. Shatner has said he tried to perform certain tracks "as though I were drugged." One listen to the LP confirms the veracity of that statement.

Produced by **music** industry veteran **Don Ralke**, *The Transformed Man* is an intensely personal aural journey through the works of playwrights, poets, and pop lyricists. The album is highlighted by Shatner's staccato spoken-word renditions of such rock classics as Bob Dylan's **"Mr. Tambourine Man"** and The Beatles' **"Lucy in the Sky with Diamonds."** "I wanted to show the various ways writers express themselves at different times on universal themes," Shatner said by way of an explanation. Three decades later, he was still clarifying his intentions to a baffled world. "When a cut is played without any context you'll be puzzled by what I'm doing, but my hope is that you'll know what I'm doing if you listen to the whole record." Some have suggested the record was Shatner's attempt to assimilate, through speech and song, his close encounter with **aliens** in the Mojave Desert.

Dismissed as the product of a bad acid trip by most listeners at the time, today *The Transformed Man* is considered a camp classic. Rhino Records included two of the cuts on *Golden Throats*, a 1990 novelty album celebrating tone-deaf celebrity caterwauling. *Entertainment Weekly* called the LP "the most ear-splitting album of all the former cast members [of *Star Trek*]"—no small distinction, if you have heard any of **Leonard Nimoy**'s records. In 1991, authors Jimmy Guterman and Owen O'Donnell included TTM in their book *The Worst Rock 'n' Roll Records of All Time*. The American Booksellers Association even offered Shatner $100,000 to sing **"Mr. Tambourine Man"** at its 1991 convention. He wisely declined.

However dubious its artistic merits, *Transformed Man* did lay the groundwork for much of Shatner's mid-'90s career revival. Echoes of the record can be detected in his TV commercials for **Priceline.com**, turn-of-the-century recordings with **Ben Folds**, and musical-themed appearances in the feature film **_Free Enterprise_** and the animated TV series **_Futurama_**.

Over the years, Shatner's opinion of his groundbreaking first studio album has changed dramatically—and then changed back again. In 1968, soon after the record's release, he compared **Transformed Man** favorably to such other career milestones as the first time he received star billing and the rave notices he elicited for **The World of Suzie Wong** on Broadway. "When I listen to this record, I have the same thrill," he said. Below is a sampling of his ever-changing thoughts about **The Transformed Man**:

"This, to me, is a work of art."
—to biographers in 1979

"Some cuts worked, some didn't. I haven't heard it in a long time."
—to Playboy in 1989

"I think the album is very meritorious. I'm not embarrassed by The Transformed Man at all. Am I living in a fool's paradise?"
—to the Rocky Mountain News in 1997

"I knew all along that we were treading a very fine line between buffoonery and bravery."
—to Billboard in 2000

TRINITY AND BEYOND ✴ ✴

In the first of two nuclear-themed narration assignments (the other is 1999's *Nukes in Space*), Shatner hosts this feature-length 1995 documentary commemorating the fiftieth anniversary of the dropping of the atomic bombs on Hiroshima and Nagasaki. The spectacular examination of the nuclear age relies on impressive visual effects and a score by the Moscow Symphony Orchestra, with Shatner's ponderous voiceovers as an appropriate counterpoint.

TRUSKOLASKI, JEFF

This burly former auctioneer is America's premier William Shatner impersonator. Truskolaski, who performs under the name "J. Trusk," frequently appears in character as Captain Kirk at roasts, bar mitzvahs, and corporate functions across the United States. In recent years, he has added a **Denny Crane** impression to his repertoire.

Truskolashi began "doing" Shatner in the mid-1990s after friends remarked on his resemblance to the actor. He appeared alongside original crewmembers **George Takei**, **Nichelle Nichols**, **James Doohan**, and **Walter Koenig** at Trek Con '96 in Hartford, Connecticut and was featured in *Trekkies*, a 1997 documentary about *Star Trek* fandom. Truskolaski's finest moment of Shatner imposture came on May 31, 1995, when he beamed on to *The Tonight Show* for a meeting with the man himself. Anyone interested in hiring out Truskolaski's unique services can visit him on the web at jtrusk.com.

TWENTY-FIVE YEAR MISSION TOUR

This series of joint appearances made by Shatner and Leonard Nimoy celebrated twenty-five years of *Star Trek*. The shows played to sellout crowds in eleven cities across the United States in the summer of 1992. Engaging in lighthearted banter designed to play off commonly held perceptions of themselves (Shatner as an overbearing egotist, Nimoy as a brooding iceman), the erstwhile costars developed an extemporaneous rapport that left audiences howling with approval. The duo regaled **fans** with anecdotes from their days on the TV and movie series, including the oft-repeated bicycle story.

"We're in the smelling-of-the-roses phase of our life," Shatner said of the tour. "So we're enjoying each other more and more. He makes me laugh, and I get him to giggle sometimes." The pair later reconvened in Nimoy's garden for a more subdued iteration of the same routine, released to DVD in 2001 as *Mind Meld*.

20,000 PYRAMID ✳ ✳ ✳ ✳

During his **game show** heyday in the mid-1970s, Shatner often appeared as a celebrity player on this daytime staple, variously hosted by Bill Cullen and Dick Clark. The concept was simple; contestants paired with celebrities to solve seven word association puzzles in six categories displayed on an enormous pyramid.

Pyramid was a game of peace, but for some reason Shatner's appearances had a tendency to devolve into mayhem. On one occasion, now widely circulated as an online video clip, Shatner played the game's playoff round solo, frantically leaping from chair to chair as his non-celebrity partner cheered him on from outside the winner's circle. In another, more infamous appearance, Shatner experienced a violent on-air meltdown that apparently got him banned from the show for life. Shatner was appearing alongside fellow celebrity **Leonard Nimoy**, taping one of the five days' worth of shows they would complete in a single afternoon, thanks to the magic of wardrobe changes. Shatner's dexterity with a clue had once again carried his partner into the playoff round, earning her a chance at $20,000. However, he froze up on the final answer, reading out part of the name of the category, blowing the victory at the last possible second. Then, still on camera, Shatner went berserk, lifting up his plush swivel chair from the show's futuristic set and heaving it over a railing. The show quickly cut to a commercial. The nervous gasps of the audience soon turned to laughter, however, as the camera cut back in on Shatner and Nimoy standing together holding the broken bits of chair between them, with broad smiles on their faces. Pressure from a grueling schedule, frustration over his moribund career, and his own fondness for practical jokes offer some rationale for Shatner's outburst, but a completely satisfactory explanation has never come to light. In any case, he was never asked to return to the program.

TWILIGHT ZONE, THE ✳ ✳ ✳ ✳

Shatner appeared in two episodes of the classic fantasy anthology series, hosted by Rod Serling. In "Nick of Time," he plays Don Carter, a newlywed who becomes obsessed with a bobbing-head fortune-telling machine in an Ohio diner. The episode, tidily scripted by master fanta-

"There's a man on the wing of his plane!" Shatner plays the consummate nervous flyer in a classic episode of *The Twilight Zone*.

sist Richard Matheson, is one of the understated gems of the series. More well known is "Nightmare at 20,000 Feet," in which Shatner gives a memorably twitchy performance as Bob Wilson, a disturbed airline passenger who keeps spotting a gremlin on the wing of the airborne plane. Incredibly cheap make-up effects are the only blemishes in this otherwise gripping episode, also written by Matheson.

BOOK ANOTHER FLIGHT, SHATNER'S ON THE PLANE!

Next time you're traveling, check the seat next to you for a burly seventy-something man with a curiously full head of hair. It could be Shatner, and that spells danger for your flight/cruise/train ride. Because on screen, wherever Shatner goes, disaster follows, as this handy chart indicates.

OPUS	SHATNER ROLE	DISASTER
Twilight Zone "Nightmare at 20,000 Feet"	Jittery airline passenger	Gremlin on wing causes near fatal disaster
Horror at 37,000 Feet	Jittery airline passenger	Ghosts from the cargo hold terrorize passengers
Perilous Voyage	Drunken cruise ship passenger	Ship is hijacked by South American revolutionaries
Disaster on the Coastliner	Con man on board high-speed train	Demented engineer sets train on collision course

The cauliflower gremilin bedevils Shatner in a publicity still from *Nightmare at 20,000 Feet*.

ULTIMATE SURVIVORS: WINNING AGAINST INCREDIBLE ODDS ✳✳

Wannabe lawman Shatner hosts this inspirational 1991 video, which profiles law enforcement personnel who survived near-death experiences. The eighty-five-minute program plays off Shatner's reassuring *Rescue 911* persona. Reenactments show a police officer being shot in the face by a deranged motorist, a U.S. marshal escaping an armed ambush, and a state trooper trapped inside a burning squad car. The cumulative effect, as the *Hollywood Reporter* observed, is to promote the idea that "a long-term outlook on life and its rewards is necessary to recover from physical and psychological trauma."

UNIVERSE ✳✳

This 1976 documentary, narrated by Shatner, examines man's place in the cosmos. The twenty-eight-minute, NASA-sponsored film uses animation to chronicle cosmic history forward from the big bang. A shorter, punchier precursor to Carl Sagan's *Cosmos*, *Universe* was nominated for an Academy Award for Best Documentary Short. The following year, Shatner explored similar terrain—this time from a crackpot science perspective—in *Mysteries of the Gods*.

VANISHED ✳✳

Billed as a "long-form TV movie," this four-hour long, two-part 1971 production is actually one of the first TV miniseries. Based on the novel by Fletcher Knebel, *Vanished* concerns the sudden disappearance of a top presidential advisor. Shatner plays Dave Paulick, a military aide, but he is just a small part of an all-star cast that includes Richard Widmark, Tom Bosley, E. G. Marshall, and Robert Young. Widmark and Young received Emmy nominations for their work. Somewhere in the sea of familiar faces is Neil Hamilton, who played police commissioner Gordon on TV's *Batman*.

VAN PATTEN, DICK

This genial, bald, squeaky-voiced actor, best known as the Bradford family patriarch on TV's *Eight Is Enough*, is a longtime friend of Shatner's. He appears as a harried UFOlogist in Shatner's 2002 film **Groom Lake** and has been one of the actor/director's regular tennis partners for many years. In fact, Van Patten's son, Nels Van Patten, is a renowned tennis pro who counts Shatner among his celebrity clients. Asked by *Sports Illustrated* to describe the experience of learning the "love game" at the hands of a Hollywood scion, Shatner responded: "It's not so much being taught to play tennis by a Van Patten. It's playing Dick Van Patten that is really objectionable. He lobs everything, and it drives you nuts."

VEGETARIANISM

Like his friend and fellow **Star Trek** cast member **Leonard Nimoy**, Shatner is a longtime vegetarian. While he's rarely spoken about it in interviews, his commitment seems to have both an ethical and a medical basis. Shatner explores both these concerns, along with the spiritual element of vegetarianism, in the 1982 documentary **The Vegetarian World**.

> "Vegetarianism isn't just a diet. It's an entire approach to life."
> —*Shatner, in 1982's* The Vegetarian World

THE VEGETARIAN WORLD ✳ ✳ ✳

"You may be wondering exactly what a vegetarian is," Shatner says at the beginning of this 1982 documentary, which he hosts and narrates. While most of us could probably solve that imponderable in about five seconds, the actor spends the next 30 minutes taking viewers on an earnest guided tour of the world of meatless dining. This brief, propagandistic feature seems more than a bit dated today ("Most major cities now feature several vegetarian restaurants," Shatner informs us at one point). However, it is enlivened by numerous gory scenes of cattle being slaughtered. Shatner appears on-camera periodically throughout, wearing ill-fitting chinos and a powder blue sport shirt, browsing the supermarket produce aisle and reminding his audience about the wide range of tasty vegetarian meal options. "There's chow mein, and curry, enchiladas, and my favorite: eggplant parmigiana," he intones over a well-stocked buffet table. In another scene, he dons a jogging suit to counter the common misconception that vegetarians are "weak and anemic." While it's no *Supersize Me*, *The Vegetarian World*'s classroom-film-strip feel makes it worth a look for Shatner completists. Once relegated to the VHS cutout bin, it's now easily accessible via the Internet.

VIRGIN GALACTIC

In 2006, Shatner turned down a chance to fulfill Captain Kirk's mandate "to boldly go where no man has gone before" when he rebuffed British entrepreneur Richard Branson's invitation to visit outerspace in a celebrity-filled space shuttle. Two years earlier, news reports had first begun to circulate that Shatner and Sigourney Weaver, among others, had offered to pony up the British equivalent of $210,000 in exchange for a lift on Branson's *Virgin Galactic* shuttle. There was just one problem. Shatner had never agreed to any such arrangement. He accused Virgin officials of using his name to drum up free publicity for the venture. "I do want to go up, but I need guarantees I'll definitely come back," Shatner announced in a press statement in which his fears of zero-gravity vomit figured prominently. In the end, *Virgin Galactic* remained stuck in space dock. Lance Bass of the boy band 'N Sync did undergo astronaut training for a possible voyage, but reneged on the trip when he failed to come up with the money. As of this writing, **James Doohan**, whose cremains were blasted into orbit and came crashing down in the New Mexico mountains in 2007, remains the only member of the **Star Trek** cast to travel in space.

> "Throwing up is a lonely sickness and not
> something I'd like to pay for."
> —*Shatner, on the prospect of actually traveling in space with* Virgin Galactic

VISITING HOURS   ✳

"So frightening you'll never recover!" blared the posters for this 1982 slasher movie. That may well be true. The Canadian-made cheapie is so repugnant it could put you off your feed for days. Lee Grant stars as a crusading telejournalist who runs afoul of the local homicidal maniac, played with gusto by glowering *Scanners* weirdo Michael Ironside. Shatner has a thankless supporting role as Gary Baylor, Grant's devoted producer/amanuensis. Most of the action takes place inside a hospital—hence the title. Ironside's character goes by the none-too-frightening name Colt Hawker. The film is also known as *The Fright* and *Get Well Soon*.

VOICE OF THE PLANET   ✳ ✳ ✳

In this ten-hour ecological **television** special, Shatner stars as a writer whose computer channels Gaia, the spirit of Planet Earth. As the deliciously named William Hope Planter, Shatner appears from his home in a Himalayan monastery. Faye Dunaway provides the voice of Gaia, who rails against animal experimentation while espousing the benefits of mandatory sterilization for third world citizens.

Shatner and Lee Grant must outwit a crazed killer in 1982's *Visiting Hours*.

Filmed on location in Nepal, the bizarre new age "documentary"—which *People* magazine dubbed "the longest infomercial ever made"—aired over five nights on TBS beginning October 15, 1990. Shatner was proud of his work on the series, going so far as to cite *Voice of the Planet* as the one performance of his that he would most like to pass on to his grandchildren. In an ironic sidelight, the monastery where the series was filmed burned down a short time later when a group of American visitors blew out a circuit while hooking up an electrical generator.

VON PUTTKAMER, JESCO

This scientist, futurist, and space flight planner was interviewed extensively by Shatner for his 1977 opus **Mysteries of the Gods**. A **Star Trek** aficionado (he actually penned his own **Trek** novella), Von Puttkamer also served as a technical adviser on **Star Trek: The Motion Picture**.

VULCAN SALUTE

Fictitious hand gesture used on **Star Trek**, in which the thumb and forefinger, middle and ring fingers are held apart. **Leonard Nimoy** originated the salute, which he based on a rabbinical blessing offered to Jewish congregations during prayer. Shatner is unable to perform the **Vulcan salute**, which he was required to give for a humorous scene in **Star Trek III: The Search for Spock**. Director Nimoy's solution was to tie Shatner's fingers into the proper positions with fishing line.

WANT A RIDE, LITTLE GIRL?

See **Impulse**.

WAR (BOOK SERIES)   ✴ ✴

To date, Shatner has written two books in his *War* science-fiction series, featuring dyspeptic twenty-second century diplomat Benton Hawkes. *Man o' War* kicked things off in 1996, with *The Law of War* following two years later. Borrowing elements from such revered sources as Ray Bradbury and Robert Heinlein, Shatner spins the tale of a human-settled Mars beset by labor squabbles and political machinations. The protagonist, a cranky middle-aged dog lover, seems like a stand-in for Shatner himself. "One can hardly quarrel with Shatner's spritely pacing or abundant and well-handled action scenes," *Publishers Weekly* enthused. The publication also wondered of the prolific author/actor: "Wherever does he find the time?"

WEIGHT

Shatner has long struggled to keep down his earthly body weight. Early in his career, it was not even an issue. "I never thought much about having a good body," he recalled of his younger days, "because I was gifted by having a good body. I didn't do much in the way of care, nor did I ever abuse it by drinking or smoking very much."

By the time Shatner started working on **Star Trek** in the late 1960s, however, his Battle of the Bulge was raging. On the set, he carped constantly about his captain's tunics, which seemed to get smaller each time they were cleaned. While he exercised strenuously during the summer months to arrive fit and trim for the start of each season, over the course of the season's filming he allowed his waistline to balloon. The problem became so serious by the show's third season that memos were exchanged between producers about the possibility of putting together a clip reel of Shatner at his heaviest in order to shame him into slimming down. Even though the reel was never made, Shatner did embark on a crash diet after viewing some unflattering dailies.

Certainly the plush velour costuming favored by **Star Trek** wardrobe man William Theiss did not help matters any. But then, uncomfortably-tailored outfits have followed Shatner wherever he has gone in his career, from the skin-tight pajamas he had to pour himself into for **Star Trek: The Motion Picture** to the bulging police sergeant's uniform he wore on **T. J. Hooker**. "We had twelve shirts made for Shatner [for *Star Trek III*]," explained costume designer Robert Fletcher. "He diets before a movie and shows up looking terrific. But he would slip as it went along." Later in his career, according to the eyewitness testimony of **Claudia Christian** (among others), Shatner addressed the problem of extra tonnage by donning a cumbersome **corset** to hold in his enormous belly. "Every inch of bloat shows on camera," he told the *Washington Post* in 1991.

WEST HILL HIGH SCHOOL

Shatner graduated class of 1948 from this Montreal high school. The archetypal jock, Shatner was, at one time or another, a member of the skiing, wrestling, and football teams. "I had aspirations of being a football player and at the same time I wanted to act," he once said. "As a result, I was torn in two directions. The actors don't play football and the football players think the actors are sissies." Only his religious commitments kept him from advancing on the gridiron, where he once missed being chosen for the team because of his observance of the Jewish holy days. Not that Shatner has any regrets about the way things turned out. "I was a bit small for a pro football career," he has said.

WHALE OF A TALE, A ✳

Shatner must have been hard up to take part in this low-budget 1976 children's feature about a boy and his whale. Filmed at Marineland in California, the rarely seen movie was also released as *Joey and the Whale*. Shatner plays Dr. Jack Fredericks, a marine biologist who hires young Joey (Scott Kolden) to haul buckets of chum for him. The lad gets lost at sea and is rescued by a trained porpoise. The G-rated confection costars the insipid trio of Abby Dalton, Andy Devine, and Marty Allen.

"I'm not terribly proud of some of the features I've made," Shatner once explained to an interviewer, "but they were offered to me at various times when better movies weren't being offered." Shatner could have been speaking of *A Whale of a Tale* or any of a half dozen other movies he made during these, his **lost years** of the 1970s.

"WHALES WEEP NOT"

Apparently Shatner has a thing for whales. There's **Star Trek IV**, of course, and the aforementioned **A Whale of a Tale**, plus his affinity for this erotic poem by D. H. Lawrence, which he recited before rapt audiences at his **one-man shows** in the 1970s. Filled with phallic imagery, "Whales Weep Not" combines Shatner's concern for the environment with another of his passions, male sexuality. He invariably performed the poem to a backing track of actual humpback whale sounds. "Their sounds were like a song as they filtered through the water, a beautiful song that repeated over and over again," Shatner told the *New York Times*. "The whale sounds were a form of music that gave new meaning to the poetry of Lawrence." Shatner often followed up his reading of "Whales Weep Not" with a passage from H. G. Wells' *The War of the Worlds* describing a Martian emerging from his spacecraft. "Our theme was how are we going to be able to deal with creatures from outer space if we are not able to get along with creatures from inner space."

The whale/martian routine would prove a highlight of the late '70s live shows that people who were present still comment on more than 30 years later. For those interested in recapturing a taste of the experience, Shatner (as Captain Kirk) recites a portion of "Whales Weep Not" in *Star Trek IV: The Voyage Home*.

"It was like hearing a singer coming in and out of sounds of the deep—in front of 18,000 people who thought it was crazy. And it was!"
—*Shatner, on his performance of "Whales Weep Not" at the Hollywood Bowl*

WHITE COMANCHE ✶ ✶ ✶

Shatner sinks his teeth into a juicy **dual role** as biracial twins bent on destroying each other in this 1968 western feature. As Notah, the titular Comanche, he gets to wear war paint and issue high-pitched whoops from atop his galloping charger. As Notah's brother Johnny Moon, who was raised by whites, he mostly broods and makes cryptic pronouncements like "Next time, don't eat the peyote." (If only the director and screenwriter had taken his advice!) All hell breaks loose when Johnny Moon is charged with a murder committed by Notah. In a climactic duel, Shatner gets to shoot at himself while mounted on identical rampaging stallions. Ancient Joseph Cotten is on hand to help sort it all out. Shatner spent three months in Spain working on the low-budget production, putting considerable strain on his already creaky **marriage** to **Gloria Rand**.

WHITNEY, GRACE LEE

This shapely blonde actress played Yeoman Janice Rand during the first TV season of *Star Trek*. The original Chicken of the Sea mermaid in a series of popular tuna fish commercials, Whitney had an impressive resume but a reputation for wild behavior on the set. She quickly soured on the way her character was developed. "I was hired as a sexy, ballsy woman," she told an interviewer. Nevertheless, most of her screen time was spent in menial tasks, such as bringing Kirk soup or preparing his uniform shirts for wear. Before the first episode even aired, *Star Trek*'s creators were working on ways to write her out of the show. One of her only supporters on the set was Shatner. When he lobbied for her not to be fired, rumors began to circulate that the two were lovers. Both parties have always denied these claims. In effect, Whitney says, their relationship was a lot like the one their fictional characters enjoyed. "There was no sexuality between Rand and Kirk. The relationship was never consummated. He was married to the ship. Supposedly, she was in love with him, and supposedly he was very fond of her, but I don't think they ever really got together." After being let go from the show midway through the first season, Whitney went into a self-confessed personal and professional tailspin, before finally righting herself with some AA assistance in the late 1970s.

WILD, THE ✳ ✳ ✳

In the first of two ecologically-themed animated features for which he did voiceover work in 2006 (the other is **Over the Hedge**), Shatner plays Kazar. As the power-hungry **king** of the wildebeests, he schemes to lead his species to the top of the food chain. While the film itself received mixed reviews, critics were almost universally charmed by Shatner's over-the-top performance. Several detected an homage to Captain Kirk's most famous big-screen nemesis. As the *San Francisco Chronicle* put it: "William Shatner shows up as a bad-guy wildebeest and finally answers the question: 'What would happen if Shatner played the Ricardo Montalban role in *Star Trek II: The Wrath of Khan*?'"

"WILLIAM FUCKING SHATNER"

This derisive nickname was hung on Shatner by actor Wil Wheaton, who played Ensign Wesley Crusher on *Star Trek: The Next Generation*. Wheaton cooked up the profane moniker after a particularly unpleasant encounter with Shatner on the set of **Star Trek V** in 1988. The two actors were working on adjacent soundstages one day when **Star Trek** creator **Gene Roddenberry** facilitated an impromptu introduction. Sixteen-year-old Wheaton was thrilled to be meeting one of his boyhood idols, but Shatner was less than cordial. He refused to shake the boy's hand and mocked the Starfleet uniform Wheaton was wearing. "What is that, your spacesuit?" Shatner chortled. A mortified Wheaton tried to explain his role on *Star Trek: The Next Generation*, but Shatner would have none of it. "I'd never let a kid come onto my bridge," he reportedly declared, and walked away. Roddenberry later had Shatner

Shatner tries to horn in on some of Bryan Ferry's action with this publicity shot for his 1977 album *William Shatner: Live*.

send the lad a note of apology for his boorish behavior, but from then on Wheaton knew him only as "William Fucking Shatner."

WILLIAM SHATNER: LIVE ✱✱✱✱

This 1977 live album captures Shatner's performance of his **one-man show** in the mid-1970s. Recorded at Hofstra University, the two-record set was produced by Shatner and released through his company, Lemli Music (named after his daughters **Leslie**, **Melanie**, and **Lisabeth**). A remarkable performance before a mostly stoned college audience, *William Shatner: Live* features the actor performing excerpts from *War of the Worlds* and *Cyrano de Bergerac*, as well as his own musings on space travel.

Shatner is the only *Star Trek* crew member whose albums consistently place on critics' lists of the Fifty Worst Rock 'n' Roll Albums of All Time. But that's only because so few people have heard the abominable LPs released by **Leonard Nimoy**, **Nichelle Nichols**, and **Grace Lee Whitney**. Even Brent Spiner of *Star Trek: The Next Generation* has chimed in with an album of pop standards. Behold the roundup of misguided solo projects:

NICHELLE NICHOLS

Uhura Sings **(1986):** Have you heard "Ode to the Space Shuttle"? Seen the video? Don't worry, you have plenty of company.

LEONARD NIMOY

Leonard Nimoy Presents Mr. Spock's Music from Outer Space **(1968):** **Gene Roddenberry** tried to stop Nimoy from using the Spock name on this turkey. Nimoy should have considered removing his own moniker as well.

Two Sides of Leonard Nimoy **(1969):** An album of original tone poems set to music. If it weren't so consistently boring, it might actually be worse than "The Transformed Man."

The Way I Feel **(1969):** This time, Nimoy breaks up the poetic tedium with cover versions of famous tunes. "If I Had a Hammer" is a real lowlight.

The New World of Leonard Nimoy **(1970):** Yet another album of pop classics disemboweled by the master. This one features a positively constipated rendition of "Proud Mary."

Outer Space, Inner Mind **(1976):** God help us, it's a double album. Need we say more?

BRENT SPINER
Ol' Yellow Eyes Is Back **(1991):** Spiner can actually carry a tune (he starred in the 1997 Broadway revival of *1776*). But did he have to invite his *Next Generation* costars to warble backing vocals on "It's a Sin to Tell a Lie"?

GRACE LEE WHITNEY
Disco Trekkin' **(1976):** Actually a 45 rpm (backed with "Star Child"), this one just feels like an LP.

WILLIAM SHATNER MASK
Mask worn by crazed slasher Michael Myers in the classic 1978 horror movie *Halloween*. Because of the film's shoestring budget, the prop department had to use the cheapest mask they could find in the local costume store: a William Shatner mask. They then spray-painted the face white and teased out the hair to create the eerie effect required.

In a case of life imitating art, Shatner himself has taken to donning two William Shatner masks on Halloween trick or treat excursions with his grandchildren. "I take one off, and I've still got the mask on," he told carrot-topped TV gabber Conan O'Brien in 1997. "Then I take the other off," he continued, pointing to his face, "and I've still got the mask on!"

WILLIAM SHATNER'S A TWIST IN THE TALE ✳ ✳
Shatner is your host for this syndicated 1999 **television** series consisting of high-concept ghost stories for children. According to

Homicidal ghoul Michael Myers gazes out at his victims from the eyeholes of a William Shatner mask in *Halloween*.

Shatner, the series was designed to provide parents with spooky dramas "that you can enjoy with your youngster, secure in the knowledge there will be nothing you would not want the child to see." Did anyone ask the roomful of kids if they wanted to see Shatner mugging and capering at the beginning of each episode?

Ask Shat

Q: Can you give us any financial advice, oh great one?
A: Don't buy anything on time, and that includes cars and houses.

WILLIAM SHATNER'S FULL MOON FRIGHT NIGHT ✴ ✴

Shatner hosted this short-lived TV series for the Sci-Fi Channel in 2002. Billed as being "in the tradition of *Elvira* and *Mystery Science Theater 3000*," the weekly program presented low-budget horror films from the vaults of Full Moon Features, a schlock factory run by B-movie auteur Charles Band. Shatner assumed the classic Vampira/Zacherley role, appearing in humorous wraparound segments, either as a tuxedoed master of ceremonies or a costumed ghoul in monster-themed sketches. He occasionally conducted interviews with horror and sci-fi luminaries, such as Marvel Comics creator Stan Lee.

WILLIAM SHATNER'S SPPLAT ATTACK ✴ ✴

"The ammunition may be paint, but the danger is very real," Shatner intones at the outset of this pay-per-view **paintball** tournament, later released on DVD. Staged in conjunction with the Society of Paintball Players and Teams (SPPLAT) in August of 2002, the event combined two of Shatner's favorite pursuits: **paintball**; and raising money for charity, in this case his Hollywood Charity Horse Show. Billed as the biggest sci-fi-themed **paintball** game ever, *Spplat Attack* pitted three teams of paintballers against one another in an intense competition combining elements of the classic ***Star Trek*** episodes "The Squire Gothos" and "The Gamesters of Triskelion." Shatner himself secured permission from Paramount for the use of *Trek*-related characters and insignia. Participants included **paintball** legend Tom Kaye and syndicated **radio** shock jock Erich "Mancow" Muller.

WOMEN

Shatner has never been coy about spelling out the attributes he desires in a woman. He once defined a good female figure as "the Greek ideal. Venus de Milo. 36-24-36." And in 1989, when asked which heavenly body he'd like most to visit, Shatner replied, "How about Melanie Griffith?" He's even detailed hairstyle and fashion guidelines for his potential conquests. "I am definitely in favor of the long hair trend in women," he told *Photoplay* magazine in 1968. "One of the glories of being a woman is long, luxuriant hair, whether it is used to run barefoot through or tie in pigtails. A girl who is particularly well built should wear miniskirts, if she has the right legs. If not, she should consider getting clothes to overcome these defects, not show them off for all to see."

Beyond good looks and a spectacular body, a woman, if she wishes to hold Shatner's attention, must also possess a quality he calls "magnetism." "If a woman is not pretty, but she has that magnetism, that special something, it can be dynamite," he has said. "And if she's pretty and she has that special something—that's wild." A certain homey orientation and a few shared interests catch his eye as well. Shatner looks for "a girl who's capable of giving love as well as receiving. One who can cook but also eat her own food with relish, one who plays tennis, has a sense of humor to counter my straitlaced manner, and one who likes to go horseback riding."

Shatner claims to have been a male chauvinist even in his high school and college years. "During my day and age one took a girl out and tried to make a pass and tried to make out. That was the big deal," he once remembered. However, by the late 1970s, Shatner believed he had arrived at "a point beyond women's lib" where his belief in the dominance of society by alpha males and the imperatives of equality could harmonize. "I really do intrinsically

Shatner shows off his latest accessory at the 1968 premiere of Francis Ford Coppola's musical turkey *Finian's Rainbow*.

and insightfully believe in the equality of a woman and a man's mind," he told biographers in 1979. "I do also believe that there is greater upper body strength in a man, that nature gave him more musculature. But while there are those few areas where nature has provided variations in our bodies, I really do believe in the equality of man and woman, and in equal pay for equal work."

There is one area where Shatner claims to be skittish about equal opportunity, however—**television** news. "I find it hard to accept a young girl as a newscaster," he once declared, "as against an older man with gray hair telling me the news." In 1989, Shatner, by then an older man with fake hair, began telling viewers the news about emergency phone calls and rescue operations as host of the **television** reality program *Rescue 911*.

WORLD OF SUZIE WONG, THE

Shatner won numerous awards in 1958 for his performance in this Broadway play. Then 27, he abandoned his burgeoning Hollywood career to take the lead role in the **stage** production, which opened at the Broadhurst Theatre on October 14, 1958.

Based on the novel by Richard Mason, *The World of Suzie Wong* concerns a Canadian architect who falls in love with a Chinese prostitute while living in Hong Kong. Shatner won the part of Robert Lomax (the architect) after a fifteen-minute audition. His female lead was French actress France Nuyen, a twenty-two-year-old ingenue with whom he clashed repeatedly over preparation and approach. In fact, it was commonplace for actors on the *Wong* set to be bullied by Shatner, who took control of the elaborately mounted show with the tenacity of a man who believed this play could make or break his entire career. The atmosphere became so poisonous that director Joshua Logan simply stopped showing up for rehearsals.

The ill wind of backstage strife no doubt affected the critical reception as well. "It opened as a turkey," Shatner remembered years later. "It got seven bad notices. It was directed as a turgid drama. People walked out in the middle of it—you could hear whole rows of people getting up and walking out." At best, the players were damned with faint praise. "William Shatner gives a modest performance that is also attractive," wrote Brooks Atkinson in the *New York Times*, "a little wooden, perhaps, which is one way of avoiding maudlin scenes."

The play seemed destined for the scrap heap. However, Shatner had too much at stake to let it slide into oblivion. He began subtly changing the pace and tenor of the show, turning it from a turgid drama into a fluffy romantic confection. Audiences began to respond. A play that was slated to close after three months got a new lease on life. Amazingly, *The World of Suzie Wong* lasted a year and a half on Broadway. For his part, Shatner was rewarded with **acting** honors from Theater World, the Theater Guild, and the Drama Circle. Thereafter, he never could shake the reputation of being a behind-the-scenes control freak, and that may have factored into the decision not to cast him in the ensuing 1960 film version. Shatner's leading man part went to William Holden, who was a bigger star than Shatner at the time. Shatner was crushed at being passed over, but he would soon get used to seeing plum roles go to screen actors with more bankability.

In a strange case of chickens coming home to roost, two disgruntled members of the *Suzie Wong* cast would cross paths with Shatner later in life. William Windom, Shatner's understudy in the role of Lomax—whom he mistreated badly—returned to grind his gears as Captain Decker in the classic second season **Star Trek** installment "The Doomsday Machine." France Nuyen, with whom Shatner warred constantly during the Broadway run, sparred with him once more, this time in the role of Elaan, a petulant alien princess who beams aboard the starship *Enterprise* in the third-sea-

"Do I get egg roll with that?" Shatner ogles one of his co-stars in Broadway's *The World of Suzie Wong*.

son episode "Elaan of Troyius." Both she and Shatner most certainly must have drawn on their *Suzie Wong* experience in playing many scenes of bickering and recrimination. They were able to work past the bad blood, however, and they went on to do two more **television** projects together in the early 1970s.

WRITING

A true Renaissance man, Shatner has pursued writing in addition to **acting**, **directing**, and **producing**. Throw in his musical dabblings, and you have the entertainment industry equivalent of baseball's rare five-tool player. His writing aspirations go back to his earliest days in show business.

Shatner began submitting script ideas for **Star Trek** soon after he was hired for the TV series in 1966. Creator **Gene Roddenberry** related one instance when the actor forced him, as executive producer, to read one of his story treatments. "He wouldn't let me take it home to read," Roddenberry recalled. "He insisted on reading it right there. So I fortified myself with a Scotch and prepared to suffer. But the story flowed and was so damned poetic I caught myself wishing I could write that well." Nevertheless, Roddenberry passed on this supposedly brilliant script, for reasons he left unstated. Beyond piddling script changes, Shatner did not get a chance to put words into the mouths of **Star Trek** characters until 1989, when he cowrote and directed the feature film **Star Trek V: The Final Frontier**.

For Shatner, writing, **acting**, and his other disciplines form one gorgeous artistic mosaic. "I've learned a great deal about acting from writing," Shatner explained in 1967. "An actor interprets a writer's work just as a musician interprets a composer's work. The criterion of a good actor is how well he interprets the work of the writer. Even the writer may not know exactly what he has written. This is the nebulous area in which the actor works."

WYNDER, DR. ERNST

This nutritionist and fitness expert served as Shatner's health guru for a time during the late 1970s. Shatner met Wynder, the director of the American Health Foundation, at a dinner party in 1978. At the time, the actor was desperately trying to get in shape for his triumphant return to the big screen in **Star Trek: The Motion Picture**. Wynder convinced him to abandon such luxuries as sugar and coffee and embrace a rigorous workout regimen. By the next year,

Shatner was noticeably trimmer (though some have hinted that other methods, such as liposuction, may have had something to do with that). In 1979, the star served as celebrity spokesperson for Wynder's "Know Your Body" program, which endeavored to help young people stay fit.

ZMED, ADRIAN

This swarthy, boyish-looking actor played brash patrolman Vince Romano on *T. J. Hooker* from 1982 to 1985. A virtual unknown when he joined the show, Zmed went on to star in the feature film *Grease 2* and serve as host of the syndicated televised disco party *Dance Fever* from 1985 to 1987. He is included here mainly because his name begins with the letter *Z*.

Adrian Zmed appears mesmerized by the size of Shatner's baton on the set of the police drama *T. J. Hooker*.

I have awarded "Kirk Points" for each episode on the following basis:

One (1) point if Kirk gets action (KGA) from a female admirer.

One (1) point if Kirk is seen with his shirt off or his shirt partially torn (SO).

One (1) point if Kirk's blood is spilt during the episode (KB).

One (1) point if Kirk engages in hand to hand combat (HHC).

One (1) point if Shatner plays a dual role (DR).

One (1) point if Kirk unplugs or outwits a supercomputer (SC).

One (1) point if Kirk gives a long, moralizing speech to an alien or enemy (LMS).

One (1) point if Kirk is annoyed by the presence of a persnickety bureaucrat (PB).

One (1) point if Kirk refuses to kill an enemy for moral reasons (RTK).

One (1) point if Kirk commits an egregious violation of the Prime Directive (EV).

Because Shatner has set the bar so high, I have added a five-point bonus for episodes where five of the above conditions apply. A perfect ten represents the ultimate in Shatner performances, the nirvana of Shatnerica.

FIRST SEASON, 1966-67

(NBC-TV, each episode 60 minutes) **Regular Cast:** William Shatner (Captain James T. Kirk); Leonard Nimoy (Mr. Spock); DeForest Kelley (Dr. Leonard "Bones" McCoy); George Takei (Lt. Hikura Sulu); Nichelle Nichols (Lt. Nyota Uhura); James Doohan (Engineer Montgomery "Scotty" Scott).

EPISODE 1: "THE MAN TRAP"

Original Air Date: 9/8/66 **Director:** Marc Daniels; Telewriter: George Clayton Johnson **Guest Cast:** Grace Lee Whitney (Yeoman Janice Rand); Alfred Ryder (Professor Crater) **Synopsis**: A shapeshifting "salt vampire" begins stalking the corridors of the *Enterprise*, draining crewmembers of their sodium chloride. **Kirk Points:** 0 (More of a McCoy episode) **Friends of Bill:** Telewriter George Clayton Johnson costarred with Shatner in the 1962 film *The Intruder*.

EPISODE 2: "CHARLIE X"

Original Air Date: 9/15/66 **Director:** Lawrence Dobkin **Telewriter:** D.C. Fontana
Guest Cast: Grace Lee Whitney (Yeoman Janice Rand); Robert Walker Jr. (Charlie Evans). **Synopsis:** Charlie Evans, an insufferable brat with super powers, tries to take over the *Enterprise*. **Kirk Points:** 1 (LMS)

EPISODE 3: "WHERE NO MAN HAS GONE BEFORE"

Original Air Date: 9/22/66 **Director:** James Goldstone; Telewriter: Samuel A. Peeples **Guest Cast:** Gary Lockwood (Lt. Comdr. Gary Mitchell); Sally Kellerman (Dr. Elizabeth Dehner). **Synopsis:** A mysterious force field at the edge of the galaxy gives Comdr. Gary Mitchell awesome destructive powers. **Kirk Points:** 4 (SO, KB, HHC, LMS) **Friends of Bill:** Paul Fix (Dr. Piper) appeared with Shatner in the 1964 film *The Outrage*.

EPISODE 4: "THE NAKED TIME"

Original Air Date: 9/29/66 **Director:** Marc Daniels **Telewriter:** John D. F. Black
Guest Cast: Grace Lee Whitney (Yeoman Janice Rand); Majel Barrett (Nurse Christine Chapel); Bruce Hyde (Lt. Kevin Riley). **Synopsis:** A strange disease infects the *Enterprise*, bringing out the emotional insecurities of the crewmembers. **Kirk Points:** 1 (SO)

EPISODE 5: "THE ENEMY WITHIN"

Original Air Date: 10/6/66 **Director:** Leo Penn **Telewriter:** Richard Matheson **Guest Cast:** Grace Lee Whitney (Yeoman Janice Rand). **Synopsis:** A transporter malfunction splits Kirk into two people: "Good" Kirk is kind and gentle; "Bad" Kirk is rude, boorish, and steals McCoy's brandy. **Kirk Points:** 4 (KGA, SO, HHC, DR)

EPISODE 6: "MUDD'S WOMEN"

Original Air Date: 10/13/66 **Director:** Harvey Hart **Telewriter:** Stephen Kandel
Guest Cast: Roger C. Carmel (Harry Mudd) **Synopsis:** Intergalactic rapscallion Harry Mudd and his crew of Amazon beauties cause a commotion on a remote mining planet. **Kirk Points:** 0

EPISODE 7: "WHAT ARE LITTLE GIRLS MADE OF?"

Original Air Date: 10/20/66 **Director:** James Goldstone **Telewriter:** Robert Bloch

Guest Cast: Majel Barrett (Nurse Christine Chapel); Michael Strong (Dr. Roger Korby) **Synopsis:** Dr. Korby, a mad scientist, fashions an android duplicate of Kirk in an effort to win the love of Nurse Chapel. **Kirk Points:** 1 (DR)

EPISODE 8: "MIRI"
Original Air Date: 10/27/66 **Director:** Vincent McEveety **Telewriter:** Adrian Spies **Guest Cast:** Grace Lee Whitney (Yeoman Janice Rand); Kim Darby (Miri); Michael J. Pollard (Jahn). **Synopsis:** Kirk and his crew encounter a group of ragamuffins who have a strange disease that kills them at puberty. **Kirk Points:** 8 (SO, KB, LMS, plus a special 5-point bonus for the priceless scene in which the children surround Kirk and chant "Bonk bonk on the head" in unison). **Friends of Bill:** Kim Darby (Miri) went on to costar with Shatner in the 1972 TV movie *The People.*

EPISODE 9: "DAGGER OF THE MIND"
Original Air Date: 11/3/66 **Director:** Vincent McEveety **Telewriter:** Shimon Wincelberg **Guest Cast:** James Gregory (Dr. Tristan Adams); Morgan Woodward (Dr. Simon van Gelder); Marianna Hill (Dr. Helen Noel). **Synopsis:** Kirk must outwit the sadistic director of a Federation penal colony. **Kirk Points:** 0

EPISODE 10: "THE CORBOMITE MANEUVER"
Original Air Date: 11/10/66 **Director:** Joseph Sargent **Telewriter:** Jerry Sohl **Guest Cast:** Grace Lee Whitney (Yeoman Janice Rand); Clint Howard (Balok) **Synopsis:** The fearsome alien who has been menacing the *Enterprise* turns out to be the child-like Balok. Once he discards his disguise, he kicks back a brew with Kirk and his crew and teaches everyone a lesson about prejudice. **Kirk Points:** 1 (SO)

EPISODE 11: "THE CONSCIENCE OF THE KING"
Original Air Date: 12/8/66 **Director:** Gerd Oswald **Telewriter:** Barry Trivers **Guest Cast:** Arnold Moss (Anton Karidian); Barbara Anderson (Lenore Karidian); Bruce Hyde (Lt. Kevin Riley). **Synopsis:** The lead player in a troupe of actors traveling on board the *Enterprise* turns out to be a notorious mass murderer. **Kirk Points:** 1 (KGA)

EPISODE 12: "BALANCE OF TERROR"
Original Air Date: 12/15/66 **Director:** Vincent McEveety **Telewriter:** Paul

Schneider **Guest Cast:** Grace Lee Whitney (Yeoman Janice Rand); Paul Comi (Lt. Andrew Stiles); Garry Walberg (Commander Hansen) **Synopsis:** Kirk engages in a duel of wits with a Romulan commander during an encounter in the Neutral Zone. **Kirk Points:** 0 (Still a great episode) **Friends of Bill:** Larry Montaigne (Decius) had appeared with Shatner in the *Outer Limits* episode "Cold Hands, Warm Heart" in 1964.

EPISODE 13: "THE MENAGERIE"
Original Air Dates: 12/17/66, 12/24/66 **Director:** Marc Daniels **Telewriter:** Gene Roddenberry **Guest Cast:** Jeffrey Hunter (Captain Christopher Pike); Susan Oliver (Vina). **Synopsis:** Spock is put on trial for diverting the *Enterprise* to the forbidden planet of Tabs IV. **Kirk Points:** 1 (PB) **Friends of Bill:** Malachi Throne (Commodore Mendez) played a doctor who treats Shatner in the *Outer Limits* TV episode "Cold Hands, Warm Heart" in 1964.

EPISODE 14: "SHORE LEAVE"
Original Air Date: 12/29/66 **Director:** Robert Sparr **Telewriter:** Theodore Sturgeon **Guest Cast:** Shirley Bonne (Ruth); Oliver McGowan (Caretaker). **Synopsis:** While on shore leave, the *Enterprise* crew finds their memories and nightmares brought to life by a mysterious caretaker. **Kirk Points:** 4 (KGA, SO, KB, HHC)

EPISODE 15: "THE GALILEO SEVEN"
Original Air Date: 1/5/67 **Director:** Robert Gist **Telewriters:** Oliver Crawford and Shimon Wincelberg **Guest Cast:** John Crawford (High Commissioner Ferris); Don Marshall (Lieutenant Boma). **Synopsis:** Spock saves the crew of the shuttlecraft Galileo when it crash-lands on a planet populated by hostile ape creatures with spears. **Kirk Points:** 1 (PB)

EPISODE 16: "THE SQUIRE OF GOTHOS"
Original Air Date: 1/12/67 **Director:** Don McDougall **Telewriter:** Paul Schneider **Guest Cast:** William Campbell ("General" Trelane) **Synopsis:** The *Enterprise* crew encounters Trelane, a whimsical and impetuous alien child with strange powers and baroque taste in clothing. **Kirk Points:** 1 (LMS)

EPISODE 17: "ARENA"

Original Air Date: 1/19/67 **Director:** Joseph Pevney **Telewriter:** Gene L. Coon **Guest Cast:** Carole Shelyne (Metron); Gary Coombs and Bobby Clark (Gorn). **Synopsis:** All-powerful aliens force Kirk to fight the Gorn, a hissing lizard-like creature. **Kirk Points:** 10 (SO, KB, HHC, LMS, RTK + 5-point "nirvana" bonus)

EPISODE 18: "TOMORROW IS YESTERDAY"

Original Air Date: 1/26/67 **Director:** Michael O'Herlihy **Telewriter:** D.C. Fontana **Guest Cast:** Roger Perry (Captain John Christopher). **Synopsis:** The *Enterprise* is thrown backward in time to late 1960's America, where they must deal with an incredulous Air Force pilot. **Kirk Points:** 0

EPISODE 19: "COURT-MARTIAL"

Original Air Date: 2/2/67 **Director:** Marc Daniels; Telewriters: Don M. Mankiewicz and Stephen W. Carabatsos. **Guest Cast:** Richard Webb (Lt. Comdr. Benjamin Finney); Elisha Cook Jr. (Samuel T. Cogley). **Synopsis:** Kirk is court-martialed for allegedly causing the death of a crewman. **Kirk Points:** 2 (KGA, SO)

EPISODE 20: "THE RETURN OF THE ARCHONS"

Original Air Date: 2/9/67 **Director:** Joseph Pevney **Telewriter:** Boris Sobelman **Guest Cast:** Charles Macaulay (Landru) **Synopsis:** The *Enterprise* visits the planet Beta III, run by the supercomputer Landru, whose inhabitants worship it as a god. **Kirk Points:** 1 (SC)

EPISODE 21: "SPACE SEED"

Original Air Date: 2/16/67 **Director:** Marc Daniels; Telewriters: Gene L. Coon and Carey Wilbur **Guest Cast:** Ricardo Montalban (Khan Noonien Singh); Madlyn Rhue (Lt. Marla McGivers). **Synopsis:** Kirk and company thaw out a cadre of cryogenically frozen ubermenschen led by Ricardo Montalban. **Kirk Points:** 5 (special bonus for setting the stage for the ultimate battle of ham versus ham fifteen years later in *Star Trek II: The Wrath of Khan*).

EPISODE 22: "A TASTE OF ARMAGEDDON"

Original Air Date: 2/23/67 **Director:** Joseph Pevney **Telewriters:** Robert Hamner and Gene L. Coon **Guest Cast:** Gene Lyons (Ambassador Robert Fox) **Synopsis:**

Kirk must talk some sense into the heads of a race that fights war cleanly, via computer. **Kirk Points:** 3 (SC, LMS, PB)

EPISODE 23: "THIS SIDE OF PARADISE"
Original Air Date: 3/2/67 **Director:** Ralph Senensky **Telewriter:** D.C. Fontana **Guest Cast:** Jill Ireland (Leila Kalomi) **Synopsis:** Spock and the rest of the crew are infected by alien spores that liberate repressed emotions. Kirk alone remains immune. **Kirk Points:** 2 (KB, HHC)

EPISODE 24: "THE DEVIL IN THE DARK"
Original Air Date: 3/9/67 **Director:** Joseph Pevney **Telewriter:** Gene L. Coon **Guest Cast:** Janos Prohaska (Horta). **Synopsis:** Kirk and company investigate a series of mysterious deaths in an underground mining colony. **Kirk Points:** 1 (RTK)

EPISODE 25: "ERRAND OF MERCY"
Original Air Date: 3/23/67 **Director:** John Newland **Telewriter:** Gene L. Coon **Guest Cast:** John Colicos (Commander Kor). **Synopsis:** Kirk acts to stem a Klingon invasion of Organia, a planet populated by passive, elderly men. **Kirk Points:** 2 (LMS, EV)

EPISODE 26: "THE ALTERNATIVE FACTOR"
Original Air Date: 3/30/67 **Director:** Gerd Oswald **Telewriter:** Don Ingalls **Guest Cast:** Robert Brown (Lazarus). **Synopsis:** The *Enterprise* takes in two versions of a man named Lazarus—each from different universes and unable to coexist without causing destruction. **Kirk Points:** 0

EPISODE 27: "THE CITY ON THE EDGE OF FOREVER"
Original Air Date: 4/6/67 **Director:** Joseph Pevney **Telewriter:** Harlan Ellison **Guest Cast:** Joan Collins (Sister Edith Keeler). **Synopsis:** Kirk falls in love with doomed social worker Joan Collins while trapped on Earth in the 1930s. **Kirk Points:** 6 (KGA + 5-point bonus for putting up with Harlan Ellison.)

EPISODE 28: "OPERATION: ANNIHILATE"
Original Air Date: 4/13/67 **Director:** Herschel Daugherty **Telewriter:** Stephen W. Carabatsos **Guest Cast:** Majel Barrett (Nurse Christine Chapel). **Synopsis:** Kirk's

brother and his family are wiped out by fuzzy flying bats that disrupt the central nervous system. **Kirk Points:** 1 (DR, as Kirk and, in different hairpiece and false mustache, as his brother's corpse.)

SECOND SEASON, 1967–68

(NBC-TV, each episode 60 minutes) **Regular Cast Addition:** Walter Koenig (Ensign Pavel Chekov)

EPISODE 29: "AMOK TIME"
Original Air Date: 9/15/67 **Director:** Joseph Pevney **Telewriter:** Theodore Sturgeon **Guest Cast:** Majel Barrett (Nurse Christine Chapel); Arlene Martel (T'Pring) **Synopsis:** Spock's sexual drive reasserts itself, forcing him to return to Vulcan for a marriage ceremony. Unfortunately, part of the festivities involves swinging a large axe at Kirk. **Kirk Points:** 3 (KB, SO, HHC) **Friends of Bill:** Larry Montaigne (Stonn) had appeared with Shatner in the *Outer Limits* episode "Cold Hands, Warm Heart" in 1964; Arlene Martel (T'Pring) went on to costar with Shatner in the 1974 TV movie *Indict and Convict.*

EPISODE 30: "WHO MOURNS FOR ADONAIS?"
Original Air Date: 9/22/67 **Director:** Marc Daniels **Telewriters:** Gilbert A. Ralston and Gene L. Coon **Guest Cast:** Michael Forest (Apollo); Leslie Parrish (Lt. Carolyn Palamas) **Synopsis:** The *Enterprise* is waylaid by the Greek god Apollo, an ancient space traveler now dwelling on the planet Pollux IV. **Kirk Points:** 0

EPISODE 31: "THE CHANGELING"
Original Air Date: 9/29/67 **Director:** Marc Daniels **Telewriter:** John Meredyth Lucas **Guest Cast:** Majel Barrett (Nurse Christine Chapel); Vic Perrin (the voice of "Nomad") **Synopsis:** Nomad/Tan-Ru, a hybrid computer/alien probe, invades the *Enterprise* and mistakes Kirk for its creator. **Kirk Points:** 6 (SC + 5-pont bonus for being the ultimate "Kirk destroys a supercomputer" episode.)

EPISODE 32: "MIRROR, MIRROR"
Original Air Date: 10/6/67 **Director:** Marc Daniels **Telewriter:** Jerome Bixby **Guest

Cast: Barbara Luna (Lt. Marlena Moreau) **Synopsis:** A transporter malfunction deposits an *Enterprise* away team in an alternate universe where Spock has a cool-looking goatee. **Kirk Points:** 9 (KGA, KB, HHC, RTK + 5-point "tunic" bonus)

EPISODE 33: "THE APPLE"
Original Air Date: 10/13/67 **Director:** Joseph Pevney **Telewriters:** Max Ehrlich and Gene L. Coon **Guest Cast:** Celeste Yarnall (Yeoman Martha Landon) **Synopsis:** Kirk pulls the plug on a supercomputer that the inhabitants of Gamma Trianguli IV have been worshipping as a god. **Kirk Points:** 1 (SC)

EPISODE 34: "THE DOOMSDAY MACHINE"
Original Air Date: 10/20/67 **Director:** Marc Daniels **Telewriter:** Norman Spinrad **Guest Cast:** William Windom (Comdr. Matthew Decker) **Synopsis:** The *Enterprise* rescues a ruined starship and its half-cracked commander, Matthew Decker, who is ridden with guilt over the destruction of his vessel by a huge calzone-shaped "doomsday machine." **Kirk Points:** 5 (special bonus for the debut appearance of Kirk's dress tunic) **Friends of Bill:** William Windom (Decker) was Shatner's understudy on Broadway in *The World of Suzie Wong* (1958).

EPISODE 35: "CATSPAW"
Original Air Date: 10/27/67 **Director:** Joseph Pevney **Telewriter:** Robert Bloch **Guest Cast:** Antoinette Bower (Sylvia); Theo Marcuse (Korob). **Synopsis:** Kirk and company encounter two alien pipe cleaners in human form. Using a transmuter device, they turn Scott and Sulu into drooling, pasty-faced zombies. **Kirk Points:** 0

EPISODE 36: "I, MUDD"
Original Air Date: 11/3/67 **Director:** Marc Daniels **Telewriters:** Stephen Kandel and David Gerrold **Guest Cast:** Roger C. Carmel (Harry Mudd); Kay Elliott (Stella Mudd). **Synopsis:** The *Enterprise* is hijacked by Harry Mudd and his army of androids. **Kirk Points:** 1 (SC)

EPISODE 37: "METAMORPHOSIS"
Original Air Date: 11/10/67 **Director:** Ralph Senensky **Telewriter:** Gene L. C0011 **Guest Cast:** Elinor Donahue (Ambassador Nancy Hedord); Glenn Corbett

(Zefram Cochrane). **Synopsis:** The *Enterprise* crew encounters Zefram Cochrane, the 180-year-old inventor of warp drive, being kept young and healthy by a mysterious cloud entity known as "The Companion." **Kirk Points:** 1 (PB)

EPISODE 38: "JOURNEY TO BABEL"

Original Air Date: 11/17/67 **Director:** Joseph Pevney **Telewriter:** D.C. Fontana **Guest Cast:** Majel Barrett (Nurse Christine Chapel); Mark Lenard (Ambassador Sarek); William O'Connell (Thelev) **Synopsis:** While en route to a Federation conference, the *Enterprise* plays host to a series of intrigues involving ambassadors both real and disguised. **Kirk Points:** 1 (PB)

EPISODE 39: "THE DEADLY YEARS"

Original Air Date: 12/8/67 **Director:** Joseph Pevney **Telewriter:** David P. Harmon **Guest Cast:** Charles Drake (Comm. George Stocker); Sarah Marshall (Dr. Janet Wallace); Beverly Washburn (Lt. Arlene Galway). **Synopsis:** The *Enterprise* becomes infected with a disease that accelerates the aging process. **Kirk Points:** 1 (PB)

EPISODE 40: "OBSESSION"

Original Air Date: 12/15/67 **Director:** Ralph Senensky **Telewriter:** Art Wallace **Guest Cast:** Majel Barrett (Nurse Christine Chapel); Stephen Brooks (Ensign Garrovick) **Synopsis:** Kirk goes nutzoid when the *Enterprise* is infiltrated by a hovering cloud creature that, years earlier, had decimated the crew of his first starship. **Kirk Points:** 0

EPISODE 41: "WOLF IN THE FOLD"

Original Air Date: 12/22/67 **Director:** Joseph Pevney **Telewriter:** Robert Bloch **Guest Cast:** John Fiedler (Commissioner Hengist) **Synopsis:** Scotty is implicated in a series of brutal knife murders on a pleasure planet. **Kirk Points:** 1 (PB)

EPISODE 42: "THE TROUBLE WITH TRIBBLES"

Original Air Date: 12/29/67 **Director:** Joseph Pevney **Telewriter:** David Gerrold **Guest Cast:** Stanley Adams (Cyrano Jones); William Schallert (Nilz Bans) **Synopsis:** While on a mission to protect grain storehouses on Space Station K-7, the *Enterprise* crew is pestered by trader Cyrano Jones and his stock of purring, rapidly multiplying Tribbles. **Kirk Points:** 1 (PB) **Friends of Bill:** William Schallert (Nilz Barris) went on to play Shatner's father-in-law in the 1978 TV movie *Little Women*.

EPISODE 43: "THE GAMESTERS OF TRISKELION"
Original Air Date: 1/5/68 **Director:** Gene Nelson **Telewriter:** Margaret Armen **Guest Cast:** Joseph Ruskin (Galt); Angelique Pettyjohn (Shahna) **Synopsis:** Kirk, Uhura, and Chekov are forced to engage in gladiatorial combat by a race of oozy, brain-like beings called the Providers. **Kirk Points:** 3 (KGA, SO, HHC)

EPISODE 44: "A PIECE OF THE ACTION"
Original Air Date: 1/12/68 **Director:** James Komack; Telewriters: David Harmon and Gene L. Coon **Guest Cast:** Anthony Caruso (Bela Oxmyx); Victor Tayback (Jojo Krako) **Synopsis:** Kirk and the crew get caught up in a mob war on a planet modeled after 1920s gangland Chicago. **Kirk Points:** 0

EPISODE 45: "THE IMMUNITY SYNDROME"
Original Air Date: 1/19/68 **Director:** Joseph Pevney **Telewriter:** Robert Sabaroff **Guest Cast:** Majel Barrett (Nurse Christine Chapel). **Synopsis:** The *Enterprise* confronts a gigantic space virus that eats starships. **Kirk Points:** 0

EPISODE 46: "A PRIVATE LITTLE WAR"
Original Air Date: 2/2/68 **Director:** Marc Daniels **Telewriter:** Gene Roddenberry **Guest Cast:** Majel Barrett (Nurse Christine Chapel); Michael Witney (Tyree); Nancy Kovack (Nona). **Synopsis:** Kirk interferes with life on an undeveloped planet in order to prevent the Klingons from interfering with life on an undeveloped planet. **Kirk Points:** 1 (EV)

EPISODE 47: "RETURN TO TOMORROW"
Original Air Date: 2/9/68 **Director:** Ralph Senensky **Telewriter:** Gene Roddenberry **Guest Cast:** Majel Barrett (Nurse Christine Chapel); Diana Muldaur (Dr. Ann Mulhall) **Synopsis:** Three disembodied alien brains attempt to appropriate the forms of Kirk, Spock, and Dr. Anne Mulhall. **Kirk Points:** 1 (SO)

EPISODE 48: "PATTERNS OF FORCE"

Original Air Date: 2/16/68 **Director:** Vincent McEveety **Telewriter:** John Meredyth Lucas **Guest Star:** David Brian (John Gill); Skip Homeier (Melakon). **Synopsis:** Kirk and his crew join the resistance movement on a planet modeled after Nazi Germany. **Kirk Points:** 1 (LMS)

EPISODE 49: "BY ANY OTHER NAME"

Original Air Date: 2/23/68 **Director:** Marc Daniels **Telewriters:** D. C. Fontana and Jerome Bixby **Guest Cast:** Majel Barrett (Nurse Christine Chapel); Warren Stevens (Rojan) **Synopsis:** The *Enterprise* is subdued by the Kelvans, a race of emotionless aliens who enjoy turning people into little dodecahedrons. **Kirk Points:** 1 (KGA)

EPISODE 50: "THE OMEGA GLORY"

Original Air Date: 3/1/68 **Director:** Vincent McEveety; Telewriter: Gene Roddenberry **Guest Cast:** Morgan Woodward (Captain Ronald Tracey); Roy Jensen (Cloude William) **Synopsis:** Kirk intervenes in a planetary conflict eerily similar to the Vietnam War. **Kirk Points:** 7 (HHC, LMS + 5-point bonus because the long, moralizing speech is the Preamble to the Constitution.)

EPISODE 51: "THE ULTIMATE COMPUTER"

Original Air Date: 3/8/68 **Director:** John Meredyth Lucas; Telewriter: D.C. Fontana **Guest Cast:** William Marshall (Dr. Richard Daystrom) **Synopsis:** Kirk bristles when he is relieved of command so that Dr. Richard Daystrom can test out his new starship-commanding computer on the *Enterprise*. **Kirk Points:** 2 (SC, PB)

EPISODE 52: "BREAD AND CIRCUSES"

Original Air Date: 3/15/68 **Director:** Ralph Senensky **Telewriters:** Gene L. Coon and Gene Roddenberry **Guest Cast:** William Smithers (Captain R. M. Merik/Merikus). **Synopsis:** Kirk and company are forced to engage in gladiatorial combat on a planet modeled after imperial Rome. **Kirk Points:** 3 (KGA, HHC, EV)

EPISODE 53: "FRIDAY'S CHILD"

Original Air Date: 3/22/68 **Director:** Joseph Pevney **Telewriter:** D.C. Fontana **Guest Cast:** Julie Newmar (Eleen); Tige Andrews (Kras); Michael Dante (Maab).

Synopsis: Kirk and company meddle in the affairs of the planet Capella in order to prevent the Capellans from aligning with the Klingons. **Kirk Points:** 1 (EV)

EPISODE 54: "ASSIGNMENT: EARTH"
Original Air Date: 3/29/68 **Director:** Marc Daniels **Telewriters:** Gene Roddenberry and Art Wallace **Guest Cast:** Robert Lansing (Gary Seven); Teri Garr (Roberta Lincoln). **Synopsis:** The *Enterprise* travels back in time to 1968 Earth to stop an interstellar super agent from sabotaging a rocket launch and altering history. **Kirk Points:** 0

THIRD SEASON, 1968–69

(NBC-TV, each episode 60 minutes) **Regular Cast Addition:** Majel Barrett (Nurse Christine Chapel).

EPISODE 55: "SPOCK'S BRAIN"
Original Air Date: 9/20/68 **Director:** Marc Daniels **Telewriter:** Lee Cronin **Guest Cast:** Marj Dusay (Kara) **Synopsis:** Amazon women swipe Spock's noodle and use it to power their planet. **Kirk Points:** 0

EPISODE 56: "THE ENTERPRISE INCIDENT"
Original Air Date: 9/27/68 **Director:** John Meredyth Lucas **Telewriter:** D. C. Fontana **Guest Cast:** Joanne Linville (Romulan Commander). **Synopsis:** Kirk appears to be going nuts, but it is all part of a plan to get him on board a Romulan ship to steal their cloaking device. **Kirk Points:** 1 (DR)

EPISODE 57: "THE PARADISE SYNDROME"
Original Air Date: 10/4/68 **Director:** Jud Taylor **Telewriter:** Margaret Armen **Guest Cast:** Sabrina Scharf (Maramanee); Rudy Solari (Salish). **Synopsis:** Kirk gets bonked on the noggin and thinks he's the chief of an alien Indian tribe. **Kirk Points:** 10+ (KGA, SO, KB, HHC, DR, RTK, EV + 5-point "nirvana" bonus and Special Award for Excellence; this is the ultimate Kirk showcase.)

EPISODE 58: "AND THE CHILDREN SHALL LEAD"

Original Air Date: 10/11/68 **Director:** Marvin Chomsky; Telewriter: Edward J. Lasko **Guest Cast:** Melvin Beli (Gorgan) **Synopsis:** A fat, evil angel named Gorgan uses a band of orphans to incapacitate the *Enterprise* crew and take over the ship. **Kirk Points:** 1 (LMS)

EPISODE 59: "IS THERE IN TRUTH NO BEAUTY?"

Original Air Date: 10/18/68 **Director:** Ralph Senensky; Telewriter: Jean Lisette Aroeste **Guest Cast:** Diana Muldaur (Dr. Miranda Jones); David Frankham (Lawrence Marvick) **Synopsis:** Dr. Miranda Jones arrives on the *Enterprise* with a nefarious sidekick and a box containing a telepathic alien who makes Spock go blind. **Kirk Points:** 0

EPISODE 60: "SPECTRE OF THE GUN"

Original Air Date: 10/25/68 **Director:** Vincent McEveety **Telewriter:** Lee Cronin **Guest Cast:** Rex Holman (Morgan Earp); Ron Soble (Wyatt Earp); Charles Maxwell (Virgil Earp); Sam Gilman (Doc Holliday) **Synopsis:** After violating Melkotian space, the *Enterprise* crew is sentenced to participate in a reenactment of the Gunfight at the O.K. Corral. **Kirk Points:** 1 (RTK)

EPISODE 61: "DAY OF THE DOVE"

Original Air Date: 11/1168 **Director:** Marvin Chomsky **Telewriter:** Jerome Bixby **Guest Cast:** Michael Ansara (Kang); Susan Howard (Mara) **Synopsis:** The crews of the *Enterprise* and a Klingon battle cruiser are set at odds by an invisible entity that feeds on hatred. **Kirk Points:** 1 (RTK) **Friends of Bill:** Michael Ansara (Kang) went on to play Diamond Jack Bassitter alongside Shatner in the 1975 TV movie pilot for *The Barbary Coast*.

EPISODE 62: "FOR THE WORLD IS HOLLOW AND I HAVE TOUCHED THE SKY"

Original Air Date: 11/8/68 **Director:** Tony Leader **Telewriter:** Rick Vollaerts **Guest Cast:** Kate Woodville (Natira) **Synopsis:** A terminally ill McCoy falls in love with a High Priestess who holds the key to curing his disease. **Kirk Points:** 0

EPISODE 63: "THE THOLIAN WEB"

Original Air Date: 11/15/68 **Director:** Ralph Senensky **Telewriters:** Judy A. Burns and Chet L. Richards **Guest Cast:** Barbara Babcock (voice of the Tholians) **Synopsis:** Kirk is stranded on a "ghost ship" that rematerializes at regular intervals. A bickering Spock and McCoy must find a way to get him back. **Kirk Points:** 0

EPISODE 64: "PLATO'S STEPCHILDREN"

Original Air Date: 11/22/68 **Director:** David Alexander **Telewriter:** Meyer Dolinsky **Guest Cast:** Michael Dunn (Alexander); Liam Sullivan (Parmen). **Synopsis:** Telekinetic Greeks in space force Kirk and his crew to hit one another and perform musical comedy. **Kirk Points:** 10 (KGA, SO, HHC, LMS, RTK + 5-point "nirvana" bonus)

EPISODE 65: "WINK OF AN EYE"

Original Air Date: 11/29/68 **Director:** Jud Taylor **Telewriter:** Arthur Heinemann **Guest Cast:** Kathie Browne (Deela, Queen of Scalos) **Synopsis:** Kirk drinks some tainted water that sends him into a weird, speeded-up dimension populated by gorgeous women who need reproductive partners. **Kirk Points:** 1 (KGA)

EPISODE 66: "THE EMPATH"

Original Air Date: 12/6/68 **Director:** John Erman **Telewriter:** Joyce Muskat **Guest Cast:** Kathryn Hays (Gem); Willard Sage (Thann); Alan Bergmann (Lab) **Synopsis:** While investigating a planet about to be destroyed by a supernova, Kirk, Spock, and McCoy are subject to experimentation by two hydrocephalic aliens. **Kirk Points:** 0

EPISODE 67: "ELAAN OF TROYIUS"

Original Air Date: 12/20/68 **Director/Telewriter:** John Meredyth Lucas **Guest Cast:** France Nuyen (Elaan); Jay Robinson (Lord Petri); Tony Young (Kryton). **Synopsis:** While transporting the beautiful Elaan to her marriage ceremony on the planet Troyius, Kirk falls in love with the alien queen. **Kirk Points:** 1 (KGA, PB) **Friends of Bill:** France Nuyen (Elaan) played Shatner's love interest on the New York stage in *The World of Suzie Wong* in 1958.

EPISODE 68: "WHOM GODS DESTROY"

Air Date: 1/3/69 **Director:** Herb Wallerstein **Telewriter:** Lee Erwin **Guest Cast:** Steve Ihnat (Garth of Izar); Yvonne Craig (Marta). **Synopsis:** A shapeshifting psychotic imprisons Kirk and Spock in a Federation insane asylum. **Kirk Points:** 1 (DR, as Kirk and Garth-as-Kirk)

EPISODE 69: "LET THAT BE YOUR LAST BATTLEFIELD"
Original Air Date: 1/10/69 **Director:** Jud Taylor **Telewriter:** Oliver Crawford **Guest Cast:** Lou Antonio (Lokai); Frank Gorshin (Bele). **Synopsis:** The *Enterprise* picks up alien minstrel show oddities Bele and Lokai, who chase each other endlessly around the ship, teaching everyone a lesson about racism. **Kirk Points:** 2 (LMS, PB) **Friends of Bill:** Lou Antonio (Lokai) appeared with Shatner in the 1970 TV movie *Sole Survivor.*

EPISODE 70: "THE MARK OF GIDEON"
Original Air Date: 1/17/69 **Director:** Jud Taylor **Telewriters:** George F. Slavin and Stanley Adams **Guest Cast:** Sharon Acker (Odona); David Hurst (Hodin). **Synopsis:** Attempting to beam down to an overpopulated planet, Kirk finds himself on what appears to be a completely empty *Enterprise.* **Kirk Points:** 1 (KGA)

EPISODE 71: "THAT WHICH SURVIVES"
Original Air Date: 1/24/69 **Director:** Herb Wallerstein **Telewriter:** John Merdyth Lucas **Guest Cast:** Lee Meriwether (Losira) **Synopsis:** While exploring an uncharted planet, Kirk and his crew are hunted by a beautiful woman whose touch is deadly. **Kirk Points:** 1 (SC)

EPISODE 72: "THE LIGHTS OF ZETAR"
Original Air Date: 1/31/69 **Director:** Herb Kenwith **Telewriters:** Jeremy Tarcher and Shari Lewis **Guest Cast:** Jan Shutan (Lt. Mira Romaine). **Synopsis**: A cloud of twinkling lights takes over the body of Scotty's main squeeze. **Kirk Points:** 0

EPISODE 73: "REQUIEM FOR METHUSELAH"
Original Air Date: 2/14/69 **Director:** Murray Golden **Telewriter:** Jerome Bixby **Guest Cast:** James Daly (Flint); Louise Sorel (Rayna Kapec). **Synopsis:** Kirk falls in love with the beautiful android ward (Rayna Kapec) of Flint, an immortal alien who has lived many past lives, such as Johannes Brahms and Leonardo da Vinci. **Kirk Points:** 1 (KGA)

EPISODE 74: "THE WAY TO EDEN"

Original Air Date: 2/21/69 **Director:** David Alexander **Telewriter:** Arthur Heinemann **Guest Star:** Skip Homeier (Dr. Thomas Sevrin); Mary-Linda Rapelye (Irina Galliulin); Victor Brandt (Tongo Rad). **Synopsis:** The *Enterprise* allow aboard a band of space hippies who attempt to commandeer the starship. **Kirk Points:** 0

EPISODE 75: "THE CLOUD MINDERS"

Original Air Date: 2/28/69 **Director:** Jud Taylor **Telewriter:** Margaret Armen **Guest Cast:** Jeff Corey (Plasus); Charlene Polite (Vanna); Diana Ewing (Droxine); Fred 'The Hammer' Williamson (Anka). **Synopsis:** Kirk and his crew become embroiled in a labor dispute between troglodyte miners and their overlords, who live in an ethereal cloud city. **Kirk Points:** 2 (EV, PB)

EPISODE 76: "THE SAVAGE CURTAIN"

Original Air Date: 3/7/69 **Director:** Herschel Daugherty **Telewriter:** Gene Roddenberry and Arthur Heinemann **Guest Cast:** Janos Prohaska/voice of Bart LaRue (Yarnek); Lee Begere (Abraham Lincoln); Barry Atwater (Surak); Philip Pine (Colonel Green); Carol Daniels Dement (Zora); Nathan Jung (Genghis Khan); Robert Herron (Kahless). **Synopsis:** Yarnek, an alien rock, attempts to decide the issue of Good vs. Evil by having Abraham Lincoln and Genghis Khan battle each other. Yeah, that's a fair fight. **Kirk Points:** 1 (HHC)

EPISODE 77: "ALL OUR YESTERDAYS"

Original Air Date: 3/14/69 **Director:** Marvin Chomsky **Telewriter:** Jean Lisette Aroeste **Guest Cast:** Ian Wolfe (Mr. Atoz); Mariette Hartley (Zarabeth) **Synopsis:** Spock and McCoy leap through a time portal and wind up stranded in an ice age where Spock reverts to early Vulcan savagery. **Kirk Points:** 0

EPISODE 78: "TURNABOUT INTRUDER"

Original Air Date: 6/3/69 **Director:** Herb Wallerstein **Telewriter:** Arthur H. Singer **Guest Cast:** Sandra Smith (Dr. Janice Lester); Harry Landers (Dr. Arthur Coleman). **Synopsis:** Resentful Janice Lester uses a machine to place her mind in Kirk's body, and vice versa. **Kirk Points:** 6 (DR + 5-point bonus for playing the ultimate dual role as a member of the opposite sex.)

BIBLIOGRAPHY

PERIODICALS

"Actor's Wife Drowns." *New York Times*. August 11, 1999.

"All-Bran Adds a Bit of Protein To Go with Fiber." *Grocer*. May 26, 2007.

"Beamed Up Again." *Variety*. January 10, 1994.

Beauregard, Sue-Ellen. Review of the Videotape Ultimate Survivors: Winning Against Incredible Odds. *Booklist*. January 1, 1992.

Benson, John. "Folds Puts Shatner CD on the Front Burner." Billboard.com. June 23, 2004.

Bianculli, David. "'Tek' Another Look." *New York Daily News*. January 5, 1995.

Bierly, Mandi. "Set To Stun." *Entertainment Weekly*. April 13, 2007.

Boulton, Marsha. "Shatner Keeps on Trekkin." *Maclean's*. December 10, 1979.

Brady, James. "In Step with William Shatner." *Parade*. March 2,1986.

Brooke, Jill. "Shatner Captains Real Life Drama." *New York Post*. April 18, 1989.

Brown, Peter H. "Embattled Enterprise." Washington Post. December 18, 1986.

Buchalter, Gail. "*Star Trek*'s Straight Arrow." *People*. July 5, 1982.

Buckler, Grant. "*Star Trek*'s Kirk Beams Up to CEO Role." *Newsbytes News Network*. February 21, 1995.

"The Captains." *TV Guide*. August 24, 1996.

Castro, Peter. "Chatter: Star Search." *People*. July 10, 1989.

Cavanaugh, Tim. "Happy 40th Birthday, *Star Trek*." *Reason*. August 1, 2006.

Challender, Mary. "Captain Kirk Has Lost Faith, but *Star Trek* Has Its Faithful?" *Gannett News Service*. August 22, 1996.

Chatter column: "Walking Tall." *People*. April 5, 1982.

Chidley, Joe. "Captain of Enterprise." *Maclean's*. November 28 1994.

Cohen, Charles E. "The Trek to Tek." *TV Guide*. January 15, 1994.

Dick, Jeff. Review of the Video I Am Become Death. *Booklist*. August, 1997.

Eisenberg, Lawrence. "William Shatner Finds Heroism a Touchy Enterprise." *TV Guide*. December 16, 1989.

Engel, Joel. "Bad News for Captain Kirk in the 24th Century." *New York Times*. July 25, 1994.

Fessier, Michael. "No One Ever Upsets the Star." *TV Guide*. October 15, 1966.

Finn, Robin. "Star's Trek: Spaceship to Show Ring." *New York Times*. November 8, 1986.

Flamm, Matthew. "Maiden Voyage for Kirk." *New York Post*. June 4, 1989.

Fowler, James E. "Dammit Jim, I'm Just a Cowboy." *Los Angeles Times*. April 18, 1996.

"Galaxy of Trek Stars." *TV Guide*. November, 1997.

Gardella, Kay. "Riding Herd on Troublemakers." *New York Daily News*. November 12, 1985.

Gliatto, Tom. "Show Me the Money." *People*. November 27, 2006.

Graham, Jefferson. "Shatner Finds a New Frontier as Director of Star Trek V." *USA Today*. June 8, 1989.

Hammond, Sally. "CBS Prosecutor Won't Win 'Em All." *New York Post*. January 3, 1965.

Higgins, Robert. "The Intergalactic Golden Boy." *TV Guide*. June 22, 1968.

Hill, Sandy. "At 63, Shatner Has All Systems Engaged." KnightRidder/Tribune News Service. April 21, 1994.

Holsom, Laura. "What Shatner Hath Wrought; The Intersection of the Internet and Celebrity." *New York Times*. June 6, 2000.

Hughes, Mike. "Shatner Finds New Space." Gannett News Service. January 20, 1994.

Jones, Steven. "Shatner's 'Trek.'" *USA Today*. November 9, 1993.

Keck, William. "Celebrities' Pets Get Star Treatment." *National Enquirer*. October 21, 1997.

Kempley, Rita. "*Star Trek VI* Boldly Going." *Washington Post*. December 4, 1991.

Kenny, Glenn. Review of the Book *Star Trek Memories*. *Entertainment Weekly*. February 16, 1996.

Kiester, Edwin, Jr. "A Star's Trek." *TV Guide*. August 14, 1982.

Koltnow, Barry. "Shatner Looks Back on 30 Years as Kirk." KnightRidder/Tribune News Service. November 17, 1994.

Lee, Luaine. "Now An Admiral, Shatner Hopes to Keep on Trekkin." *New York Daily News*. June 20, 1982.

Mann, Rick. "Warp Speed Ahead." *TV Guide*. July 24, 1993.

Model, Betsy. "Full Speed Ahead." *Cigar Aficionado*. December 1, 2006.

Moran, W. Reed. "Shatner Builds Hope for Recovering Women." *USA Today*. January 22, 2001.

Monthly Film Bulletin. February 1975.

Neuhaus, Cable. "Geek Love." *Entertainment Weekly*. March 11, 1994.

Noth, Dominique Paul. "*Star Trek* Hero a Busy Man." *Biography News*. August, 1974.

Oldenburg, Ann. "Kirk Out?" *USA Today*. October 26, 1994.

"Out of This World!" *Globe*. December 12, 1997.

Peck, Harvey. "Shatner on Stage." *New York Daily News*. May 18, 1969.

Prevetti, C.A. Review of the Video "It Didn't Have to Happen: Drinking and Driving" in *School Library Journal*. March 1995.

Queenan, Joe. Review of the Television Movie *Prisoner of Zenda, Inc*. *People*. September 30, 1996.

Raddatz, Leslie. "*Star Trek* Wins the Ricky Schwarz Award." *TV Guide*. November 15, 1967.

Rensin, David. "A Farewell to Kirk." *TV Guide*. October 8, 1994.

Richter, Erin. "Counterfeit Bills." *Entertainment Weekly*. October 13, 1995.

Romanelli, Alex. "Shatner's New Image." *Television Week*. August 20, 2007.

Roush, Matt. "TekWar Treks To Future-Cop Territory:" *USA Today*. January 17, 1994.

Sager, Mike. "What I've Learned: William Shatner." *Esquire*. February 1, 2006.

Sanz, Cynthia. "Beam Him Down." *People*. November 28, 1994.

Schnaufer, Jeff. "Coping: Sound of Silence." *People*. May 19, 1997

Shatner, William. "What I Watch." *TV Guide*. April 10, 1993.

"Shatner Gets Bigger Play." *Fairfield County Business Journal*. June 10, 2002.

"Shatner in Palimony Suit," *Los Angeles Times*. January 26, 1990.

"Shatner's Ex-wife Sues over Horse Semen." Salon.com. May 7, 2003.

"Shatner To Aid Mideast via 'Therapeutic Riding.'" *Deseret News*. May 31, 2006.

Shepard, Richard E "A Tale of Two Media:" *New York Times*. August 10, 1958.

Simonetti, Karen. Review of the Book *Ashes of Eden*. *Booklist*. May 1, 1995.

Smith, Eric J. "Shatner, 'Invasion' Suffer Identity Crisis. *Multichannel News*. March 28, 2005.

"*Star Trek*: The Geritol Generation." *Entertainment Weekly*. November 20, 1992.

"*Star Trek*'s Stars Trek." *People*. July 20, 1992.

Steffens, Daneet. "The Pen Is Mightier Than the Phaser." *Entertainment Weekly*. June 23, 1995.

Svetky, Benjamin. "I'm Typing As Fast As I Can." *Entertainment Weekly*. January 15, 1993.

Swertlos, Frank. "Did Shatner Finance Raid into Laos?" *TV Guide*. February 12
    1983.

Teubner, Gary. "Beam Me Out, Scotty!' *New York Post*. February 4, 1994.

Thomas, Rochell. "A Chat with William Shatner." *TV Guide*. May 21, 2007.

"Tongue-Thai'd." *New York Post*. January 7, 2007.

Towle, Patricia and Alan Smith. "William Shatner Branded a Sex Maniac."
    National Enquirer. October 10, 1995.

TV Teletype Feature: "New *Star Trek* Series Planned." *TV Guide*. February 7, 1981.

Viens, Stephen and Melissa Key. "Beam Me Up." *Star*. December 2,1997.

"What's Up with William." *TV Guide*. May 5, 1990.

Wilkins, Mike. "It May Be Music to Your Ears . . . But Not Mine." *TV Guide*.
    October 3, 1987.

"William Shatner Sells Kidney Stone." *USA Today*. January 17, 2006.

"William Shatner Treks Down the Aisle." *National Enquirer*. December 12, 1997.

Wilson, David S. "Captain Kirk Comes Down to Earth," *TV Guide*. October 13, 1990.

Witchel, Alex. "Contemplating Death and the Sequel." *New York Times*.
    November 23, 1994.

BOOKS

Alexander, David. *Star Trek Creator: The Authorized Biography of Gene
    Roddenberry*. New York: Penguin Books, 1994.

Beckley, Timothy Greene. *UFOs Among the Stars*. New York: Global
    Communications, 1992. pp. 8–11.

Berlin, Joey. *Toxic Fame: Celebrities Speak on Stardom*. Detroit: Visible Ink,
    1996. pp. 171 and 499.

Bly, Robert W. *The Ultimate Unauthorized Star Trek Quiz Book*. New York:
    Harper Perennial, 1994.

Contemporary Theatre, Film, and Television, vol. 3. Detroit: Gale Research,
    1983. pp. 336–38.

Current Biography Yearbook. New York: H. W. Wilson, 1987. pp. 504–507.
    Engel, Joel. *Gene Roddenberry: The Myth and the Man Behind* Star Trek.
    New York: Hyperion, 1994.

Funt, Marilyn. *Are You Anybody?* New York: Dial Press, 1979. pp. 292–310.

Gould, Jodie. *Heather! An Unabashed, Unauthorized Celebration of All Things
    Locklear*. New York: Citadel Press, 1995.

Gross, Edward and Mark A. Altman. *Captain's Logs*. Boston: Little, Brown, 1995.

Hauck, Dennis William. *Captain Quirk*. New York: Pinnacle Books, 1995.

Hauck, Dennis William. *William Shatner: A Bio-Bibliography*. Westport, CT: Greenwood Press, 1994.

Hill, Marilyn and Rabbi Jerome Cutler, editors. *Celebrity Kosher Cookbook*. New York: Parker, 1975. p.16.

Koenig, Walter. *Warped Factors: A Neurotic's Guide to the Universe*. New York: Taylor, 1998.

Luckman, Mike. *Alien Rock*. New York: MTV Books, 2005

Marill, Alvin H. *Movies Made for Television: 1964–2004*. Lanham, MD: Scarecrow Press, 2005.

Nemecek, Larry. *The Star Trek: The Next Generation Companion*. (rev. ed.) New York: Pocket Books, 1995.

Nichols, Nichelle. *Beyond Uhura*. New York: G. P. Putnam's Sons, 1994.

Nimoy, Leonard. *I Am Not Spock*. New York: Hyperion, 1975.

Nimoy, Leonard. *I Am Spock*. New York: Hyperion, 1995.

Okuda, Michael and Denise Okuda. *The Star Trek Encyclopedia* (revised edition). New York: Pocket Books, 1997.

Parish, James Robert and Vincent Terrace. *The Complete Actors' Television Credits, 1948-1988*. Metuchen, NJ & London: Scarecrow Press, 1989. pp. 437–39.

Rioux, Terry Lee. *From Sawdust to Stardust: The Biography of DeForest Kelley, Star Trek's Dr. McCoy*. New York: Pocket Books, 2005.

Robbins, Ira A. *The Trouser Press Record Guide*. New York: Macmillan, 1991.

Sachs, Margaret. *UFO Encyclopedia*. New York: G. P. Putnam's Sons, 1980. p. 289.

Shatner, Lisabeth with William Shatner. *Captain's Log: William Shatner's Personal Account of the Making of Star Trek V*. New York: Pocket Books, 1989.

Shatner, William with Chris Kreski. *Star Trek Memories*. New York: HarperCollins, 1993.

Shatner, William with Chris Kreski. *Get a Life!* New York: Atria, 1999.

Shatner, William, Sondra Marshak, and Myra Culbreath. *Shatner: Where No Man*. New York: Grosset & Dunlap, 1979.

Solow, Herbert and Robert Justman. *Inside Star Trek: The Real Story*. New York: Pocket Books, 1996.

Takei, George. *To the Stars!* New York: Pocket Books, 1994.

Trimble, Bjo. *Star Trek Concordance*. New York: Citadel Press, 1995.

PRESS RELEASES

December 1, 1959. Sunday Showcase (NBC)

October 8, 1963. Man of Decision (ABC)

January 13, 1965. For the People (CBS)

April 10, 1967. William Shatner's Trek to Stardom (NBC)

August 31, 1968. William Shatner: Captain James Kirk in *Star Trek* (NBC)

February 2, 1968. Shatner and Captain Kirk Share Common Traits (NBC)

November 11, 1968. William Shatner Cuts a Different Kind of Record (NBC)

March 28, 1972. William Shatner, Host of the ABC Sports series "Challenge" (ABC) July 14, 1976. The Tenth Level (CBS)

October 19, 1977. William Shatner Joins Guest Star Cast of "How the West Was Won" (ABC)

February 6, 1980. William Shatner Signed for Second Six Programs in "This Was America" Series (BBI)

June 30, 1981. Shatner to Appear on "Over Easy" (Over Easy)

1983. William Shatner, Sgt. T J. Hooker in the ABC Television Network's *T. J. Hooker* (ABC)

December 11, 1986. William Shatner Host on Dec. 20 Edition of NBC's *Saturday Night Live* (NBC)

April, 1989. William Shatner: A Biography (Rogers & Cowan, Inc.)

October 25, 1993. William Shatner to Be a Guest on CNBC's "Tom Snyder" Oct. 26 (CNBC)

January 17, 1994. William Shatner Guest Stars on "sea Quest DSV" on NBC (NBC) November, 1994. William Shatner, Executive Producer/Director/Guest Star "TekWar" action dramas (Showtime)

November 30, 1994. William Shatner in "Eck the Cat Christmas Special Airing December 5 on Fox (Fox)

December 22, 1994. William Shatner Stars As *Columbo*'s Crafty Adversary Jan. 10, 1995 (ABC)

March 8, 1995. Beam Me Up Scotty. . . . William Shatner on CNBC's "Charles Grodin" (CNBC)

June 5, 1995. William Shatner on A-T Show "Straight Forward with Roger Ailes" (NBC)

INDEX

ACKNOWLEDGMENTS

The author would like to think the following people for their help in making this sequel possible: Nicholas Robinson, Chris Whelan, Hannah and Rena Rosenthal, Jane Klain, Jason Rekulak, Margaret McGuire, and Doogie Horner.